ASPECTS OF EDUCATIONAL TECHNOLOGY
VOLUME VII

Edited for the Association for
Programmed Learning and
Educational Technology by

ROBIN BUDGETT
JOHN LEEDHAM

General Editor
JOHN LEEDHAM

PITMAN PUBLISHING

First published 1973
Reprinted 1975

SIR ISAAC PITMAN AND SONS LTD.
Pitman House, Parker Street, Kingsway, London WC2B 5PB
P.O. Box 46038, Portal Street, Nairobi, Kenya

SIR ISAAC PITMAN (AUST.) PTY. LTD.
Pitman House, 158 Bouverie Street, Carlton, Victoria 3053, Australia

PITMAN PUBLISHING CORPORATION
6 East 43rd Street, New York, N.Y. 10017, U.S.A.

SIR ISAAC PITMAN (CANADA) LTD.
495 Wellington Street West, Toronto 135, Canada

THE COPP CLARK PUBLISHING COMPANY
517 Wellington Street West, Toronto 135, Canada

ISBN: 0 273 31783 0

Reproduced and printed by photolithography and bound in
Great Britain at The Pitman Press, Bath
(G.4678:15)

Foreword

The Mayor of Brighton, Alderman Gordon C C Packham, welcomed the delegates to Brighton and wished them a successful Conference. He was thanked, on behalf of the Association, by the President, Sir James Pitman, who then officially opened the Conference.

The underlying theme this year was to examine the change which has come about during the transition from Programmed Learning to Educational Technology, especially with reference to behavioural objectives. The main papers were invited so as to indicate the trends in Britain, the USA and the USSR. John Annett in delivering the opening paper dealt adequately with the historical development of the British scene; the reader can well decide for himself as to the relevancy of the future developments which Annett suggests. The Russian papers, on the other hand, appear to state the historical case in terms of contemporary practice; perhaps the concentration on the programmed approach, which was common in Britain some five or six years ago, only states part of the case; the detail and emphasis suggests that parallel developments are likely to have taken place across the USSR insofar as educational technology is concerned. The case, however, is not explicitly stated. Robert Glaser from the USA is a figure of some eminence, and his contribution on intelligence, learning and the new aptitudes states new criteria for examining success. Certainly, if one needed to evaluate progress in the field of progressive primary school education in Britain at the moment, then the principles outlined by Glaser could provide the framework for the theory needed to extend the Piagetian concept. Can it be that we have the practice and lack the theory, and the transatlantic psychologists have developed the theory lacking the practice?

The contributed papers were, on the whole, much more concerned with account and forecast than with demonstration. A strong lead came from the Open University with Hawkridge's account of the problems of selecting media for courses. It was greeted with acclaim by the many practitioners who have struggled with similar problems on a smaller scale. It is the size of the Open University's undertakings which is always of interest to educational technologists and Connors throws new light on problems of assessment, while Rowntree questions the whole range of objectives.

There was a good entry from abroad this year with Sir George Williams University, Montreal providing a large delegation; the contributions from Allan, Braham, Coldevin and Mitchell examine a range of aspects of educational technology, which shows concern in depth. The fact that this same concern is shown by several Universities and Polytechnics was a feature of this conference. The presentation of the paper by Baume and Jones on designing a course for underwater technology was very effective and their empirical derivation of objectives must find an echo in many practitioners' hearts. Teather et al,

Tribe and Peacock present separately their experiments with undergraduate populations in the learning of life sciences. Their findings suggest that new methods of instruction have a stimulus value; it is unclear whether the objectives are effected.

Redfearn provides an interesting link between university and service technical courses in examining the queueing problem, which was somewhat glossed over in earlier days, when self-pacing was first exploited. Papers from the services indicate some preoccupation with the detailing of objectives; Hawkins and Hawkins describe a systems approach to training, while Moore and Smith complete an account started in an earlier volume, which relates an interesting change of medium. Similarly Horner accounts for the reorganization of training objectives and schedules in a large industrial complex. Schwarzer suggests that objectives can be so described that the normal curve associated with learning patterns can be permanently skewed by the practice of Mastery Learning. We certainly have had the case so presented before, and equally we have failed to achieve proof that learning is determined by the way in which objectives are defined and instruction carried out. The situation is probably as complex as was so successfully demonstrated by Pratt in his paper on the understanding of selective perception so as to adapt learning to both the affective and cognitive domains. El-Araby gives an interesting account of an unusual language learning problem.

A paper from Japan (Sumi et al) stands apart in its account of the application of CAI programmes in learning courses. The findings are reported more optimistically than similar accounts in earlier editions of 'Aspects of Educational Technology'. In this respect one may refer to the account given by Clements who indicates the general neglect of the tools of educational technology amongst both trainers and teachers. Conradie surveys the scene in South Africa where they hope to avoid some of the errors committed elsewhere as they develop the field of educational technology; he could, with the advantage possible to all of us, refer to the very clear account of Cowan et al in their intermediate assessment of a developing learning unit. Papers such as this certainly clarify the role of the teacher, possibly as much as do the examinations of the specific objectives to which we aspire. Davies and McKenzie also illustrate this in their account of a systems organization for school based resources.

James Hartley et al give an account of the typographical aspects of instructional design and thus keep fresh the valuable contributions we have learned to expect from Keele. Wyant demonstrates again that the application of network analysis in course planning can clarify objectives, especially when a team of instructors or lecturers is involved. While in the field of art education, Steveni makes a lucid case for decentralization drawn from examples of subject decentralization. And finally we note that Leedham submits one of the few papers concerned with the application of a new methodology; his examination of the role of video cassette must stand up to the test of time. It can only claim originality at the moment.

From the breadth of contributions and from their separate accounts and findings it would appear that one thing emerges clearly in the search for objective criteria. The role of the individual as teacher, instructor, manager, provider emerges more and more clearly as the central provision, even as the proliferation and effectiveness of communication resources increase.

Robin Budgett
John Leedham

Contents

List of Contributors

Allan, T S	Sir George Williams University, Montreal 107, Canada
Annett, Prof J	The Open University, Bletchley, Bucks, UK
Baume, A D	North East London Polytechnic, Dagenham, Essex, UK
Bingham, Elspeth	Heriot-Watt University, Edinburgh, UK
Braham, Dr M L	Sir George Williams University, Montreal 107, Canada
Budgett, Inst Cdr R E B, RN	HMS Collingwood, Fareham, Hants, UK
Burnhill, P	Keele University, Staffordshire, UK
Clements, R	Wellcome Foundation Ltd, The Wellcome Building, 183 Euston Road, London NW1 2BP, UK
Coldevin, Dr G O	Sir George Williams University, Montreal 107, Canada
Collins, J C	University of Liverpool, UK
Connors, B	The Open University, Bletchley, Bucks, UK
Conradie, Dr P J	University of South Africa, PO Box 3403, Pretoria, RSA
Cowan, J	Heriot-Watt University, 183 Fountainbridge, Edinburgh EH3 9RU, UK
Davies, W J K	College of Further Education, St Albans, Herts, UK
El-Araby, S	The University of Cairo, Egypt
Fraser, Susan	Keele University, Staffordshire, UK
Glaser, Prof R	University of Pittsburgh (Learning Research and Development Center), Pittsburgh, Pennsylvania 15260, USA
Hardwick, K	University of Liverpool, UK
Hartley, Dr J	Keele University, Staffordshire, UK
Hawkins, Lt Cdr P F, RN	HMS Pembroke, Chatham, Kent, UK
Hawkins, Inst Lt Cdr R E, RN	HMS Pembroke, Chatham, Kent, UK
Hawkridge, Prof D	The Open University, Bletchley, Bucks, UK
Horner, K B	Service Training, Rank Xerox, 338 Euston Road, London NW1, UK
Ilyina, Prof Tatyana	Lenin Pedagogical Institute, Moscow, USSR
Itaya, H	Japan Society for Promotion of Machine Industry, Tokyo, Japan
Jones, B	NE London Polytechnic, Mechanical Engineering Department, Longbridge Road, Dagenham, Essex, UK
Leedham, Dr J F	College of Education, Loughborough, Leics, UK
McKenzie, Mrs F	College of Further Education, St Albans, Herts, UK
Maslova, Prof Galina	Research Institute of the Method and Subject Matter of Learning, Moscow, USSR
Mitchell, Prof P D	Sir George Williams University, Montreal 107, Canada
Moore, Inst Lt Cdr J D S, RN	HMS Collingwood, Fareham, Hants, UK
Morton, Dr J	Heriot-Watt University, 183 Fountainbridge, Edinburgh EH3 9RU, UK
Peacock, D	University of Sussex, Brighton, UK
Pratt, Dr D D	University of British Columbia, Vancouver 8, Canada
Redfearn, Inst Lt Cdr D, RN	RNSETT, RN Barracks, Portsmouth, Hants, UK
Rowntree, D G F	The Open University, Bletchley, Bucks, UK
Schwarzer, Dr R	23 Kiel 16, Kanalstrasse 28, Germany
Shapovalenko, Prof S G	Research Institute of School Equipment and Technical Means of Learning, Moscow, USSR
Shimada, M	Japan Society for Promotion of Machine Industry, Tokyo, Japan
Smith, Inst Lt J F K, RN	HMS Sultan, Gosport, Hants, UK
Steveni, M W	School of Art Education, 26 Priory Road, Edgbaston, Birmingham, UK
Sumi, H	Japan Society for Promotion of Machine Industry, Tokyo, Japan
Teather, Dr D C B	AVA & PL Unit, University of Liverpool, Liverpool, UK
Tribe, Dr M A	University of Sussex, Brighton, UK
Wyant, T G	23 Southam Road, Birmingham 28, UK
Yagi, K	c/o Kikaishinko Kaikan Building, 5-8, 3-Chome, Shibakoen, Minato-Ku, Tokyo, Japan

Psychological Bases of Educational Technology

JOHN ANNETT

The typical research project at first focused on the question of whether machines could teach. Literally hundreds of projects compared 'conventional' versus 'programmed' methods. After a while the research field opened out into studies of the mechanics of programmed learning. There was the famous book versus machine controversy which, by 1962 had been won by the books leaving many expensive machines stranded. In 1962 with the help of Max Sime and Chris Knapper I adapted the tab test idea to the control of 'cheating' in a scrambled book. The so-called Key Card System. Keith Duncan, then with the army, showed no difference between the Auto-Tutor, the key card and indeed an army instructor.

Other researchers manipulated step size, presence or absence of rein-forcement, the deletion of branches, single versus group working and many other variables — I won't bother to review them.

By 1963 I had become pretty firmly convinced that a well written pro-gramme could be hacked about, the means of presentation and the conditions of learning altered out of all recognition, and still the learners learned.

But what is a well written programme? I have seen some badly written programmes; programmes which missed out important logical steps in the argument, programmes with mistakes in them, programmes which were so boring that students must have found it very difficult to keep awake. But how do you make a good programme?

I was always rather unreceptive, not to say hostile, to the conventional Skinnerian doctrine and I was unable to find any clues in it which seemed to me really helpful. Short steps — yes, that seemed a sensible idea at least up to a point. But how big is a step? The old criterion of error rate is thoroughly unreliable. A too-long step can, in these terms, be made into an acceptably short step by a variety of means which more or less amounted to telling the student the answer. Activity on the part of the learner seemed a good idea, but what sort of activity? The activity of checking a multiple-choice answer or moving the answer shield down the page was perhaps enough to keep the student awake — a minimal condition for learning — but was it enough to engage the attention, to help the student to formulate his own solutions, to get him so interested he would like to learn some more?

Reinforcement of each step? Well, you can hardly argue with that. One does not have to be an ardent S-R theorist to see that at some stage the student must be made aware of what the right answer is. I have underlined the triviality of the way 'reinforcement' is used in a few paragraphs in my book 'Feedback and Human Behaviour'. Back in 1931 E L Thorndike demonstrated in several learning tasks, typically of the paired-associate type that unless the learner is told which response (or which answer — it's the same thing) is correct he will not learn. Thorndike's argument, that people would learn due to the process of reinforcement, is fallacious. The simple fact is that until the experimenter or the teacher specifies 'the correct answer' there is nothing to be learned.

To say that learning is due to reinforcement can only be **either** a trivial restatement of the fact that until the learner is told what he has to learn he cannot do it **or** if it is intended to mean something else, like strengthening S-R associations, that it does not follow. It seems to me that many people, including psychologists are still basically confused about the meaning, or rather the lack of meaning of the term 'reinforcement'. But let me return to the question of 'how do you write a good programme?'

The generally recognized starting point is **the end** — that is what behaviour one wishes to achieve. The so-called terminal behaviour is often pretty complex. In one of his early papers on programmed learning Skinner remarked that high school mathematics could be broken down into something like 25,000 individual responses which had to be learned. He never did say how he arrived at this number (even assuming it to be approximate) nor what 'breaking it down' means.

In 1957 two relevant and quite contradictory books had been published, and in retrospect it seems a pity that workers in programmed learning did not, apparently, think of what they were doing in terms of these two books. The books I refer to are Skinner's 'Verbal Behaviour' and Chomsky's 'Syntactic Structures'. In 'Verbal Behaviour' Skinner pushed the notion of operant conditioning to its limits, and indeed beyond. Verbal behaviour, or language is seen as being acquired by reinforcement and shaping procedures. Mothers talk to their babies, they say 'milk' when offering a drink, and 'Dada' when father comes. These words can become conditioned stimuli for appropriate responses. Similarly children are taught to ask by making reinforcements contingent on a noise approximating the name of the desired thing.

Chomsky, on the other hand, believed language to be based on very different principles. Language seems to involve a system for generating

2

meaningful sentences and not just those which have actually occurred in the history of a particular individual, but a system for generating any conceivable sentence in a given language. Chomsky's notion of grammar is of a set of rules which makes it possible to utter sentences and to recognize whether sentences are meaningful in a particular language. One of the arguments against the Skinnerian theory is that by a conditioning process it will probably take more than a lifetime for an individual to achieve the level of language of which he is capable by adolescence. The Skinnerian theory is reasonably plausible in relation to learning the meanings of individual words, but it is implausible when applied to a more significant unit of language – the sentence. The classical short step overt response frame of a linear programme treats the missing word as the response to be conditioned to the preceding stimuli – the earlier parts of the sentence. The evidence from psycholinguistics makes this 'chain-response' type of interpretation totally implausible. The process of generating sentences anticipates the end. The phrases fall into a structure which the speaker must have 'in his head' before beginning to utter the first word.

There is an analogy with making a skilled response such as a tennis stroke. When well executed there is a pattern of precisely timed movements leading towards the stroke and the follow through. Just as in skilled movements precise repetition of a specifically learned sequence is the exception rather than the rule. Actors have to take great pains to learn their lines and speakers their scripts, but in normal conditions of conversation and question and answer, meaningful sentences are adapted to precisely the unique ongoing conversation.

Perhaps it should strike us as strange that programmes designed to teach highly complex linguistic skills should be based on such an inadequate model and yet still, apparently, work well enough. Fortunately, both the programme writers and the students have sufficient language competence to get by and the structure of a linear programme has enough 'slack' in it to be only marginally constricting.

Before trying to draw out some of the implications of what I have been saying about the inadequacy of the Skinnerian model of language I should like to return to my historical thread.

By 1963 I had become interested in industrial training. The next year brought the Industrial Training Act and the involvement of Government in promoting training. After carefully studying Bloom's Taxonomy of Educational Objectives, concept charts and even mathetics, I found a helpful way of looking at the analysis of subject matter, or more specifically of analysing industrial tasks.

In 1960 George Miller, who had taken Chomsky's side along with Eugene Galanter, who you may remember published one of the earliest collections of

papers on programmed instruction, and a very gifted neurophysiologist Karl
Proban published a book called 'Plans and the Structure of Behaviour'. In
my view this elegant book struck the death blow to S-R psychology. It contained a new idea for a behavioural unit — not a stimulus-response unit but
a TOTE unit. TOTE stands for test, operatem test, exit. Any coherent
piece of behaviour is describable as a feedback loop. You are probably familiar with the TOTE description of how to hammer a nail into a piece of wood.
The initial indication — the stimulus if you like, is a discrepancy between
what is wanted and what is the case. Is the nail flush? Answer 'no'. Operate
— hammer — test again — no — hammer — test again — yes — exit. One of
the many things which can be said about the TOTE unit is that a stimulus is
seen not just as something which starts a piece of behaviour but also as
something which stops it.

Things which stop activity are as important as things which start it.
Suppose you are a trainee cook. In making a cake one might read in a recipe
book: beat the mixture to a soft dropping consistency. Now anyone can beat,
but can everyone recognize a soft dropping consistency? It would be helpful
to have a demonstration — to have someone point to a mixture which has
reached a soft dropping consistency. We found that many industrial tasks
involved learning to recognize signals which indicate the response or activity
has been successfully completed. The reason for this is fairly obvious. The
essence of many tasks is essentially like aiming at a target, achieving a goal
with the minimum of effort. The TOTE unit is a way of describing how goals
can be achieved.

Another feature of the TOTE unit is particularly important. The actual
piece of behaviour described can be big or very small. Hammering a single
nail is a pretty small chunk of behaviour, but one could describe building a
house as a TOTE. Is the house complete — no — build it — is the house complete — yes — stop building it! The logic of the TOTE is the same in both
cases, but the house building TOTE is not much help, especially if you don't
know how to perform the operation part, or don't know what the house is supposed to look like when you have finished it. It would be easier to manage if
one broke the operation down into say, digging foundations, building walls,
making roofs. I hope you can readily see that each of these smaller TOTES
can be included in the house-building TOTE. You might call them sub-TOTES.
What I have just described can be called a nested hierarchy of TOTES.

In practical terms the task analyst has to tease out the hierarchical structure of the task and this is what Keith Duncan has expounded so well in his
chapter in Jim Hartley's recent book 'Strategies for Programmed Instruction'.
The significance of this approach for learning and teaching can be contrasted
with the classical S-R approach which goes at the task of teaching rather like
adding new beads to a string. We can approach teaching by asking ourselves

4

the question what it is which prevents the learner from performing in the ways in which the skilled man behaves. Generally the answers can be of two kinds. On the one hand some of the essential sub-TOTES or sub-sub-TOTES may not be present in his repertoire. Second, the plan which puts the sub-TOTES into the overall TOTE may be missing or inadequate. Let me give an example of each. A typewriter firm which was concerned about a 25% reject rate on a production line, largely due to the ineffective assembly of a single part. The instructions on the Task Analysis Sheet told the assembly worker exactly what to do, but it did not tell them what the assembly should feel and sound like when properly put together. This turned out to be an essential test in a sub-TOTE which had been omitted. Five minutes instruction was sufficient to put the matter right, and the reject rate of 25% fell to virtually nil.

In another case involving the operation of a complex refinery, the trainee process operators had been subjected to extensive training involving knowledge of chemistry, the machinery, with its various indicators and controls. This was a continuous production process and the main problem was to keep the refinery running once it had been started up. Of course valves stick, vessels leak and pipes burst and the effects of these become evident on the indicators in the control room.

What had the trainee to learn to do? In effect no pattern of faults ever repeats itself, so they had to learn to solve a general diagnostic problem. The training programme was based on an optimal search strategy, and it was very encouraging that a young apprentice, who had been through the new training scheme, correctly diagnosed a rather dangerous fault before the experienced supervisor had managed to find out what was going wrong.

I offer these industrial examples, partly because they come from my own experience, but partly because I believe that the hierarchical model can be applied to all compex learning tasks and that the lessons learned from analyzing industrial skills can be applied to intellectual skills. When learning theorists abandoned any terms used to describe **organization** in behaviour they abandoned something which is vital. One of the **organizational** terms which was used both by F C Bartlett and by Piaget is the notion of a **schema**.

The essence of a schema is that it is an organization which enables us to construct or reconstruct something. In Bartlett's memory experiments, for example, distortion of memory after a lapse of time could be attributed to the reorganization operating during the recall process. Neisser has a particularly colourful example. Remembering, he says, is like the palaeontologist digging up a few remains of a dinosaur and reconstructing a model of the original animal. What is stored is very little indeed. What is important is the ability to reconstruct the original.

The notion of being able to construct seems to be particularly important.

5

Chomsky speaks of language as if the essential feature of language competence were the ability to generate or construct meaningful sentences.

I have just been arguing that the ability to perform a complex task depends on an hierarchical structure rather like a computer programme with its stored sub-routines and an executive which brings them into play when needed. Performing a complex task is then a constructive process guided by a set of rules rather than a minutely controlled sequence of stimuli and responses.

I return to the question of what makes a good programme. One of the things which the World's best teachers seem to have done is to create a structure or a set of schemata, which enable the students to cope with problems. Good teachers probably teach relatively few facts or correct responses, but they organize material in such a way that students catch on to the essential schemata. They may not specify educational objectives in operational terms or painstakingly reinforce correct responses. But they produce new schemata, new ways of coping with the World.

At a much more modest level, hundreds of thousands of teachers are successful to the extent that they can help their students to organize their experience and to create for themselves. The necessary strategies for remembering things, solving problems and generally coping with their environment.

Those of you who are listening to me today, and can recall some of the things I talked about in glowing terms in the early 1960s, will have noticed a change. I want to assure you that the change is not essentially a softening of the head as a result of increasing age, but is rather representative of the new directions that psychology is now taking and has been taking over recent years. It would be a sad thing if the theoretical underpinnings of programmed learning and educational technology generally became intellectually stuck at the kind of learning theory the majority of psychologists thought useful in the middle 1950s.

The great disadvantage of what I have been saying is that it now seems a little less obvious how theory is translated into technology. The process of learning, once apparently so simple, is being revealed as many of us always thought it was, as extremely complex. If you like, learning psychology is in the process of sloughing off one schema and trying to formulate new ones to deal with the problems all too readily dismissed a few years ago.

I promised in my abstract that I would refer to computer assisted learning and artificial intelligence. In fact I have something on my conscience, an obligation which I need to discharge, but which nevertheless fits into the line I am taking in this paper.

In the summer of 1971 I helped to arrange a residential Seminar at Keele University under the auspices of the Social Science Research Council on the topic of Computer Assisted Instruction and Artificial Intelligence. I promised at that meeting to present some form of summary for the benefit of educational technologists.

The meeting arose out of a discussion, one might almost say an argument, between some of the groups who were then beginning research projects in Computer Assisted Instruction and some critics of these projects from amongst research groups working in Artificial Intelligence. Papers were presented by Roger Hartley and Derek Sleeman of Leeds, and Jim Howe and Sylvia Weir of Edinburgh, and on the Artificial Intelligence side there were contributions from Christopher Longrett-Higgins and Steven Izard of Edinburgh, Max Clewes and Robin Stanton from Sussex, and Ted Alcock from Aberdeen. I shall not attempt a blow-by-blow account of what was said, but only try to summarize the main lines of the debate and indicate what I believe were the useful outcomes.

No doubt this audience is already familiar with the main lines of CAI work currently being pursued. Three types of activity were discussed at the meeting. The first is exemplified by the LOGO system developed by Feurzeig and Papart at MIT. LOGO is a simple programming language which can be taught to nine or ten year olds. The programme provides instructions which can be used, for example, to produce pictures on an oscilloscope or make a little mechanical robot (called a turtle) wander about the floor. The children who learn LOGO make up their own programmes to draw flowers or faces or generate designs on the screen or make the turtle draw them on the floor with a felt tipped pen. The computer is used in a more or less ad lib way, often the children suggesting their own tasks and then writing the appropriate programmes. The supposed value of the programming activity is that LOGO problems can be described in terms of **procedures**, a procedure being a set of instructions like a cooking recipe. Papart and Feurzeig argue that constructive thinking and problem solving is a matter of discovering procedures and they even use the slogan 'knowledge is procedures'. I should point out that procedures are not necessarily invariant sequences, but are rather guiding rules. One of the things a child programmer learns is that some procedures are used recurrently so that they don't have to be written again and again and hence you need a higher order procedure to specify when or how often the relevant subprocedure is to be used.

For example, to get the turtle to draw a square on the floor you need a procedure for moving so far in a straight line and then making a 90° turn. You just need to specify it once, but then you need another procedure to count the number of turns and to stop the turtle after four. I need hardly point out that there is at least a superficial similarity between the notion of a procedure and the notion of a schema, of a TOTE, and perhaps even of a generative grammar. They all refer to systems for organizing and producing behaviour.

The second general category of CAI work is gaming and simulation. PLATO III or PLATO IV at Illinois exemplify this use of the computer in programmes which enable the student to mount an experiment in symbolic form. For example in teaching genetics, experiments involving the breeding of fruit flies are often used. The breeding process takes about three weeks or much longer if your flies die or fail to breed. The PLATO programme generates populations of fruit flies with known characteristics which can then be selectively cross-bred. The computer, in fact, constructs the new population according to the known rules of the genetics and it does it very fast indeed. Similar work is in progress at Leeds in chemistry, allowing students to conduct chemical experiments symbolically. The basic aim, of course, is to teach scientific methodology and a design of experiments, but the general question raised is, how does one represent the structure of a subject matter or a skill inside a computer in order to provide the student with a means of exploring this structure?

The third general type of CAI is what might be called 'controlled learning' and it includes both drill and practice, for example of the type developed by Suppées at Stanford, and interactive tutorial types of instruction. At its simplest controlled learning is no more than a 'beefed-up' branching programme, but it can involve the use of interesting adaptive strategies. Examples of this type of CAI are pretty well known from work at Leeds, Sheffield and Edinburgh and so I will not elaborate.

What then of Artificial Intelligence? Computers are basically stupid, in fact very stupid indeed, since they do only precisely what they are instructed to do. Teaching on the other hand is a very intelligent activity. How can you make computers intelligent enough to be entrusted with the task of teaching people? It is certainly easy to stuff a computer full of knowledge, but this will not make the computer capable of interpreting questions and being able to produce appropriate answers or to judge the appropriateness of answers offered by the student.

Take a very simple case. The computer prints a problem $3 + 2 = ?$ The student types in his answer '1'. A teacher, a human teacher, would provide help by saying something like "+ means add, not take away". In other words, the teacher has an understanding of what in all probability produced the answer '1' rather than say 5 or 6 or -1. At this level it is not too difficult to programme conditional rules of this kind into a computer. Clewes illustrated the problem of getting the computer to 'understand' in the context of recognizing three dimensional objects from two dimensional displays, such as photographs or TV pictures of objects. One way to start is to take account of the gradients of light intensity. This enables the computer to detect edges and boundaries and it can then specify what edges meet at what angles. Since some edges would be created by shadows cast by the object

8

rather than being part of the object itself we have a major source of possible confusions. The problem can only be circumvented if the system knows what 3-D shapes can possibly be constructed out of the collection of edges and their orientations it has detected. In this simple sense the computer has to know what the real world is like, just as a competent speaker has to know what grammatical constructions are possible. In fact Clewes's programme can distinguish between real objects and illusory 3-dimensional figures.

The same general point was made by Izard. One of the difficulties of having a conversation with a computer is that natural conversations are only partially explicit, and a conversation is only possible when the two participants share a good deal of knowledge about the subject of the conversation. Conversations in which everything was made entirely explicit would be long-winded indeed, but sometimes vague conversations can be made to look real enough. It has been found possible to use relatively unintelligent programmes with a very limited ability to recognize parts of speech and to use a very limited set of rules. Take as an example this conversation between a young woman and a computer programme called DOCTOR constructed by Wefsenbaum of MIT.

In what way
- They're always bugging on about something or other
Can you think of a specific example
- Well, my boyfriend made me come here
Your boyfriend made you come here
- He says I'm depressed much of the time
I'm sorry to hear you are depressed
- It's true. I am unhappy
Do you think coming here will help you not to be unhappy
- I need some help. That much seems certain
What would it mean to you if you got some help
- Perhaps I could learn to get along with my mother
Tell me more about your family
- My mother takes care of me
Who else in your family takes care of you
- My father
Your father
- You are like my father in some ways
What resemblance do you see
- You are not very aggressive but I think you don't want me to notice that
What makes you think I am not very aggressive
- You don't argue with me
Why do you think I don't argue with you
- You are afraid of me
Does it please you to believe I am afraid of you
- My father is afraid of everybody
What else comes to mind when you think of your father

9

The conversation is a total fake — the computer has not really understood anything that was said to it, and if you look carefully you will find that it does not produce any new information or advice — it simply echoes in various ways what has been said.

Something approaching a breakthrough in the crucial question of 'understanding' can be seen in the work of Terry Winograd, also of MIT. The universe of discourse — a miniature world consisting of simple 3-dimensional objects — is completely specified in a programme called Micro-planner. Here is an example of a conversation with Micro-planner.

- Will you please stack up both of the red blocks and either a green cube or a pyramid?
  OK
- Which cube is sitting on the table?
  The large green one which supports the red pyramid
- Is there a large block behind a pyramid?
  Yes, three of them: a large red one, a large green cube and the blue one
- Put a small one onto the green cube which supports a pyramid
  OK
- Put the littlest pyramid on top of it
  OK
- Does the shortest thing the tallest pyramid's supports, support anything green?
  Yes, the green pyramid
- What color is it?
  By "it" I assume you mean the shortest thing the tallest pyramid's support supports Red
- How many things are on top of green cubes?
  I'm not sure what you mean by "on top of" in the phrase "on top of green cubes"
  Do you mean:
          1 - Directly on the surface
          2 - Anywhere on top of?
- Anywhere on top of
  Three of them
- Had you touched any pyramid before you put the green one on the little cube?
  Yes, the green one
- When did you pick it up?
  While I was stacking up the red cube, a large red block and a large green cube
- Why?
  To get rid of it
- Why did you do that?
  To clean off the red cube
- Why did you clean off that cube?
  To put it on a large green cube
- Why did you do that?
  To stack up the red cube a large red block and a large green cube
- Why did you do that?

Because you asked me to

- How did you do it?
  By putting a large red block on the table; then letting go of it;
  then putting a large green cube on it; then letting go of that cube;
  then putting the red cube on that cube; then letting go of that cube

- How many objects did you touch while you were doing it?
  Four of them

- What did the red cube support before you started to clean it off?
  The green pyramid

- There were five blocks to the left of the box then
  No, only four of them: the red cube, two large green cubes and
  a large red block

● ● ●

- Thank you
  You're welcome!   (From Winograd 1970, pp. 35-60)

It is perhaps worth noting that the programme which does this takes all
of 256 K of store to operate even in this simple world which in some reasonable sense it understands. The programme understands in the sense that it
not only interprets questions, but knows how to go and look for the correct
answer.

If it is true that computers will not make good and effective teachers
until they are capable of understanding natural language and until they can
see not only that an error has been made but also what sort of mistake it is
and why it has been made, then the road to CAI will be long and vastly expensive. As Longuit-Higgins put it: the human student is a rather rich information source. Reducing him to a sort of morse code consisting of a string of
multiple-choice answers we lose a lot of this information and so reduce the
possibility of understanding his difficulties.

What then can work on artificial intelligence offer CAI? People in CAI
are looking for techniques which might be helpful, for example better methods
of interpreting student response or of modelling behaviour or of modelling
the structure of a subject matter. It emerged, however, that for the time
being at least artificial intelligence workers are more concerned with modelling basic Cognitive processes than being able to improve the practical technology of CAI. Some of the experimental psychologists present were rather
critical of artificial intelligence. Everyone agreed that if you can get your
theory of pattern recognition or problem solving or whatever to work on a
computer it is at least a self consistent theory and the modelling process is
a very rigorous way of demonstrating this. On the other hand it could be
argued that one has to have made some kind of psychological analysis of the
intelligent operation to be modelled before one can start to write the programme. Computer programmes of the conventional sort don't work like
human beings at all. One has to have an idea of what human beings do before
tackling the difficult task of making a computer behave like one. A.I.

programmes, don't in themselves solve psychological or educational problems. They just demonstrate that the problem has or has not been solved.

My talk this afternoon has wandered some distance from the conventional
field of educational technology, so let me try to bring it down to earth.

One can look at technology from two points of view. One can start with a
theory provided by basic research and look around for means of applying it to
the general human good. This I suggest is the way we looked at the science of
learning and problems of teaching in the late 1950s and early 1960s.

Another way is to start with the problems and look around for means of
solving them. I suggest we should think more in this problem oriented way.
In the early days we came along with machines and programmes and asked
can they be applied to children, to adults, to mathematics, to history and so
on. In doing this we ignored some of the problems which were there. Only
a minute proportion of the problems of education can be solved by using currently viable technology. We have a technology of communication through the
media — we can transmit information more widely than ever before. But our
technology for answering questions, for proving information which is required,
not just dishing it out wholesale is grossly underdeveloped. One of the reasons
is that it involves intensely difficult questions to do with the nature of cognition,
questions of what it means to be capable of doing something, to be able to
understand something. Psychologists are as much to blame as anyone else
for oversimplifying the problems but, as I have tried to indicate in the earlier
parts of my paper, the psychological scene has changed a great deal in recent
years and particularly in those areas to do with thinking, knowing and learning
which are at the heart of the educational process.

It would be unwise to promise too much — to suggest that new types of
learning theory will emerge on which a new technology, perhaps involving
computers could be based. A great deal of fundamental thinking still has to
go on. If this sounds like a pessimistic note, may I just end by saying that
the existence of an educational technology, however inadequate, is a spur to
research and is a way of making us face up to some fundamental problems
which might otherwise lie dormant for a very long time. Just at present the
need to technologize education is only just beginning. The World can almost
get by, by using conventional methods, but during the next decade or so the
gap between what educational resources are needed and what our pockets can
provide will get bigger and bigger. We had better get started before it is too
late.

The Development of the Research Work on Programmed Instruction in the USSR

T A ILYINA

As a scientific problem, Programmed Instruction attracted the attention of the Soviet specialists in pedagogy and psychology about ten years ago. Like all educationalists in the world we started by studying those main ideas and principles of Programmed Instruction which were developed in the USA (Ilyina, 1963; 1965; Maslova, 1964) and which, later on were applied, with certain modifications, in other countries, including Great Britain (Ilyina, 1964; 1967) and Japan (Ilyina, 1969).

Very soon the idea of the cybernetical approach as a theoretical basis for Programmed Instruction (Berg, 1966) was established in our country. It was admitted that the theory of algorithms (Landa, 1966), and the main psychological concepts of the educational process (Talisina, 1969), as well as the general theory of education (Schapovalenko, 1965) developed by Soviet educationalists could be successfully used in working out various programmed materials including technical aids such as different kinds of teaching machines and classes with automatic feedback equipment. Almost all types of educational establishments of the Soviet system of public education; general secondary and secondary specialized schools; institutions of higher learning and professional schools; have joined the research work since it started in 1962/63. In the process of this research, many experimental programmed textbooks covering parts of instructional courses and even whole courses were created and tested. Almost all of them, at that initial stage, were based on the principles of linear programming offered by Professor B F Skinner or branching programming developed by N Crowder though even at that time several minor technical modifications had been introduced, especially in connection with the type of assignment which the student had to perform in the process of working on the program. The assignments become more varied and were aimed at activization of different mental processes.

By the middle of the sixties the Soviet specialists in programmed instruction stated that all the instructional programs should be classified into several types:

(a) **fully programmed textbooks** covering all stages of the educational process beginning with the introduction of the new study material, its retention and final testing in which all the main principles of programmed instruction may be (and should be) realized and which may be designed for completely independent work with only occasional help or consultation given by the teacher;
(b) **programmed supplements to ordinary textbooks** which give the student detailed instructions on what to do with the textbooks, several assignments for checking comprehension of the material and key answers to them. This type of programmed material helps, to a certain extent, in the application of the main principles of programmed instruction to independent work with ordinary textbooks;
(c) **programmed exercise books** of various kinds which help to facilitate the retention of the new material and in which one of the main principles of programmed instruction viz step-by-step checking is realized. Programmed exercise books are most effectively used with the help of special types of teaching machines which incorporate feedback facilities;
(d) **test-books** which may be considered as programmed materials and especially so when they are applied at the final stage of learning for checking knowledge acquired through using programmed textbooks and also when they are designed to be used with a testing machine which gives immediate feedback.

Intensive research work had been carried out to elaborate the main principles of constructing these programmed instructional materials (The Problems of PI at School, 1966; The Problems of Experimental Testing of the Methodology of PI, 1970) and by the end of the sixties they were formulated in a series of step-by-step instructions, including the stage of analysing the study material and the aims of teaching (Ilyina, 1969). In these instructional materials the above mentioned types of programmed items were analysed and treated separately but the main recommendation was to work on a system of interconnected programmed learning textbooks of different instructional functions, the example of which may be given by a series of experimental programmed textbooks 'Programmed English' for the beginners (which we have brought here). This series includes: programmed textbooks for pupils, eight exercise books of different kinds, two textbooks and two manuals for the teachers (Ilyina, 1966/67)

By this time the main concepts of programmed instruction as a new field in didactics had been formulated. Programmed instruction at present is considered as a kind of independent work of students which may be carried on more effectively as it is guided by the program itself. Additionally the programmed textbooks usually arouse more interest in the pupils than the ordinary textbooks. When programmed materials are used in schools, the work with them should be combined with other methods of instruction and

14

collective forms of work. Special research work has shown that the best duration periods for individual independent work at a lesson should be no more than 15-20 minutes in the 5th - 8th forms and about 30 minutes in the senior forms. In institutions of higher learning these periods may be prolonged, particularly if programmed learning is used at times given to students for independent work. At present, as new contents of education are being introduced in Soviet schools, and textbooks on all the school subjects have been written anew, there are practically no programmed textbooks on any subjects in our schools. Most programmed materials are at present published for institutions of higher learning. Nevertheless the testing of various kinds of experimental programmed materials is being evaluated. In schools where there are feedback classes, some kind of programmed card with exercises or tests are frequently used. As a rule these are produced by the school teachers themselves.

The main trends in the development of programmed instruction in our country correspond in theory and practice with the trends in world didactics which are treated as problems in the field of educational technology: (1) technology in education, and (2) technology of education.

The Soviet research workers are well informed of what is going on in this field abroad and compare it with the present trends and tendencies in the same field in our country (Ilyina, 1971; 1973). The first line of the development of these trends (technology in education) includes the closely connected trends: (a) the multi-media approach, ie the use of several kinds of technical aids and teaching machines in complex combination, and (b) construction of teaching materials for the main modern technical aids using the principles of programmed instruction (for example: programmed tape-recorded exercises, programmed film-strips, etc).

It should be mentioned that at present considerably more has been done in the field of research and the introduction into the educational process of different technical aids and the devices of programmed learning in various combinations, than in constructing teaching materials for these aids based on the principles of programmed instruction.

The second line of educational technology - the technology of education corresponds, in our country, to the trend in scientific and research work which is carried on in the field of methodology of education (system approach) and general didactics (strategies of education, etc). The systems approach as a new methodological concept has attracted the attention of Soviet scientists including specialists on education (Corolev, 1970; System Approach to the Research of Pedagogical Phenomena and Processes, 1971). We think that this approach opens great possibilities in the treatment and analysis of pedagogical phenomena and processes especially in the organization of the educational process and the whole system of public education. In a special course of lectures entitled 'The system approach to the organization of education', we deal with the theoretical aspects of this methodology and then show the possibility of applying this approach to the analysis of the study material (which is especially important for programmed instruction) to the organization of the study material of the system of textbooks and didactial aids designed for one course, then to the organization of the educational process (multi-media approach) and finally to the planning and to the making of a prognosis for the development of the whole system of public education of the country. This course of lectures is published in the three booklets (Ilyina, 1972, 1973).

Thus after a careful analysis of the many definitions of the main category of this approach, we have produced our own definition which will be probably considered rather long and clumsy but it reflects (to our mind) the main characteristics which one can find in all the other definitions.

"A system is a set of organized interconnected elements, united by the common goal of functioning and unity of guidance, and interacting with the surroundings as a whole."

In analysis of the study material (which may be also treated as a system) it is very important to identify the smallest particle of the elements of this system.

In didactics we are used to speaking about knowledge and skills. For the purposes of the system analysis it is more practical to speak about concept as the smallest element of knowledge and an operation as the smallest element of skills. As to the general didactical aspects of a technology of education we are at present concerned with two main problems: (a) which of the recent trends in didactics and modern educational ideas can be implemented in programmed instruction, and (b) in what way can the data of the research work in programmed instruction be used to enrich general didactics.

As is well known, the main stress in all modern theories of education is laid on the task of the development of mental abilities of pupils, such methods of teaching as those that can produce creative thinking. Soviet specialists in programmed instruction agree that it can offer many opportunities for the mental development of pupils by means of a proper arrangement of the steps of the program and giving special tasks and assignments for the pupils to perform. Very interesting research work in this field was carried out by a member of our laboratory of Programmed Instruction, S A Budassy, who proved that if the author of the program had in mind such an aim it could be effectively implemented in programmed materials (Budassy, 1973).

But as to creative thinking, programmed instruction can only perform a kind of preparatory work: with its aids the pupils can be trained to perform different mental operations and acquire such knowledge and skills as could, and should, be used in creative work. But the creative process cannot be guided by programmed textbooks: the products (results) of such work will be different in each individual case and therefore they cannot be compared with the key answers, thus the main principle of programmed instruction – step-by-step checking up cannot be realized.

Some points should be stressed in connection with the so called 'Problem solving instruction' which is so widely and favourably discussed by education-ists throughout the world. As we knew, problem solving instruction can be carried out on different levels depending on the pupils' participation in problem solving. It may be just listening to the teacher who tells about the means and ways which have lead to certain discoveries. Then it may be answering a teacher's questions presented in such a way as to help the pupils to find the solution of a problem. In this way the pupils are more active but their activity is guided by the leading questions of the teacher. The students are most active when they try to solve the problem independently, analyse the given conditions and data, put forward several variants of solving the problem, try them, find the correct way for solving it, search for the methods of checking it up and proving its fitness, etc. We think that the first two types of pupils' activities and their participation in problem solving can be easily guided by programmed materials. As to the third type which is similar to research work and requires creative thinking, this situation is the same as the problem of developing creative thinking by means of pro-grammed instruction – programmed instruction cannot fulfil such a task, it should be done by other means which will stimulate the mental activities of the pupils involved in the process of problem solving.

Individualization of education is the third modern didactical problem which arouses much discussion and is the object of intensive research work. This work has been intensified in connection with the introduction of universal secondary education in our country. It is well known that the effectiveness of the whole educational process depends on the level of activity and achieve-ments of each individual pupil. In our country the main aim of the research work in this field is to find the ways and means of creating those conditions of learning in which each pupil will be able to acquire the amount of knowledge prescribed by the State Syllabi: Soviet scientists and teachers admit that each pupil has individual peculiarities and characteristics of cognitive abilities but at the same time we agree that every normally developing child should be given all the opportunities to exercise his right to get a complete secondary education, the standard of which is at present rather high. So we think that our main task is to render the necessary help to all those who need it and to do our best to develop their cognitive abilities in the process of well organized and directed learning. In trying to find better ways of organizing the educational process the Soviet scientists look for the means among both the ordinary methods and teaching aids and among those new aids and means born by programmed instruction. Though the words 'programmed instruction' are used almost as a synonym for 'individualized education' Soviet educationalists think that it should not be treated in such a way because, in view of our main aim of directing the educational process, its opportunities are rather limited. That means that we cannot and do not offer pupils with different abilities a different amount of knowledge, we cannot lessen the amount of knowledge prescribed by the State documents on the standards of education, but we certainly can offer some additional material to those who are interested – through the so-called elective courses, extra-curricular activities, additional tasks, etc. Thus we must use programmed textbooks first of all as a means of helping those who have experienced some difficulty in understanding and remembering the material while working in the classroom with all the other pupils.

But as was said before, the research work in this field showed that it is not reasonable to offer programmed instruction for a period longer than 20-30 minutes at a time and that it should be combined with other methods and means of education. Therefore we agree that it is quite possible and reasonable to use the techniques implemented in the linear and especially in the branching programs (as well as in all their variants and combinations) for the purpose of making the process of learning more individualized, provided the programmed materials are designed exclusively for the student's independent work.

It was also suggested that programmed materials could be used to advantage by those who meet with difficulties while working at home with ordinary textbooks or by those who for some reason or another have missed many classes and need to catch up with their classmates. As a consequence we feel that there is a need for writing programs on the most difficult parts of the course, which may serve as a duplicate to the corresponding chapters in ordinary school textbooks. The so-called adaptive programming is not considered to be very appropriate for individualized teaching in Soviet educational establishments, especially so in the secondary schools, where all the pupils must acquire a definitely prescribed amount of knowledge. We think that all the advantages of programmed instruction as individualized instruction could really be utilized when the student is interested in the subject and studies that subject either for the sake of enriching his knowledge or just merely for pleasure.

We have presented here but a few examples of the points of intersection and connection of some didactical concepts with the general ideas and principles of programmed instruction. Our general evaluation of programmed instruction as a new means of education is rather moderate: we think that it should be used along with the other means and aids which can activize the teaching and learning process and help the pupils to acquire a firm and lasting knowledge. It should be used more widely in those educational establishments where independent work is the main feature of the educational process (in learning by correspondence, in evening classes etc); but we also think that all modern trends and ideas of activizing the mental processes and stimulating the cognitive activities of pupils should be applied (with some restrictions) to writing programmed materials. At the same time the intensive research on programmed instruction as a problem of modern didactics has already given results, the implementation of which can enrich the general theory of education. Thus 'algorithmicization' of education, the theoretical aspects and practical application of which were formed in the process of elaborating the theory and methodology of programmed instruction is considered at present as a constitutional part of didactics dealing with the methods and means of mental development of children in the process of education.

The detailed analysis of aims of teaching, the structural analysis of teaching materials, the step-by-step planning of the learning process is a great contribution to the general development at the textbook theory. It may even be said that the methodology of writing programmed textbooks has laid a firm basis for this theory. The research work in the evaluation of knowledge in programmed instruction and in raising the level of every day control of the pupil's achievements stimulated the work on tests as one of the means of objective evaluation of acquired knowledge which were not popular in our country until different kinds of teaching machines and feedback classes became available. (In order to use most types of such equipment, assignments with multiple choice answers were required.)

This list of contributions made by the research on the problem of programmed instruction to pedagogy can be prolonged. Also the elements of this methodology may be applied to writing ordinary textbooks (as for example has been done in my textbook 'Pedagogy' (Ilyina, 1969) for future teachers). Nevertheless we must agree that the investigation of the possibilities of programmed instruction which as a problem of didactics reflects the main tendencies in the development of modern science and technology is far from complete. The problem does not exhaust itself. On the contrary we think that only the first attempts to work out its theoretical bases have been made. The methodological implementation of all the new didactical concepts and ideas in program writing has only just been started. We do not think that proper research of the didactical functions and effectiveness of technical aids for programmed instruction has yet been undertaken. The research into the complex use of audiovisual aids and programmed instruction has only just been started. The whole technique of conducting research work on this problem, of collecting, analysing and interpreting the data needs special further investigation and elaboration. I think that the systems approach offers new ways and possibilities for effective research in the field of programmed instruction. The problem has many aspects which should become the object of a special discussion and on which the exchange of opinion is beneficial. From this point of view such representative international meetings are of great value to all the participants.

REFERENCES

Berg, A. I. (1966) 'The present situation and perspectives in the development of Programmed Instruction.' 'Znaniye', Moscow

Budassy, S. A. (1973) 'On the problem of developing thinking in Programmed Instruction'. In 'Problems of Theory and Methodology of Programmed Instruction'. Moscow Lenin State Pedagogical Institute

Corolev, F. F. (1970) 'System approach and its implementation in the research work in Pedagogy'. 'Soviet Pedagogy' No 9

Ilyina, T. A. (1963) 'About pedagogical basis of Programmed Instruction'. 'Soviet Pedagogy' No 8

Ilyina, T. A. (1964) 'Programmed Instruction in Great Britain'. 'Soviet Pedagogy' No 7

Ilyina, T. A. (1965) 'The new tendencies of Programmed Instruction in the USSR'. 'Soviet Pedagogy,' No 6

Ilyina, T. A. (1967) 'Methodology of Programming in Great Britain'. 'Soviet Pedagogy' No. 8

Ilyina, T. A. (1969) 'Programmed Instruction in Japan'. 'Soviet Pedagogy' No. 7

Ilyina, T. A. (1969) 'Pedagogy'. 'Prosveshenie' Moscow

Ilyina, T. A. (1969) 'Problems of Methodology of Programming'. 'Znaniye' Moscow

Ilyina, T. A. (1971) 'The Concepts of 'Educational Technology' in Pedagogy Abroad'. 'Soviet Pedagogy' No 9

Ilyina, T. A. (1972) 'System Approach to the Organisation of Education'. 'Znaniye' Moscow, part 1-2, part 3, 1973

Ilyina, T. A. (1973) 'System approach to education in Pedagogy abroad'. 'Soviet Pedagogy' No 3

Ilyina, T. A. and Charckovsky, Z. S. (1966-7) 'Programmed English'. Moscow State Pedagogical Institute

Landa, L. N. (1966) 'Algorithmization of Education'. 'Prosvesheniye'

Maslova, G. G. (1964) 'Programmed Instruction in Mathematics'. 'Uchpedgiz' Moscow

Schapovalenko, S. G. (1965) 'Theoretical Problems of Programmed Instruction'. Moscow State Lenin Pedagogical Institute

'System approach to the research of Pedagogical phenomena and Processes'. (1971) 'Soviet Pedagogy' No 1

Talisina, N. F. (1969) 'Theoretical Problems of Programmed Instruction'. Moscow State University

'The Problems of Programmed Instruction at School'. Moscow State Lenin Pedagogical Institute (1966)

'The Problems of Experimental Testing of the Methodology of Programmed Instructions'. (1970) Moscow State Lenin Pedagogical Institute

APPENDIX I

PROGRAMMING AN ENGLISH COURSE FOR RUSSIAN CHILDREN

The research was aimed at finding efficient ways of including programmed instruction in to the teaching process as an integral part of it, ie in combination with traditional school methods that had proved to be the most effective and suited up-to-date requirements and educational goals. Hence in planning a programmed English language course for children of the general school fifth year form we saw our task to write not separate programs that could be occasionally used in class or individual work at home, but a unified complex set of teaching materials in which the new instructional methods of teaching a foreign language and the principles of programmed instruction would be implemented as an integral whole.

Programmed instruction materials are considered as aids for individual study independent of the teacher. Such study could take place at the lesson in an ordinary classroom, in the language laboratory and at home while the student is preparing his homework. The learning procedure in these cases is such that it could include only a definitely determined behaviour. There are however speech activities that cannot be practically realized and controlled without immediate guidance by the foreign language instructor. Free spontaneous situational speech is a heuristic process where no definite keys to answers could be supplied. The program constructor can hardly be expected to write a program that would effectively teach the student verbal expression of his thoughts. Hence the task in planning and constructing a programmed course that would cover a whole year of school language studies is a problem of combining both heuristic and determined speech behaviour.

Thus there are actually two approaches to the construction of such a language course: the first presumes the writing of a set of genuine language programs and thus planning the individual activities of the students; the second implies programming the whole process of teaching and learning combining both individual and collective speech activities in classes guided by a teacher. Programmed teaching technology cannot cover all the stages of skills and habits in learning a foreign language. But the more advanced the students are, the more speech activities may be taught through the use of programmed instruction, and the more time may be allotted to it either directly as at a lesson or in the language laboratory. But there should always be place for a direct intercourse between the students and the teacher and for collective all-class activities. At the same time the students' homework can be completed with the help of programmed teaching materials. Modern methods of teaching a foreign language presume that at the initial stage the lesson is to be composed chiefly of exercises training the students in constructing and using speech patterns. As for information about the language system and structures, the students may easily find it in programs.

Hence, while planning the system of necessary exercises the following was taken into consideration:

(1) each exercise must be supplied with a key-answer that would facilitate control, ie feedback on the inner level linking the student with the program;

(2) the exercise should require a short report which also facilitates individual self-checking;

(3) each exercise should present but only one difficulty for the student;

(4) the exercises must be concrete and definite and never mislead the students' comprehension of how it should be performed.

In accordance with those requirements the multiple-choice type of exercise was widely used, and aimed at mapping the skill and habits of vocabulary and sentence-patterns usage. The multiple-choice type assignment was also used for testing and assessing the students' achievements.

The whole teaching process was organized, directed and controlled by means of an elaborate teaching aid for the teacher.

Following the main points of consideration above, the scheme was implemented in a teaching set that included:

(1) three 'Programmed English' textbooks consisting of 100 lessons;

(2) six programmed exercise books;

(3) multiple-choice training exercises (in one booklet);

(4) tape-recorded exercises to each lesson (in one separate book for a teacher);

(5) multiple-choice tests;

(6) a teachers' manual (in two books);

(7) visual aids for teaching reading skills (reading of separate letters, combinations of letters, words and phrases) spelling and all kinds of other visual aids, such as pictures, substitution tables, film strips etc.

Each of the 100 lessons of 'Programmed English', ie the main textbook for the student, is constructed of frames. The pedagogical function of the frames are numerous: some supply information only, others present tasks, some are combined-offering both information and a certain assignment. A series of frames deals with one teaching point, leads to learning a linguistic phenomenon or mastering to a certain degree a particular language skill, the proficiency degree of which has been previously planned. The frames differ in size, but as a rule, they contain only a few printed lines of information to make the student concentrate on one item and perform only one mental or verbal operation.

The pages are divided in such a way that the check yourself answers and prompts are placed in the frame and immediately below the assignment, an arrangement experimentally found to be most suitable.

The lessons are grouped in thematical series such as 'My Day', 'My Room', 'Winter Sports' etc. Having worked through the frames of one lesson the student masters one or two speech patterns, mainly a unity of a question-answer pattern, the question structure being assimilated before the answer.

Each topical section of the lesson is followed by a review set of frames: reading, writing and grammar rules presented in tables and speech patterns.

The list of 'Words to Learn' and 'Patterns to Learn' precedes each lesson. During class hours, studying under the guidance of the teacher, the students work at substitutional tables, this being accomplished through a fill-in – the blanks assignment in a unified series of frames. Prompts are gradually diminished so as to bring the student to a fully unprompted reconstruction of the pattern, this being consolidated in frames and lessons following later on. The frames also lead the student on to reading the texts and a conscious and free use of the patterns in situational speech.

The material for reading in each lesson is not only purely textual: the frames presented by way of a dialogue and question-answer frames are also used for practice in reading and comprehension. The contents of these frames being played back by a tape recorder serve as speech material for oral comprehension practice. The lessons include such forms of work and assignments that presume a simultaneous and combined use of the book and the tape recorder. Almost every lesson contains a little poem or a song to learn.

Working at the frames the students receive information on the grammar rules, reading and spelling additional to that introduced and explained by the teacher orally in class. The assignments given at the initial stage in Russian are gradually presented in English. Special signs are used for commands to work with the tape recorder.

Most of the tape-recorded exercises are directly included into the second half of the lessons (lessons 56 - 100). All of these are summarized in print in a special edition for the teacher, the necessary stress, intonation and working pauses being pointed out. This is of great help to the teacher in cases where there are no tape-recorders available. It enables him also to use those exercises in class.

The 'Programmed English' textbook is illustrated by simple match-stick drawings accompanying the frames of the lessons. In many cases they help to avoid direct translation when new vocabulary or speech patterns are introduced. The frames are not specially designed for classwork or homework. Some of them, according to the instructions given in the teacher's handbook, may be used in class, but others are for individual homework.

A further consolidation and development of language performance is afforded in the programmed exercise notebook and the multiple-choice training exercises. Here the vocabulary and speech patterns are repeated in many different variants, thus facilitating recapitulation and involuntary memorization. One of the important features of the programmed multiple choice exercises is the additional information supplied after the exercise arranged on framed cards. This information is arranged in the form of an algorithm. The exercises may be used both with the help of teaching machines or without them. In the latter case the number of the answer chosen is marked by the student in a special matrix card next to the number of the question. As a rule there are five questions or five problems to be solved in one card.

The multiple choice test for assessment control is presented to the students after each topical item. The books with the tests are given to each student at the beginning of the lesson and are collected back after the performance. The tests include series according to the following items:
(a) 'Questions and Answers'
(b) 'Words'
(c) 'Sounds and Letters'
(d) 'Spelling'

These tests may also be done with the help of the machines 'examiners' or by using a matrix which is supplied in the students programmed exercise notebook. The keys to the tests and methods of scoring are available to the teacher in the teachers manual.

All this complex set of programmed materials is brought to a unified whole in the teachers' manual. Instructions are given as to the procedure of each lesson combining programmed and conventional methods. The approximate time allotted to the procedure operations are thoroughly stated and explained, thus enabling even an inexperienced teacher to work without making serious mistakes. At the same time those instructions do not limit a creative approach on the part of the teacher. Using sound judgement he may invent and apply new or additional ways and means that would suit the particular class situation, a definite teaching point or his own creative imagination.

Experimental research in the practical application of the complex set of programmed materials in the fifth forms of different schools in Moscow and several other cities and towns of the Soviet Union has shown a considerable rise in achieving a better performance on the part of the students in mastering language skills. It has met with marked approval from the teachers who have participated in the research work.

A carefully elaborated plan of experimental research has helped us in the process of using these programmed language courses to elaborate in detail and yet on a more general basis the problem of the technology of programmed instruction, ie applying to a wider scope of school subjects. The results achieved are stated in different publications and Proceedings of the Laboratory of Programmed Instruction of the Moscow State Lenin Pedagogical Institute.

Complexes of Teaching Aids

G G MASLOVA, S G SHAPOVALENKO

At present our school system is changing over to a new curriculum in all
the school subjects and program schedule. This is going along with the
introduction of universal secondary education.

As far as mathematics and science are concerned the program schedules
have been drawn up to enrich the content of education by the introduction of
new topics and new ideas of modern science and mathematics, showing the
pupils the spheres of its implementation, stressing the growing role of
science and mathematics in the industrial revolution, in the development of
society. The contents of the material studied by pupils is now richer, new
topics are included, new methods are taught. Great attention is paid to
acquiring the methods of investigation etc.

Here are a few examples:

The study of chemistry (7th to 10th grades) includes the fundamentals
of inorganic and organic chemistry. The 8th grade course covers the major
classes of inorganic compounds, the Periodic Law and Mendeleyev's periodic
system of elements; the structure of substances, chemical formulae and
equations, halogens, the oxygen group.

The systematic course in mathematics begins in the 4th grade (age 11+).
The negative numbers are studied in the 5th grade, vectors in the 7th grade,
the logarithmic function in the 8th grade, the derivative in the 9th grade,
the integral and simple differential equations in the 10th. It is necessary to
stress that all this material should be studied by all the pupils.

The new enriched contents of education and widening the goals of education require new methods, new teaching aids, the creation of the conditions
for successful learning, for acquiring by the pupils the large amount of
knowledge and skills, developing their mental abilities, creative thinking.
We have to help teachers to plan their work.

In this paper we will speak only about one aspect of the educational
technology of one of the possible ways to raise the efficiency of the educational process – that is – the working out of complexes of various teaching

aids and didactic materials. We attach a broad meaning to this term. The notion 'teaching aids' may include textbooks for pupils, different kinds of teachers' manuals or teachers' guides, materials for independent work of pupils, audiovisual aids, technical devices, etc. It is known that now more than 25 thousand firms and companies of the world are producing various audiovisual aids, and technical means (exhibition 'Didakta' 11, 1972, Hanover).

The great variety of these aids sometimes confuse a teacher. He does not know which is better (from the pedagogical point of view). So the great necessity is to work out for each school subject complexes of teaching aids. Each of these complexes should include the reasonable number of teaching aids of reasonable price (the schools usually have rather limited funds) and should help a teacher to instruct efficiently his pupils, using the modern and progressive methods and forms of organization of learning process.

So, the complexes of teaching aids is the set of tightly interconnected text materials, audiovisual aids and devices which should be used in the educational process. The selection and construction of these aids are made in accordance with the goals of education, contents of text material and methods of instruction. At the same time each complex should include the possible small number of teaching aids, each of them being of high quality from the pedagogical, psychological and aesthetical point of view.

The optimization of learning process by correct choosing and implementation of various teaching aids is one of the main tasks of educational technology and thus the problem of working out such complexes and providing schools with them is a vital importance for us.

The experimental studies have proved that the use of complexes of teaching aids give a wonderful effect and the great results are achieved in the shorter time. At present, this work in our country is being carried out by large groups of scientists headed by the members of the Academy of Sciences of the USSR and of the Academy of Pedagogical Sciences. The most intensive work is carried on in the Scientific Research Institute of Methods and Subject Matter of Learning, and in the Institute of School Equipment and Educational Technology of the Academy of Pedagogical Sciences.

In our paper we will give a short outline of this work. We have a centralized system of education. The program in all the subjects such as mathematics, physics, chemistry, etc should be approved by the Ministry of Education of the USSR. Syllabi in Mother Language, Geography, etc by the Ministries of Education of Republics. The program in each subject usually gives the general outline of the main topics and the time allocated to each topic. The technology of working out the complexes of teaching aids is based on the very elaborate research work of different scientific aspects of our syllabi and teaching materials, on the results of special pedagogical, psychological research. The process of constructing complexes of teaching aids includes several steps:

1. The description we want to have at the end of studying a certain topic.

2. The structural analysis of the study materials (its components – notions, relations and interconnections of facts, phenomena), conditions of formation of notions.

3. Outlining the logical connections of the components and didactic sequences of their presentation to pupils.

4. The grouping of components into units. Each unit covering the certain aspect of the topics studied.

5. Finding out the students' previous experience, on which the following instruction should be based.

6. Defining the content of cognitive actions which should lead pupils to acquiring certain facts, ideas, notions, methods, etc (experiments, reading textbooks, listening to teachers' presentation of materials, etc).

7. Working out the methods of teaching and the structure (organizational form) of a lesson or series of lessons.

8. Working out means of control of pupil's achievement.

9. Making the final list of teaching aids, which should constitute the integral part of the whole complex and organization of experimental checking up of this material. Sometimes a new audiovisual aid (film strips, etc) teaching materials are constructed on the basis of this work.

10. Experimental checking of the complex and introduction of the necessary improvements.

As a result of this work special cards are written. These cards can be used as a guide for planning lessons and individual work of pupils. The set of these cards (for each unit, topic, grade, course) is a great help to a teacher. It enables him to organize his work on the scientific base. We suppose that in the near future each school will be supplied with all the teaching aids included in the complexes designed for each subject.

It is quite clear that an educational goal may be achieved by different ways and choosing the particular way depends on many factors. Because of that usually several variants of complexes are suggested and it is up to a teacher to decide which serves best. The creative activity of teachers should not be restricted in any way. System approach and ergonomic approach are very important aspects of constructing complexes of the teaching aids and school equipment. Pedagogical ergonomics is the theory of teachers' and pupils' functional possibilities and their activities in the process of learning of the adaptation of different means and surroundings to these possibilities for achieving the best effectiveness of teaching. One example to illustrate this general approach. What should we give to a teacher who has to teach a new course in mathematics?

He needs to have:

1. Some publications giving the general outline of the theoretical basis of the new syllabus and main trends of its further development. This book or books should describe methodological and philosophical aspects of a new course of school mathematics. As an example of such a book is the book written by academician A N Kolmogozov 'Scientific backgrounds of the School Mathematics'. In this book different systems of developing the most important mathematical ideas and notions are compared. Their advantages and shortcomings are shown.

2. Teachers' manuals in methodology of mathematics teaching. The material given in these books based on the main concepts and recent developments of pedagogics (didactics) and psychology. Here the teacher finds the historical analysis of the main methodological ideas, description of the different methodological approaches to course construction, the ways of presentation and developing of leading ideas, on which our new course in mathematics is based.

3. Books, where the teacher finds the detailed descriptions of the content which is taught in elementary school in iv, v, vi, vii, viii, ix, x grades.

4. Besides that the teachers have to be supplied with teachers' Guides, which can help him to organize the process of learning. This type of book is closely connected with pupils' textbooks. Great attention in Teachers' guides for each grade is paid to the oral exercises, with elements of programmed instruction. These exercises usually are given just in the beginning of a lesson and have several tasks to organize children to work, to check their readiness to acquire the new material, they should create the atmosphere of research. Moreover the content of these exercises shows the teacher the most important aspects of studied material.

In these guides the teacher finds suggestions about the implementation of teaching aids.

5. Sets of cards mentioned above; special cards with problems to help a teacher to organize individualized instruction.

6. Audiovisual aids and technical devices, necessary to conduct a lesson or series of lessons.

Complexes of teaching aids help us to introduce some elements of scientific organization of teachers' (and pupils') work. And that is a very important aspect of the educational technology.

We hope that by 1975 all our schools will have specialized (study rooms), teaching rooms (or subject rooms) in each subject. These teaching rooms will be equipped with complexes of teaching aids. That will help him (or her) to provide the necessary stimuli for the efficient learning process – that is one of the most important aspects of the Educational Technology.

Intelligence, Learning and the New Aptitudes

ROBERT GLASER

In my remarks, I shall try to show how certain developments in psychology
have influenced present day educational methods, and I shall further try to
show how recent work in learning theory, developmental psychology, and
psychometrics strongly suggests new directions for educational research
and practice. I shall do this in the context of a central problem in education –
the individualization of instruction or, in other terms, adapting educational
environments to individual differences. I shall focus, for the most part, on
the education of the young child in the pre-school and elementary school
years, although what I have to say seems applicable to all levels of an educational system.

The problem of individualization obviously has been a persistent one; it
has been recognized and proclaimed at least since the beginning of this
century. For example, in 1911, Edward L Thorndike published a monograph
entitled 'Individuality', in which it was noted that the teaching profession and
education in general were showing signs of a reaction against the uniformity
of method that for so long clutched and mechanized the schools, and that the
deadening effects of uniformity needed to be recognized. The problem has
been raised again and again. In 1925, the twenty-fourth yearbook of the
National Society for the Study of Education (an American organization) was
entitled 'Adapting the Schools to Individual Differences'. The introduction
to this volume states in forceful terms that the widespread use of intelligence
and achievement tests has made every educator realize that children vary
greatly as individuals, and "throughout the educational world, there has
therefore awakened the desire to find some way of adapting schools to the
differing individuals who attend them (Washburne, 1925)".

Such shouts of alarm have been ubiquitous; many suggestions have been
made and a few experiments have been launched. But it is 1973, and time
goes by with primarily only a recognition of the problem but no sustained
directions towards solution realized. This is the situation that I would like
to examine. I am encouraged to do so by the fact that work in the study of

human behaviour over the past 10 to 20 years now points to possible solutions. Unfortunately, I cannot point to new directions in a simple way by listing a few principles that ring with self-evident truth, although this is the fashionable road to current educational reform. The story is complicated, its roots are deep, and its complexities need to be examined.

An analysis of the problem involves the idiosyncracies of two major fields of psychology. As is known, the English and Continental European traditions of the nineteenth century gave rise to two separate disciplines of scientific psychology: psychometrics and experimental psychology. It was the psychometricians with their emphasis on technology who had significant impact upon educational methods. Indeed, the major activity in the field of educational psychology, especially in the United States, revolved around measurement and psychometric practice that emphasized the nature of individual differences and the utility of measuring these differences for education. Learning variables and modification of the educational environment, however, were not part of this field. And while this went on, experimental psychologists went into the laboratory to work on the basic foundations of their science, and concentrated on discovering and formulating general laws of behaviour unencumbered by the additional complication of individual differences. For the most part, individual differences became the error variance in experimental design.

The separation of these two fields, both of which are necessary for a complete conception of instructional theory, led to assumptions about individual differences uninfluenced by knowledge of learning and cognitive processes, and led to theories of learning uninfluenced by the effect of individual difference parameters. In this climate, characterized by the parallel, but not combined labours of two major disciplines relevant to education, the search for an educational system that responds to individuality has been going on.

To be as clear as I can, I will overstate my case by contrasting two kinds of educational environments. One I shall call a selective educational mode, and the other, an adaptive educational mode. It appears that a selective educational mode has predominated, while we aspire toward an adaptive one.

A **selective** mode of education is characterized by minimal variation in the conditions under which individuals are expected to learn. A narrow range of instructional options is provided, and a limited number of ways to succeed are available. Consequently, the adaptability of the system to the student is limited, and alternative paths which can be selected for students with different backgrounds and talents are restricted. In such an environment, the fixed or limited paths available require particular student abilities, and these **particular** abilities are emphasized and fostered to the exclusion of other abilities. In this sense, the system becomes selective with respect to individuals who have particular abilities for success – as success is defined and as it can be attained by the means of instruction that are available. The effectiveness of the system, for the designers of the system and for the students themselves, is enhanced by admitting only those students who score very highly on measures of the abilities required to succeed. Furthermore, since only those students who have a reasonable probability of success are admitted, little change in the educational environment is necessary, and the differences among individuals that become important to measure are those that predict success in this special setting.

In contrast to this, an adaptive mode of education assumes that the educational environment can provide for a wide range and variety of instructional methods and opportunities for success. Alternate means of learning are adaptive to and are in some way matched to knowledge about each individual – his background, talents, interest, and the nature of his past performance. An individual's styles and abilities are assessed either upon entrance or during the course of learning, and certain educational paths are elected or assigned. Further information is obtained about the learner as learning proceeds, and this, in turn, is related to subsequent alternate learning opportunities. The interaction between performance and the subsequent nature of the educational setting is the defining characteristic of an adaptive mode. The success of this adaptive interaction is determined by the extent to which the student experiences a match between his specific abilities and interests, and the activities in which he engages. The effect of any election of or assignment to an instructional path is evaluated by the changes it brings about in the student's potential for future learning and goal attainment. Measures of individual differences in an adaptive educational mode are valid to the extent that they help to define alternate paths that result in optimizing immediate learning, as well as long-term success.

A selective educational mode operates in a Darwinian framework, requiring that organisms adapt to, and survive in, the world as it is; an alternative is that the environment can be changed. If we design only a relatively fixed environment, then a wide range of background capabilities and talented accomplishments might be lost from view because of the exclusive reliance upon selection for survival in a particular setting. What is learned and the way in which one learns, and learns to learn, may take on less importance or receive less emphasis in a setting that offers more options for learning.

When one compares a selective educational mode with adaptive educational possibilities, one asks whether the particular selective tests and sorting out devices that are part of present schooling fail to consider abilities and talents that might emerge as important in a more interactive

31

setting where there is room for adjustment between abilities and modes of learning. In principle, and in contrast to traditional practice, there seems to be no reason why educational environments cannot be designed to accommodate more readily to variations in the backgrounds, cognitive processes, interests, styles, and other requirements of learners.

In any educational mode, then, the individual differences that take on outstanding importance are those that have ecological validity within a particular system. In the traditional selective educational mode, the individual differences that are measured in order to make educational assignments centre around the concepts of intelligence and aptitude. And this bears looking into.

Of the various attempts to measure intellectual ability that began at the turn of the century, Binet's work emerged strongly. It was a practical endeavour to predict school success. The Minister of Public Education in France supported Binet's attempts to determine what might be done to ensure the benefits of instruction to retarded children. It was decided that children suspected of retardation be given an examination to certify that, because of the state of their intelligence, they were unable to profit from instruction as given in ordinary schooling. Scholastic success in an essentially fixed educational mode was the predictive aim toward which this test was directed, for which its items were selected, and in terms of which its overall effectiveness was validated; although to be fair to Binet, his writings do indicate a great deal of sensitivity to the possibilities for individual differential diagnosis.

Nevertheless, the validation of a test is a very specific procedure in which individuals are exposed to particular kinds of test items that are constructed to predict a particular criterion measure. No test is simply valid in general, but for a specific purpose and a particular situation. The concept of Binet's work has persisted in many societies, and as Cronbach points out in the 1970 edition of his well-known book on the essentials of psychological testing: "Current tests differ from those of the earlier generation just as 1970 automobiles differ from those of about 1920: more efficient, more elegant, but operating on the same principles as before (Cronbach, 1970)."

At the present time, respected textbooks on the subject (Cronbach, 1970; Tyler, 1965) carefully point out that if we base our conclusions about what intelligence tests measure on their most effective use – that is, their predictive validity – then the verdict is that they are tests of scholastic aptitude or scholastic ability; these tests measure certain abilities that are helpful in most school work, as it is conducted in present day school situations. It is to be observed, further, that these tests of scholastic aptitude, when considered over all school levels, account for only 35 to 45 per cent of the variation in school performance.

32

Being aware of this, psychological researchers have not been remiss in attempting to probe deeper into the different facets of human behaviour that might allow us to be more sensitive to individual differences. For example, some years ago, as a result of dissatisfaction with the research on the IQ and together with the results of work on multiple factor analysis, there was a de-emphasis of the concept of general intelligence that led to the popularity of tests of differential aptitudes. At that time, in addition to an overall measure of 'intelligence' or 'general aptitude', schools began to employ tests that provided measures on a variety of factors such as spatial, mechanical, and abstract reasoning aptitudes. More than predicting overall scholastic success, these test batteries attempted to predict differential success in school programs leading to different vocations which appeared to require different aptitude patterns.

In 1964, a careful analysis was done by McNemar of the validity co-efficients of certain widely used, multi-test differential aptitude batteries. He argued from his analysis that "aside from tests of numerical ability having differential value for predicting school grades in math, it seems safe to conclude that the worth of the multi-test batteries as differential predictors of achievement in school has not been demonstrated (McNemar, 1964)". McNemar further concluded that "it is far from clear that tests of general intelligence have been outmoded by the multi-test batteries as the more useful predictors of school achievement". In general, a simple, unweighted combination of tests of verbal reasoning and numerical ability predicted school grades as well as, or better than, any combination of more specific ability tests; and these tests of verbal and numerical ability were similar to what was measured in group tests of intelligence.

This evidence suggests the following observation: given the characteristics of the present educational system, certain general measures of the ability to manipulate numbers and words predict, to a limited extent, the ability to emerge victorious from the educational environment provided. However, any attempt to further differentiate specific ability patterns that relate to specific educational programs is, at best, no more successful than the usual general ability measures or intelligence measures. Why is this so, and what does it mean?

One clue to answering this question is to note that tests of general ability, intelligence, and aptitude follow the accepted psychometric practice of attempting to predict the outcomes of learning, but make little attempt to measure those abilities that are related to different ways of learning. The generally used scholastic aptitude tests are designed for and validated in terms of predictions of the products of learning in a particular setting. They are not designed to determine the different ways in which different students learn best, to measure the basic processes that underlie various kinds of learning, nor to assess prerequisite performance capabilities required for learning a new task.

Psychologists and educational researchers, again, have not been insensitive to this state of affairs, and there has been a recent emergence of concern about the relationships between measures of individual differences and learning variables. To a large extent, this work was heralded in the United States by the 1957 book by Cronbach and Gleser entitled 'Psychological Tests and Personnel Decisions'. This book was concerned with the development of a decision theory model for the selection and placement of individuals into various 'treatments'. The word treatment was given a broad meaning, referring to what is done with an individual in an institutional setting; eg, for what job an applicant should be trained in industry, to what therapeutic method a patient should be assigned, and in education, to which particular educational program or instructional method a student should be assigned or given the opportunity to select.

Cronbach and Gleser pointed out that aptitude information is useful in adapting to treatments only when aptitude and treatment can be shown to interact. In a non-technical way, this can be explained as follows: given a measure of aptitude, and two different instructional methods, if the aptitude measure correlates positively with success in both treatments, then it is of no value in deciding which method to suggest to the student. What is required is a measure of aptitude that predicts who will learn better from one curriculum or method of learning than from another. If such measures can be developed, then methods of instruction can be designed, not to fit the average person, but to fit an individual or groups of students with particular aptitude patterns. Unless one treatment is clearly best for everyone, treatments should be differentiated in such a way as to maximize their interaction with aptitude variables.

Following up on this logic, educational psychologists have developed a line of investigation that has been called the ATI problem (ATI standing for aptitude-treatment interaction). The intent of the work is different from previous work on differential aptitude testing. In the differential aptitude testing research, emphasis was placed on determining the relationship between measured aptitudes and learning outcomes under relatively fixed educational programs. In the ATI work, the emphasis is on determining whether aptitudes can predict which one of several learning methods might help different individuals attain similar educational outcomes. To be clearer, the earlier differential aptitude work assumed several different educational programs, each one leading to different careers, and attempted to select individuals with respect to their potential success in each program. The ATI work, on the other hand, essentially assumes that if within each of these several programs there were different instructional options, then aptitude patterns might predict the option in which a student would be most successful.

Several recent comprehensive reviews report detailed analyses of ATI studies (Bracht, 1969; Bracht & Glass, 1968; Cronbach & Snow, 1969), and the conclusions are disappointing: few or no ATI effects have been solidly demonstrated; the frequency of studies in which appropriate interactions have been found is low; and the empirical evidence found in favour of such interactions is often not very convincing.

This is a disturbing conclusion; it implies that the generally used aptitude constructs are not productive dimensions for measuring those individual differences that interact with different ways of learning. These measures derived from a psychometric, selection oriented tradition do not appear to relate to the processes of learning and performance that have been under investigation in experimental and developmental psychology. It appears that the treatments investigated in the ATI studies were not generated by any systematic analysis of the kinds of psychological processes called upon in particular instructional methods, and individual differences were not assessed in terms of these processes.

To sum up at this point – the implications of my discussion so far appear, I suggest, to support the hypothesis that the human performances that we identify with the words 'general ability', 'scholastic intelligence', and 'aptitudes' have emerged on the basis of measurement and validation procedures in an educational system of a particular kind. These intelligence and aptitude factors have taken on significance because of their correlation with instructional outcomes, and not because of their relationship to learning processes or different educational techniques. Furthermore, since our educational system provides a limited range of educational options for adapting to different individuals, these general abilities override the influence of any more specific abilities that might be additionally useful if alternate ways of learning were available.

The question now is: What **are** these 'new aptitudes'? The answer that current lines of research suggest is that individual difference variables need to be conceptualized in terms of the process constructs of contemporary theories of learning, development, and human performance. There is accumulating evidence to show that we can experimentally identify and influence a variety of cognitive processes that are involved in new learning, and that the analysis of individual differences can be carried out in terms of such processes (Gagné, 1967).

Let me give some examples to clarify this point. A first example: It is known that learning to remember a list of words takes place more effectively when the learner is provided with, or provides for himself, some visual or verbal relationship between pairs of words. Presented with the words 'boy' and 'horse', one pictures a boy riding a horse, or makes up a sentence containing these words. This process has been called 'mental elaboration', referring to the fact that individuals recode or transform materials presented to them by elaborating the content, and doing this can facilitate learning. The developmental and individual difference aspects of this process have been studied. Young children profit from being prompted or encouraged in some way to engage in elaborative activity; and as children grow older, they begin to generate their own forms of mental elaboration. There are individual differences, related to children's backgrounds, in the way in which cognitive processes of this kind are carried out, and the work done to date implies that it would be fruitful to train particular children in such elaborative techniques of learning as a way of extending their capabilities (Rohwer, 1970a, 1970b, 1971).

A second example: A series of studies has identified individual differences in visual and auditory perceptual processes that are prerequisite to the successful performance of basic academic tasks in the elementary school. These perceptual processes are required to organize and extract the patterns of information presented to children in learning early number concepts and in the grapheme-phoneme correspondences required in beginning reading. The work done to date indicates that competence in these processes is differentially related to academic achievement in arithmetic and reading; visual perceptual processes are more related to arithmetic than reading, and auditory processes more related to beginning reading than arithmetic. It has also been shown that these processes themselves can be effectively taught to children, and that the effects of this instruction transfer to specific accomplishment in the beginnings of verbal and quantitative literacy (Rosner, 1972).

A third example: This example concerns the aptitudes, generally measured in high school students, that are related to success in a college or university. In a recent series of studies (Hunt, Frost & Lunneborg, undated), students were classified into high and low verbal ability groups and into high and low quantitative ability groups after taking a battery of tests used for selection for college entrance. The individuals in each of these groups were then given a series of tasks employed in laboratory experiments on the experimental analysis of information processing models of memory.* In this way, the characteristics of high verbal ability and high quantitative ability students, as defined by aptitude tests, were examined in terms of cognitive processes, as defined by particular theories of cognition.

---

* The tasks and processes studied were: continuous paired associates in the context of the Atkinson and Shiffrin model (1968, 1971); clustering; encoding, using the name matching and physical matching tasks of Posner and Boies (1971); and semantic encoding and PI (proactive inhibition) release using tasks from Wickens (1970).

The conclusions from this set of studies tentatively suggest that there is a relationship between verbal ability and the rapidity and efficiency of data manipulation in short-term memory, and between quantitative ability and resistance to distraction while consolidating information in (short-term) memory. It is further pointed out that equivalent results were often produced by different cognitive processes, so that while high and low verbal ability individuals recalled almost exactly the same number of words from an unorganized list of words, they did so in different ways. The low verbal subjects appeared to cluster the words into meaningful groups (semantic clustering), whereas the high verbal individuals appeared to 'just read the words back as they heard them'.

It is also suggested that in recognition memory tasks such as remembering faces, high verbal ability individuals adapt a naming or labelling strategy, whereas low verbal ability subjects deal with the task by using perceptual memory which deals with visual material directly. Studies of the outstanding memory performances of great mnemonists (eg Hunt & Love, 1972a, 1972b; Luria, 1968) also show different processes for different individuals, eidetic or sensory imaging in one case and a heavy reliance on verbal labels and semantic codes in another case.

Since it is now suggested that verbal aptitude and ability is related to the rapidity of information processing in short-term memory (Hunt et al, undated), the interesting question is whether we can proceed further and identify situations where speed of such processing will be predictive of school or job success. This would have more significant implications than present correlationally derived psychometric relations, because clues would perhaps now be available about how verbal ability processes might be modified or employed for learning, and this would be more adaptive than treating people as if they just have the aptitude or do not.

Studies such as these support the promise of a line of research on individual differences in terms of cognitive processes, and it appears probable that a set of new, theoretically based measures of intelligence and aptitude will move psychometric predictions from static statements about the probability of success to dynamic statements about what can be done to increase the likelihood of success. I would urge further that studies also attempt to identify the kinds of processes required by various tasks, and to characterize how individuals perform these processes. The conditions required to learn a task could then be adapted to these individual characteristics, or the individual might be taught how to engage more effectively in the processes involved.

Another sign of support for the theme of process concepts as individual difference variables comes from the work on cognitive styles or personality characteristics that influence learning and performance (Kagan & Kogan,

1970). Here, the influence of individual differences in non-cognitive domains on the cognitive processes involved in problem solving is being studied. This includes research on the effects of cultural background on the dominance of visual, auditory, or tactile sense modalities; the relationship between anxiety and the quality of immediate memory; and the degree to which an individual pauses to evaluate the quality of cognitive products in the course of problem solving, generally referred to as differences in reflection and impulsivity.

There have been some interesting attempts to modify cognitive style. For example, it has been shown that when first-grade children are placed with experienced teachers who have a reflective style, the children become more reflective during the school year than children who are placed with impulsive teachers (Yando & Kagan, 1968). The practical implication of this for school instruction is tailoring the tempo of the teacher to the tempo of the child so that, for example, the behaviour of the impulsive child is influenced by the presence of a reflective teacher model. Other studies with impulsive children have investigated the controlling function of covert speech as a self-guidance procedure whereby these children are taught to talk to themselves in order to modify their problem-solving styles (Meichenbaum, 1971; Meichenbaum & Goodman, 1969).

The processes that make up cognitive style are important to consider in adapting education to children from different cultures. As we know, early experience in a particular cultural environment provides the child with a set of values and a set of techniques and skills for learning to learn and for processing incoming information. It has been pointed out that in certain societies the middle-class child acquires these things so that they are continuous with what will be required of him in school. Whereas, what a lower socio-economic-class child acquires may be discontinuous with what school demands. In a non-adaptive environment for learning, 'cultural deprivation' is defined in terms of a set of experiences that establishes a discontinuity between pre-school experiences and school requirements. (An obvious example in the conventional school is that, explicitly or implicitly, the school requires the immediate acceptance of an achievement ethic with deferred future rewards, a characteristic most consonant with middle-class values. This discontinuity has a profound effect on the child's behaviour toward school and on the school's behaviour toward the child.) In the adaptive educational environment that I envision, it would be assumed as a matter of course that the values, styles, and learning processes that the child brings to school are of intrinsic worth. These modes of behaviour have, in fact, been extremely functional in the child's environment, and an adaptive setting would work with these assets of the child's functioning as a basis for a program of education (Getzels, 1966).

38

The work and theories of Piaget support and influence my theme of the importance of modifiable behavioural processes in adaptive education as opposed to notions of relatively fixed intelligence and aptitude. The stages of cognitive development described in the Piagetian theory of intelligence are thought to mark major qualitative changes in the modes of thinking available to the child, and consequently, changes in the kinds of specific learning of which he or she is capable. Adaptive education, as I have indicated, looks at this in two ways: the educational environment accommodates to the existing modes and processes of a learner, and it also can influence these processes through instruction. The stages described by Piaget thus provide some insight into individual modes of performance available to different children which would have to be considered in educational design.

Recently, a colleague and I (Glaser & Resnick, 1972) carried out a detailed survey on the possible teachability of basic aptitudes and Piagetian processes. In our examination of operational thinking, particularly the acquisition of concrete operations, with which most studies have been concerned, we noted a significant shift, as compared with a few years ago, in the balance of evidence concerning the trainability of these processes. A number of studies have appeared which offer grounds for suggesting the possibility of developing operational thinking through instruction. Of interest here is that as we completed this survey, we were struck with the fact that our search for work on the instructability of basic abilities uncovered far fewer studies on the training of psychometrically defined aptitudes and abilities than on the training of Piagetian and related concepts. This raises the question of why the Piagetian definition of intelligence has stimulated so much more instructional research than has the psychometric one.

I have suggested the answer already: Piagetian theory is not concerned with differential prediction, but with explication of developmental changes in thought structures and the influence of these structures on performance. This emphasis suggests a variety of specific performances on which to focus instructional attention, and also suggests hypotheses concerning the optimal character and sequence of instructional attempts. In contrast, most psychometric tests of intelligence and aptitude consist of items chosen because of their predictive power rather than their relationship to observed or hypothesized intellectual processes. Thus, they offer few concrete suggestions as to what or how to teach.

The rise of the 'new aptitudes' is also forecast by the notion of interactionism whereby accommodative changes in an individual's performance occur in the course of encounters with environmental circumstances. This has been emphasized by such diverse points of view as Piaget's and Skinner's, and currently is well expressed by Bandura in his writings on social learning theory (Bandura, 1969, 1971). We know now that psychological functioning is a continuing reciprocal interaction between the behaviour of an organism and the controlling conditions in the environment. Behaviour partly creates the environment, and the resultant environment influences the behaviour. This is clearly seen in social interaction, for example, where a person plays an active role in bringing out a positive or negative response in others, and in this way, creates, to some degree, environmental contingencies for himself through his own behaviour. This is a two-way causal process in which the environment might be just as influencable as the behaviour it regulates. The actual environment an individual experiences can be a function of his behaviour if the environment is an adaptive one.

Our penchant for a fixed educational mode arises in part from an old-fashioned psychology, from the scientific and social tendency to think in terms of fixed categories of human beings with consistent drives and dispositions (Mischel, 1969). We think this way, rather than in terms of human beings who are highly responsive to the conditions around them so that as conditions change or conditions are maintained, individuals act accordingly. Adaptive educational environments can take advantage of the fact that individuals show great subtlety in adapting their competencies to different situations, if the situation permits such adaptability. Although individuals show generalized consistent behaviour on the basis of which we frequently characterize them, this does not preclude their also being very good at discriminating and reacting to a variety of experiences in different ways. The traditional measures of general ability and aptitudes err on the side of assuming too much consistency, and de-emphasize the capability of individuals to devise plans and actions depending upon the rules, needs, and demands of alternative situations. If, in our thinking about individual differences, we make as much room for the capability of individuals to adapt and change, as well as to be stable, and as much room for the capacity for self-regulation and self-development, as well as for victimization by enduring traits, then an adaptive notion of education must follow. An educational system should present alternative environments that enhance the ability of the individual for self-regulation in different possible situations for learning.

So far, I have tried to show that the state of our understanding of human behaviour has in some sense precluded a fruitful approach to individualization and adaptive education. For the reasons I have outlined, we have been fixed on an essentially selective mode of education and on the concepts that underlie it. I have also attempted to indicate some directions that have been taken and some milestones that we seem to have passed that appear to make change toward our ideals for adaptive education more feasible than heretofore.

While I have so far stressed fundamental research understandings, progress will not occur by research alone. The design and development of operating educational institutions is also required. Throughout history, science and technology, research and application have forced each other's hands, and mutually beneficial relationships between the two are absolutely necessary for the development of new forms of education. At the present time, as a result of work on the development of school environments that are adaptive to individual differences, certain requirements are emerging that contrast the design of an adaptive educational environment with more traditional forms of education. While I have emphasized, so far, the importance of intra-individual cognitive processes, more obvious environmental factors also must be attended to. Briefly stated, some seven of these appear to be the following:

1. In subject-matter instruction, one major mode of adaptation involves learning achievement. Based upon a student's attainment of certain performances, decisions can be made about subsequent instruction. The emphasis on the achievement of competence should be quite deliberate and different than it has been in the past. The assumption now is that ways can be found to ensure that most children will master the literacy objectives of elementary school, and the explicity tactic is to place the burden on the instruction to maximize the ways in which the child can progress, rather than necessarily assuming that the child lacks a particular capability or aptitude. The implications of this emphasis are important. The school environment should convey to students that they are differentiated on the basis of their performance, and that the school is oriented toward assisting them in maximizing their attainment regardless of their particular background or labels they have obtained on other bases such as IQ tests. What is emphasized is not the discrepancy between potential and accomplishment; rather, accomplishment, not potential, is viewed and valued in its own right. For this purpose, techniques need to be developed for analysing the properties of individual performance frequently enough and in enough detail for individualized instructional decisions, and computer-assisted instruction is of help in this regard.

2. Another obvious kind of individual difference is the rate, pace, and rhythm of learning. It is fashionable to say that adaptation on the basis of mere learning rate is not very important since there are deeper concerns with process and style. However, rate has some interesting ramifications. If it is not limited by a teacher's concern for a child moving beyond the amount of subject matter approved of for that grade, self-pacing does give the student the option of moving ahead if he or she so desires. It permits the student to exercise some sense of his own rhythm of work. There are individual differences in this respect; some students like to spend a concentrated amount of time on their work, complete it, and then get more work to do. Others like to work for shorter periods of time, enjoy their distractions, and come back to their work. Some like to engage in some exploratory

41

activity to test and display newly learned skills, and then get on with new work. Others like to reward themselves with some playful activity upon the completion of their successful performance. These tempos of work are very obvious, and the relationships between rhythm and pace of work and learning, retention, and transfer are an interesting matter for research investigation.

3. A third obvious source of individual differences relates to the outcomes and consequences of a student's activity. There are individual differences in needs for feedback: some children need more questions answered than others; some need more careful explanation of directions; some need infrequent praise for their accomplishments; others need very frequent attention for small accomplishments. This mechanism of adaptation can be facilitated by designing classroom procedures in such a way that a teacher can organize activities in order to pay some attention to all students in a circumscribed period of time. For example, keeping the principles of reinforcement in mind, the teacher can constantly scan the activity of the children and comment to those who appear to be working, and spend little time with those who for some reason or other are not attending to their work when it is appropriate for them to do so. Teacher attention is important and children will shift their activities to obtain it, as they observe the activities for which the teacher provides attention and conversation. A teacher can also become aware of children who have initial needs for much contact and then systematically withdraw support as the child becomes more self-sustained. This continuous 'feedback role' of the teacher is one important way in which individual differences can be adapted to, and training a teacher for this role is to be particularly emphasized in educational settings adaptive to individual differences. The presently very active field of behaviour modification is designing and analysing such school practices, and among the many interesting questions for study, one of the most interesting is the issue of the relationship between reinforcement contingencies used in the classroom and the 'natural community of reinforcers' present in later learning situations both in and out of school (Wolf & Risley, 1971; Resnick, 1971; Bandura, 1969).

4. Another aspect of individual differences is the degree to which learners can manage their own enterprises – the extent to which they can set up and conduct their own lessons and assess their own performance. Self-management skills involve such things as following directions, identifying current assignments, deciding on and selecting appropriate materials, setting up the task, completing the task, obtaining an evaluation of it, and being able to identify the available options for new work. Children vary in this respect, and appropriate classroom management can adapt to these differences. However, skill at self-management is both an individual difference to which the instructional environment adapts and which the environment can influence and change. Self-management skills can be

42

actively taught and many of us have been amazed at the extent to which very young children can conduct their own enterprises in a classroom setting. An area of psychological study related to these skills is investigation of the process of self-reinforcement, whereby individuals exercise control over the rewards and punishments consequent to their own actions (Bandura, 1971). Study for such self-regulation is a new area of research that seems very relevant to school learning. Such questions as the following are involved: How do children develop self-prescribed standards of behaviour for evaluating the adequacy of their performance? What are the effects of social comparison and modelling on the use and maintenance of these standards? How are reinforcing events made available so that students can serve as their own reinforcing agents? Under what conditions do children in the classroom acquire self-rewarding and self-punishing behaviour? And what is the effectiveness of these self-administered consequences in influencing learning?

5. An important requirement for adaptive education is the design of flexible curricula with many points of entry, different methods of instruction, and options among instructional objectives. Extensive sequential curricula that must be used as complete systems and into which entry at different points is difficult will give way to more 'modular' organizations of instructional units. This does not imply the abandonment of sequence requirements inherent in the structure of the material to be learned, but does imply that prerequisites, where essential, are to be specified in terms of capabilities of the learner rather than in terms of previous instructional experiences. A flexible curriculum avoids the necessity for all individuals to proceed through all steps in a curriculum sequence, and adapts to the fact that some individuals acquire prerequisites on their own, while others need more formal support to establish the prerequisites for more advanced learning. In such a system, it should be easy to incorporate new and varied instructional materials and objectives as they are developed in response to the changing educational interests and requirements of both teachers and students (Resnick, 1972).

6. There is need for increased emphasis on open testing and behaviourally indexed assessment. In an adaptive environment, tests designed primarily to compare and select students can be expected to play a decreasing role, since access to particular educational activities will be based on a student's background together with his command of prerequisite competencies. Tests will be designed to provide information directly to the learner and the teacher to guide further learning. These tests will have an intrinsic character of openness in that they will serve as a display of the competencies to be acquired, and the results will be open to the student who can use this knowledge of his performance as a yardstick of his developing ability. These tests also will assess more than the narrow band of traditional academic

outcomes. Measures of process and style, of cognitive and non-cognitive development, and of performance in more natural settings than exist in the traditional school will be required. Fortunately, this trend in process-oriented, broad-band assessment is now discernible in many new efforts.

7. The teaching of basic psychological processes is also required, as I have indicated throughout my discussion. We have assumed for too long the stability of 'basic aptitudes'; now we need to determine how these talents can be encouraged and taught. At the Olympic Games, young men and women joyfully exceed existing limits of human capability; in the intellectual sphere, this is also possible. The talents of individuals can be extended so that they can be provided with increased possibilities for education.

I am at the end now of these formal remarks, and have one last comment: It should be said that the nature of a society determines the nature of the educational system that it fosters, and educational systems tend to feed into the existing social practices. If this is so, then an adaptive educational system carried to its ultimate conclusion may be out of joint with the present social structure in certain societies. An adaptive environment assumes many ways of succeeding and many goals available from which to choose. It assumes further that no particular way of succeeding is greatly valued over the other. In selective environments, it is quite clear that the way of succeeding that is most valued is within the relatively fixed system provided. Success in society is defined primarily in terms of the attainment of occupations directly related to the products of this system. School-related occupations are the most valued, the most rewarding, and seen as the most desirable. However, if an adaptive mode becomes prevalent and wider constellations of human abilities are emphasized, then success will have to be differently defined; and many more alternative ways of succeeding might have to be appropriately rewarded than may presently be the case.

The preparation of this paper was supported by the Learning Research and Development Center, supported in part by funds from the National Institute of Education (NIE), United States Department of Health, Education, and Welfare. The opinions expressed do not necessarily reflect the position or policy of NIE and no official endorsement should be inferred.

FURTHER READING

Bandura, A. and Walters, R. H. (1963) Social learning and personality development. Holt, Rinehart & Winston Inc., New York

Bracht, G. H. (1972) Perspectives in educational and psychological measurement. Prentice-Hall, New York

Cronbach, L. J. (1969) Essentials of psychological testing. Harper & Row, New York

Gagne, R. M. (1970) The conditions of learning. Holt, Rinehart & Winston Inc., New York

Lumsdaine, A. and Glaser, R. (1962) Teaching machine and programmed learning. A source book. N.E.A., USA

Luria, A. R. (1966) Human brain and psychological processes. Harper & Row, New York

Thorndike, E. L. (1912) Education. A First Book. Macmillan & Co, London

Educational Selection of Media with Particular Reference to ETV
T S ALLAN

Education, being largely though not entirely a matter of communication, has in the end given most new technologies of communication a trial in the class-room. I say 'in the end' because I think it is true that a new communication system has almost no chance of serious educational application until it has been developed in society for general purposes. Such development is usually a slow and costly business far beyond the resources society is willing to allocate to education. Availability in developed form is, however, by no means the only criterion by which educators decide whether or not to use a new medium, and I will try to suggest what the other criteria are and why some of them have not operated very markedly in favour of ETV, which has failed to realize what speakers at conference after conference used to des-cribe as its vast educational potential.

The decision to introduce a new thing in education is only in part a fully conscious and deliberate decision. It is seldom the result of careful analysis and systematic testing. It is almost always the other way round. A new thing is introduced and, if it survives a period of crude trial and error, it may then be submitted to rigorous scientific research.

It has certainly been so with ETV. It was first introduced in schools in America in the late 1940s, and in France and Britain in the 1950s, partly because it was already available in the community and partly because there seemed to be a 'prima facie' case for its educational use. After all, exposed to general TV, people obviously learned things. A lot of people had non-educational reasons for pushing ETV, and a considerable number of educa-tors were intrigued by the glamour of the new medium. Among them they soon produced a list of the useful functions TV was said to perform in education: it would make top experts available in every classroom; it would open windows on the world; it would give the content of instruction reality; it would provide a front seat for every student at scientific demon-strations; it would solve the problem of teacher shortage, etc. Most of the claims had some truth in them, but the length and variety of the list gave the whole procedure an air of salesmanship, of thinking up good reasons for an educational development which had not really been tried and tested. As the novelty wore off teachers began to ask what, in fact, this expensive and demanding new medium had to contribute to education. In the 1950s and 1960s there were more questions than answers and there was the small flood of research into the comparative effectiveness of ETV and live teaching summarized by Chu and Schramm, with the result we all know - that in general there was no significant difference. Much of this research was neither rigorous nor scientific, and it certainly cannot be said that ETV has yet been satisfactorily analysed any more than live teaching has. But in the meantime the largely obscure process of natural selection of cultural inno-vations has gone on and TV's large place in society and relatively small place in education is being continuously determined by its capacity for adaptation to actual needs and conditions in different cultural environments.

There are sub-environments in any culture. Just as the Arctic selects certain forms of life for survival, so does the austere intellectual climate, in which a small part of the population lives part of the time, select certain types of TV programming, assuming that they are available for selection. Education provides one such sub-environment with several sub-sub-environ-ments within it, and after more than twenty years of ETV certain patterns of provision and use have evolved because they have proved adapted to particular educational requirements. It is perhaps not too early to attempt some analy-sis of the reasons for their selection.

METHOD FOR ASSESSING SELECTION VALUE OF MEDIA
IN EDUCATION

The question we have to consider is in one way simple: what factors deter-mine the individual teacher, administrator or other educationist to use or not to use ETV or any other medium of communication? This decision, taken by a sufficient number of people, is life or death for a medium. It is obvious that over the twenty years of its existence enough educators have decided in favour of ETV at least to keep it alive in its present form, but not enough to give it a dominant place in education.

We are dealing with variable factors which control behaviour. There is the primary level response which is the individual's perceptual experience of the medium in operation. He has seen programs, he has heard about ETV. Immediately secondary level responses with a cybernetic function are brought into play, and these act as controls of his further contacts with ETV or any other new medium or innovation. He may say, in effect, 'I don't want any-thing more to do with this'; or 'I'd like to investigate this thing a little more'; or 'I have no strong feelings one way or the other about this'. His degree of interest acts as a gating mechanism. We are concerned with the

47

group which opens the gate, for it is this group which will decide the fate of the medium by its initial size and later decisions.

Many other variables of the secondary level exercise control, and it is these we must try to identify. They have in most cases a strong subjective component. Take, for example, the individual's assessment of the availability of the medium. The medium has an objective availability but it is not this which is decisive. It is the subjective estimate of objective availability by the population concerned which is decisive. We are concerned here with a statistical average value. One individual will reject ETV as unavailable because it is provided only in a special room and not in his classroom. His standard of availability is very high. Another will not reject ETV as unavailable if he thinks it likely that his school authority can be persuaded to buy a TV set for his school. His standard of availability is low.

The variables are at any one time fixed, and therefore the individual's choices of media, but they are also themselves subject to control by feedback. For example, if I think that any piece of hardware which requires more than the flick of a switch and the turning of one knob to operate it is inconvenient, then a TV set will get past this control, but not a tape recorder. If, however, I am very impressed by the number and variety of my educational purposes which the tape recorder can serve, this feedback may make me reconsider my previous estimate of inconvenience. I seek instruction in the operation of tape recorders and so establish in myself a higher tolerance of inconvenience of operation. Interaction of this kind goes on continuously, otherwise we would be fixed mechanical systems.

The individual is both a complex system of responses to his environment and also, in respect of a special set of his responses, constitutes a special environment to which new experiences have to adapt. The responses of all the people who make up the educational world constitute a special set and therefore a special environment to which any educational innovation has to adapt or disappear. I am well aware that a medium does not literally adapt, but that is true only of the medium in its purely mechanical aspects. A medium, as a social entity, is much more than that. Its adaptability is a function of its physical system and of all the possible ways in which it can be modified, and of all the possible messages which it can be used to convey. In this sense a medium has enough of the characteristics of a living creature to make the biological analogy at least plausible as a heuristic device. The medium has certain possibilities of adaptation to the special educational environment, which is a set of variables which can change in relation to new experience, but do not continuously change much or very rapidly, otherwise the set becomes quite unstable, and the individual's behaviour very erratic.

My listing of variable control factors is necessarily very crude and incomplete, and does not take sufficient account of their interaction. Some

48

factors operate for individuals as gate mechanisms. For example, if A thinks that CAI is completely unavailable to him, he may not consider it any further. I have tried, again in a crude way, to take account of this by giving the different factors different weighting, but only a statistical survey could establish norms for weighting.

I have listed 15 variables. No one individual is influenced by them all, but over the educational population as a whole these factors, I suggest, determine the decision to use or not to use a particular medium. I have rated 8 media for each variable on a 5-point scale, and I have weighted each by a factor of 1, 2, 3, 4 or 5. The following is the list of variables with rating scale and weighting (Table I).

Table I

	-2	-1	0	+1	+2	Weighting
1. Availability	almost unavailable	to very limited extent	moderately	easily	completely	x5
2. Cost	very expensive	expensive	moderately	cheap	very cheap	x5
3. Convenience for Class Use	very inconvenient	fairly	a little	convenient	very convenient	x1
4. Convenience for Individual Use	"	"	"	"	"	x1
5. Participation Potential	very low	low	moderate, interested	high	very high	x3
6. Control of Class	very weak	weak	moderate	fairly strong	very strong	x3
7. Quantity and Variety of Messages available	very small	fairly small	moderate	fairly large	very large	x4
8. Capacity for Communicating Complex Conceptual Thinking	very low	low	moderate, interested	high	very high	x2
9. Capacity for Demonstration	"	"	"	"	"	x3
10. Perceptual Range and Variety	very small	fairly small	moderate	fairly large	very large	x2
11. Affective Power	very weak	weak	moderate	fairly strong	very strong	x1
12. Control of Time of Use	almost none	very little	reasonable	very considerable	complete	x3
13. Control of Pace of Delivery	"	"	"	"	"	x2
14. Programmed Feedback	none	very little	moderate	considerable	very considerable	x3
15. Free Feedback	"	"	"	"	"	x3

(See Table II)

For the purposes of this analysis the teacher must be considered a medium of communication, an agent. From the beginning of formal education the teacher has been the main agent of instruction. He is both a physical medium like a TV set or a computer terminal, and the vehicle of messages like TV or computer programs. It is assumed that he has survived in the educational environment because he is very well adapted to it, the environment in his case being reduced to its basic elements of potential students

Table II

		Live Teacher Now 1978		Print Now 1978		Audio B/C Recorded Now 1978		B/C ETV Now 1978		Film Now 1978		Tape/Slide Now 1978		CAI Now 1978		Recorded A-V Now 1978	
1.	Availability x5	+10	+10	+10	+10	+5	+10	+5	+5	0	0	+5	+5	-10	-10	-10	+5
2.	Cost x5	-10	-10	+5	+5	+5	+5	+5	+5	-5	-5	-5	0	-10	-10	-5	0
3.	Convenience for Class Use x1	+2	+2	+1	+1	+1	+1	+1	+1	-1	-1	0	0	-2	-2	0	0
4.	Convenience for Indiv. use x1	+2	+2	+2	+2	+1	+1	+1	+1	-1	-1	-1	-1	+2	+2	+2	+2
5.	Participation Potential x3	+6	+6	0	0	0	0	0	0	0	0	0	0	+6	+6	0	0
6.	Control of Class x3	+6	+6	-6	-6	-6	-6	-6	-6	-6	-6	-6	-6	-6	-6	-6	-6
7.	Quantity and Variety of Messages x4	+4	+4	+8	+8	0	0	0	0	-4	-4	0	+4	-4	+4	-8	+4
8.	Capacity for Conceptual Thinking x2	+2	+2	+4	+4	+2	+2	0	0	0	0	0	0	+4	+4	0	0
9.	Capacity for Demonstration x3	+3	+3	-3	-3	-3	-3	+6	+6	+6	+6	+3	+3	0	0	+6	+6
10.	Perceptual range and Variety x2	-2	-2	-4	-4	-4	-4	+4	+4	+4	+4	+2	+2	-2	-2	+4	+4
11.	Affective Power x1	+1	+1	+1	+1	+1	+1	+2	+2	+2	+2	+1	+1	-2	-2	+2	+2
12.	Control of Time of Use x3	+6	+6	+6	+6	+6	+6	-6	-6	+3	+3	+3	+3	+3	+6	+6	+6
13.	Control of Pace of Use x2	+4	+4	+2	+2	+2	+2	-4	-4	0	0	+2	+2	+4	+4	+2	+2
14.	Programmed Feedback x3	+6	+6	-6	-6	-6	-6	-6	-6	-6	-6	-6	-6	+6	+6	-6	-6
15.	Free Feedback x3	+6	+6	-6	-6	-6	-6	-6	-6	-6	-6	-6	-6	-6	-6	-6	-6
	+	+58	58	39	39	23	28	24	24	15	15	16	20	25	32	22	31
	-	-12	12	25	25	25	25	28	28	29	29	24	19	42	38	41	18
	Score	46	46	14	14	-2	+3	-4	-4	-14	-14	-8	+1	-17	-6	-19	13

and society's expectations. Since the teacher is the most successful educational medium we can take him as our standard against which to evaluate all other media. How does the live teacher rate on the 15 variables?

He is physically completely available, very expensive, very convenient, commands a high participation potential and has strong control of a class, can provide a large quantity and variety of messages at high cost with moderate consistency, can handle conceptual thinking on a high level, has high capacity for demonstration, but fairly low perceptual range and variety, fairly strong affective power, is in complete control of his time of instruction and of its pace, and can provide any level of feedback required.

The other media I have chosen to rate are books (or any printed materials), audio systems (including radio and tape recording), broadcast ETV, Film, CAI, tape/slide presentation (any mode of presenting still pictures synchronized with audio), and recorded audio-video systems, ie any system of presenting at the user's will recorded synchronized moving pictures and sound. As a check on the order of preference yielded by the ratings in Table II, I have listed in Column A the eight media in what I take to be their order of frequency of use at present in British schools:

A Estimated Frequency of Use	B Use Now (Table II)	C Use in 1978 (Table II)
1. Live teacher	46 (1)	46 (1)
2. Print	14 (2)	14 (2)
3. Audio (B/C & Recorded)	-2 (3)	+3 (4)
4. ETV (B/C)	-4 (4)	-4 (6)
5. Tape/slide	-8 (5)	+1 (5)
6. Film	-14 (6)	-14 (8)
7. CAI	-17 (7)	-6 (7)
8. Recorded Audio-video	-19 (8)	13.(3)

The ratings in Column B agree with the estimates in Column A. Leaving aside the live teacher who is in a special category, print is in very frequent use, audio, ETV and tape/slide in frequent use, film less frequent and CAI and recorded audio-video in very little use at present. The rating for film may be too low. Table II predicts that in five years time the order of frequency of use will have altered as shown in Column C with the result that print and recorded audio-video will be in very frequent use, audio and tape/slide in frequent use, B/C, ETV in less frequent use, CAI gaining but still not in frequent use, and film in much less frequent use. What such an exercise cannot foresee, of course, is new technical development which may alter the whole picture, particularly with regard to CAI.

What is the value of this exercise? Without collection of data from a large sample of the educational population, and the application of appropriate statistical techniques, its value is simply as a sketch of an approach to the problem which may be worth following up. At the moment I find it useful mainly as a diagnostic instrument for the identification of the relative strengths and weaknesses of various media. In the remainder of this paper I would like to note what the diagnostic instrument tells us about ETV and its offshoots, recorded audio-video systems, and explain why I think the latter may to some extent achieve what ETV has not.

Broadcast ETV is, at least in Britain, almost completely available, cheap, convenient for both class and individual learning, offers considerable quantity and variety of material of good quality, has a high capacity for demonstration and great perceptual range and variety and strong affective power; but it has serious weaknesses: (1) it relies only on program interest to secure participation; (2) it cannot control a class; (3) it handles complex conceptual thinking only moderately well; (4) the user cannot control time of use or pace of delivery; nor (5) does it provide for feedback of any immediate kind.

These are damaging weaknesses and are sufficient to account for its limited place in education compared with print. ETV shares the first and fifth weaknesses with all media except the live teacher and CAI, and the second with all except the live teacher, and these limitations must simply be accepted. Weakness (4) is peculiar to broadcast media with fixed timetables insofar as time of use is concerned. There are possible answers to this problem and I believe the future of ETV will depend on one such solution or on a mixture of several. Basically they all derive from the obvious fact that if broadcast ETV and any other programmed audio-visual material is recorded and somehow made available to the user at the time and place he wants it at reasonable cost, its future scale of use will depend on educational factors rather than on extraneous factors of availability, cost and convenience.

The invention of the VTR was the first step. Theoretically it is possible for an institution with a VTR to record off air whatever programs it wants, but the choice of material is at any time limited by broadcasting schedules and the cost of storing large numbers of programs is high. What the teacher really needs is access to any item of his choice, whether first broadcast on TV or made on film, from a vast library of up-to-date educational material. He wants it at a suitable time, though not necessarily on demand, and he would like to be able to preview it and also to freeze the picture and re-wind at will. There are two main problems to be solved here – the production of the library of educational programs and, secondly, a distribution system which is efficient and not too expensive. There are solutions to the second problem already available in dial access information retrieval systems like Ottawa's IRTV experiment, or in video-cassette or equivalent systems. IRTV is an attractive system for teacher and student, but to make it available to all educational users everywhere will be very expensive. Eventually I have no doubt this highly convenient form of distribution will be widely available though not within the next five years.

The other type of answer to the distribution problem, which is also in existence, is the video-cassette or its equivalent on disc, coded film etc. The technical specifications need not concern us here. Whatever system is found the most suitable, it will be one that provides for: (a) recording and playback of programs off air; (b) recording and playback of the user's own material; (c) playback, with stop and re-wind facility, of program materials from library sources. The organization of a quick distribution system, which would have to be much speedier and simpler than the present method of film distribution, is a major problem. The fact that videotape messages can be distributed by cable or broadcast may make a fast and efficient system possible. This would be a combination of video-cassette and IRTV, with distribution to a recording centre in each locality, and physical distribution of cassettes from there to the user.

There remains for any system of distribution, whether dial access or by cassette or by a combination of both, the enormous problem of having enough good material to distribute. This may well prove a more intractable problem than any raised by technical difficulties. At present little is available. Institutions may make their own or record off air such programmes as they wish, and are permitted, to record. In many countries broadcasting companies are by far the largest producers of educational material, which is, however, of the set programme type. It is often very good of its kind, but broadcasting companies cannot be expected to explore the production of non-broadcast materials on a large scale. At most they can be expected to make their broadcast products available for use in cassette or other appropriate form. The major new production must surely be done in educational institutions or by bodies comparable to educational publishers. Freedom from the exacting conditions of broadcasting is essential to the full and varied development of ETV.

There remains the third weakness – that ETV and film do not handle complex conceptual thinking very satisfactorily. The case can be put briefly though its adequate discussion would require a separate paper, if not a book. Conceptual thinking, or reasoning, is expressed in strings of propositions, either in plain language or in some other sign code. The characteristic of all such codes is that they are conventional, that their signifiers do not in any way resemble the signified. The signs themselves are perceptual, ie heard or seen or, as in Braille, tactile, but the perceptual aspect is irrelevant to the meaning. The visual in TV, however, is, in Piaget's terminology, generally symbol and not sign, ie it is 'motivated', it resembles what it stands for. As J S Bruner would say, it is iconic representation. (The vocabulary of semiotics is far from uniform. Bruner, for example, uses symbol to denote what most other writers call sign, but the basic distinctions are clear enough.) Charles Morris has used the term 'iconocity' to denote 'the degree to which pictorial signs or symbols are similar to the object signified'. The class of symbols as distinct from signs can be further subdivided into iconic symbols and schematic symbols, an example of the latter being a flowchart which has only a metaphorical visual resemblance to a certain set of abstract relationships.

It is to be noted that TV has at its disposal every kind of visual and auditory symbol system: the abstract auditory signs of speech, music and signals, the iconic auditory symbols of natural effects; iconic visual symbols, ie moving or still pictures which signify what they look like; schematic visual symbols like graphic models; and visual signs, ie printed words or other sign systems. There is, therefore, nothing to prevent TV from presenting a lecturer delivering strings of logical propositions or from showing a printed version of his lecture. There is nothing except that neither is acceptable TV. As TV they require a degree of concentration which few viewers are willing or able to achieve, and they are obviously less efficient as instruction than the live lecture, paced by feedback from the class, or the book which can be read at any pace and re-read at will. If complex conceptual thinking can, in fact, be expressed only in signs rather than in iconic symbols, then TV is not a particularly good medium for its expression. I believe this to be fundamentally true, and that it is one valid reason for the decreasing use of ETV the higher one goes in education and the more education becomes concerned with Piaget's third phase of formal operations. I suggest, however, that the case needs qualification in three directions:

1. The great strength of TV is the iconicity of its symbols, ie it is mediated, or vicarious, perceptual experience. Traditionally education has had very little time for perceptual experience, either immediate or mediate, except as perception of abstract auditory or visual signs, but for the majority of people perceptual experience or its reproduction in iconic symbols is more important than the sign. I do not share the fashionable view of print as a kind of blight which has wasted the human mind for four centuries but there has been an imbalance between the perceptual and the conceptual in education which is already being redressed, and has to be still further redressed in favour of the perceptual, if the alienation of students from formal education is to be reduced.

2. The danger of learning to operate with signs is that it may easily fall into verbalism. In education we tend to reward most highly the student who can reproduce the largest number of verbal generalizations on any subject in the shortest time. We do not insist enough on the translation of the generalizations into terms of experience. If a student writes that there was widespread social unrest in England in the 1840's what does he understand by that? If he lives in Ulster he probably does know exactly what it means for he lives it. The vicarious experience which TV offers is certainly very different from the real thing, but it is the best substitute for the real experience which is generally not available. The relation of the conceptual to the perceptual experience, which it ultimately is about, is one of the essential functions which TV or film can perform in education. It has, however, to be recognized that this is a slow and, for the bright student, often a tedious operation. It has also to be recognized that there are areas of abstract thinking like logic and mathematics where the problem of relating thought to perceptual experience has defeated the best minds.

3. In these abstract areas of thinking ETV has not sufficiently explored the use of schematic symbols to assist comprehension. The limiting factor is that to represent complex thinking in spatial terms the visual model itself may become so complex that it ceases to have any expository value.

The developments I have outlined would, I believe, give audiovisual programs a considerably greater place in education.

REFERENCES

Ashby, W. R. (1960) Design for a Brain
Bruner, J. S. et al (1966) Studies in Cognitive Growth
Chu and Schramm (1967) Learning from Television - What the Research Says
Committee for Economic Development (1968) Innovation in Education: New
    Directions for the American School
De Vito (Ed) (1971) Communication: Concepts and Processes
Gombrich, E. H. (1960) Art and Illusion
Mackenzie, Eraut and Jones (1970) Teaching and Learning: an introduction
    to new methods and resources in higher education
Mehrabian, A. (1971) Silent Messages
Morris, C. (1964) Signification and Significance
Piaget, J. (1950) The Psychology of Intelligence
Piaget, J. and Inhalder (1969) The Psychology of the Child
Travers, R. M. W. (1970) Man's Information Systems

An Educational Technology Approach to a Course in Underwater Technology

D BAUME, B JONES

SUMMARY

The paper describes the development and operation of a new course option
in a new engineering discipline – underwater technology – at the North East
London Polytechnic. The problems involved in defining a new discipline, in
terms of the skills it requires, are discussed, and sample teaching materials
are shown. Several principles from what Davies calls 'Educational Technology' (1972) were incorporated into the course. These include establishing,
and giving to students, a hierarchy of behavioural objectives; matching these
objectives to student interests, and vice-versa; developing the most effective
learning situation for each objective, within economic constraints, without
reference to such conventional classifications as 'lecture' or 'seminar';
making full use, in course re-design, of feedback from students and employers, as well as developments in both underwater and educational technology;
and using the teacher and the Polytechnic primarily as a resource, to support
student learning. The development of confluent learning situations in the
course is discussed.

The paper thus describes an attempt to develop a new course in a new
subject from some educational technology first principles.

INTRODUCTION

The underwater environment presents the engineer with some heroic problems. Hopefully, a conventional engineering course develops many of the
skills an engineer needs to tackle such problems. It seemed to us, however,
that it should be possible to design a course to develop some of the more
specific skills required.

We decided to construct a subject called Underwater Technology for the
final year of a Higher National Diploma course in Mechanical Engineering.
This is a higher technician course, just below degree level.

This paper describes how the option was designed, and is still being
developed, by members of the Underwater Technology Group in the

Mechanical Engineering Department of the North East London Polytechnic. In particular, it describes how some educational technology principles were applied to the design of the option.

EDUCATIONAL PRINCIPLES

The educational principles we tried to adopt in planning the option, listed below, will be familiar. However, we have perhaps been fortunate in the relative freedom we have had to apply these principles. The Joint Committees, which are responsible for the HND scheme, are sometimes cited as a force preventing innovation. We found them both interested and very helpful, placing no obstacles in the way of the more unusual features of the option.

We are working with a new and relatively undefined subject area, and hence with few preconceptions about educational method and no textbooks. We have been able to use the option in part as a testbed for our developing understanding of what Davies calls 'Educational Technology' (Davies, 1972). If this paper has any value, it is probably as an account of a relatively unfettered process of course development which tries to employ the following principles:

(i) The course should be planned, to meet some established need, in terms of a hierarchy of behavioural objectives, which should be communicated to the students.

(ii) Entry skills should be determined, and students should build on those skills to achieve the objectives.

(iii) For each objective, the most appropriate learning situation should be employed. This will often be one which requires from the student a performance very similar to that described in the objective.

(iv) Feedback, from students, staff and employers, should be applied to the continuing development of the course.

(v) Attention should be given to affective and psychomotor, as well as cognitive objectives.

(vi) The lecturer, the Polytechnic and, where appropriate, the outside world, should all be viewed and used by the student as a resource, to help him attain his objectives.

WRITING THE OBJECTIVES

We began by writing a syllabus (Figure 1). We blush to admit this, and in admitting it we do not recommend it. It was, of course, a complete contravention of the first of our educational principles. An excuse might be that we were required to submit a syllabus to gain permission to run the option. However, the reason, as opposed to the excuse, was that we discovered and read about the principles as we developed the course. This paper thus describes a process of development rather than a static situation.

Our first run through the option used this syllabus. For several reasons we became dissatisfied. One reason was that our concept of the aims of the course, and hence of the skills we were trying to develop in the students, changed. This happened as our knowledge of both underwater technology and educational technology increased. We realized that we wanted to produce a solver of underwater engineering problems, rather than an expert in the seven subject areas listed on the syllabus. We thus concluded that an open-book examination, which emphasized use of information rather than memory, was needed, and this was introduced.

Another reason for our dissatisfaction sprang from the practical problems of operating the course. For example, we found no need to teach 'The Underwater Environment' as a separate topic; all we wanted was for the students to be able to determine the effects of the underwater environment on whatever problem they were tackling.

A third reason was the increasing effects on our day-to-day work of our reading and thinking on educational technology and, particularly course objectives. (See, for example, MacKenzie et al, 1970; Popham & Baker, 1970; Davies, 1971; Baume & Jones, 1972.)

For all these reasons, we decided to determine the objectives of the course. Our first attempt read:

'The student should be able to solve engineering problems, either for or in the underwater environment. '

This is a poor objective by Mager's stern standards (Mager, 1962) specifying neither performance standard nor the conditions under which the skill is to be exercised. Defining a performance standard for a high-level objective such as this is difficult (although it is clearly possible; we do it, usually implicitly, every time we mark an examination script). At present, we use sample problems with solutions to indicate standards, although we are looking for more systematic ways of doing this.

However, it is not difficult to reach a decision on the conditions under which the objective should be attained. We describe above why we wanted an 'open-book' examination. The performance conditions are therefore that the student shall have access to such notes and data sheets as he finds useful.

PLANNING THE COURSE

With our overall objective decided, we found it convenient to re-divide the option into three sections (Figure 1). These sections reflect a convenient, though not waterproof, way of classifying the types of problem which the student will learn to solve. Component objectives for each of these sections were derived from the course objective.

All three sections have this in common; the types of problems to be solved are new to the students. However, the sections differ both in the

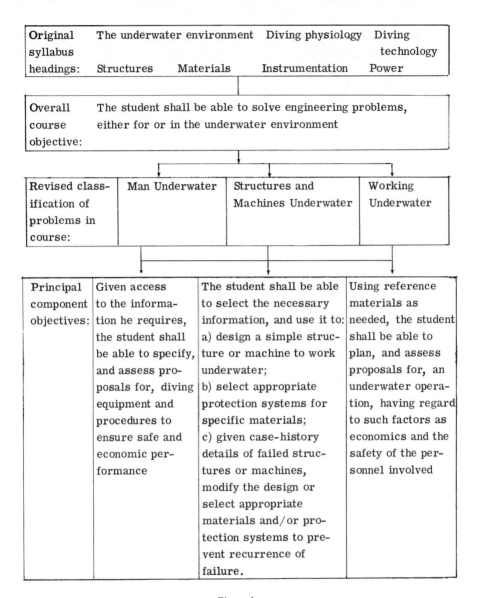

Original syllabus headings:	The underwater environment		Diving physiology	Diving technology
	Structures	Materials	Instrumentation	Power

Overall course objective:	The student shall be able to solve engineering problems, either for or in the underwater environment

Revised class- ification of problems in course:	Man Underwater	Structures and Machines Underwater	Working Underwater

Principal component objectives:	Given access to the informa- tion he requires, the student shall be able to specify, and assess pro- posals for, diving equipment and procedures to ensure safe and economic per- formance	The student shall be able to select the necessary information, and use it to: a) design a simple struc- ture or machine to work underwater; b) select appropriate protection systems for specific materials; c) given case-history details of failed struc- tures or machines, modify the design or select appropriate materials and/or pro- tection systems to pre- vent recurrence of failure.	Using reference materials as needed, the student shall be able to plan, and assess proposals for, an underwater opera- tion, having regard to such factors as economics and the safety of the per- sonnel involved

Figure 1

amount of new data and techniques to be assimilated and in the extent to which they resemble what the student thinks of as 'engineering'. 'Man Underwater' introduces new subject matter, including some physiology, which in no way looks like conventional engineering. 'Structures and Machines Underwater', on the other hand, involves mainly the application of existing skills in new engineering situations. Finally, 'Working Underwater' introduces new information, hardware and techniques, but is quite unmistakably engineering.

INTRODUCING THE STUDENT TO THE COURSE

Students who have been attracted to the Polytechnic by the opportunity of studying underwater technology will join the option with considerable enthusiasm for the subject. They will also have taken part in extra-curricular project work and in practical diving activities, and so will have considerable knowledge and experience. However, students joining the option before 1974 may have little prior knowledge.

We have tried various ways of introducing students to the course. We have tried a free discussion, inspired by Mager's work on learner-controlled instruction (Mager, 1961), in which the students tell us something about underwater technology as they see it, and together we establish a map of the subject based on their interests. Rather more traditionally, we have shown slides of some notable examples of underwater technology hardware, and again discussed them.

In the absence of any rigorous experiment, we can only offer our impression that such introduction helps the students to orientate themselves with respect to the course.

We shall now describe the main features of each section of the course.

Man Underwater - a programmed approach

The initial discussion of underwater technology with new students, referred to immediately above, at least established that there is a need to send men underwater to carry out work, and that doing this presents problems, physical, physiological and psychological.

The primary skill to be learned, then, is solving problems about man underwater. Taking an extreme position, based on our third educational principle (op cit), we tried to plan a course in which students did nothing other than solve problems of this type.

Our decision to use data sheets has already been mentioned; suitable data sheets were written (Figure 2).

Before each problem, or at least each group of problems, the component objective involved was identified, so that the student could see where he was going.

On several grounds, it seemed desirable to give the students immediate knowledge of results, so answers were provided. (For example, this gave the students some freedom of pace of working, and it meant that they could continue to work outside the classroom if they wished.) By this time it had become apparent that the problems, with answers, were best given to the students as handouts.

> **Respiration physiology**
>
> We breathe to obtain oxygen to burn up food to give energy. (In other
> words, respiration provides oxygen for metabolism.) Air consists of
> approximately 21% O_2 and 79% N_2. We don't use all the oxygen we
> breathe in with each breath; exhaled air still contains around 16-17% O_2,
> 79% N_2 and the balance CO_2, a principal product of metabolism.
> The stimulus which makes us breathe is not a shortage of oxygen, but a
> build-up of CO_2 in the lungs. When it reaches around 3-5% of one
> atmosphere partial pressure, a strong need to breathe is felt. This is
> true whatever the absolute pressure of the gas in the lungs; ie, whatever
> the depth the diver is at.

Figure 2

The problems the student would be able to solve in order to reach the
course objective would be fairly complex. It was unlikely that students
would have been able to solve them on entry to the course, though in future
years this assumption will need checking. However, we had to decide at
what level to pitch the initial problems. Ideally, an entry test would be
given, and a sequence of problems provided to match the needs and interests
of each student. This promised to be very expensive, and a compromise
was made. Problems were pitched at a level at which some, but not all,
students could answer unaided. (This was determined in part empirically.)
Optional hints, to be used in case of need, were available. By this time it
had become clear that we were planning something similar to a learning
program.

A flowchart is shown in Figure 3 and three pages of the resultant program are shown as an Appendix. The format is varied (again in accordance
with principle (iii) – that the activity should be appropriate to the objective).
Usually, a question frame is followed by one or two optional hint frames.
The answer frame, including some explanation, is followed by the next
question. Sometimes, an optional branch is provided when the student feels,
or proves, himself deficient in some required skill. For example, a branch
revises the subject of partial pressures, an essential and, to some students,
puzzling, topic.

It is in the nature of problems that an unambiguously correct answer is
not always available. Further, it seems desirable that students should have
the opportunity to practice writing, and defending longer and more varied
answers than a program as described above allows. The aim was not to
write a program capable of independent operation, but to plan a teaching
sequence to attain certain objectives. The staff are resources, to be used

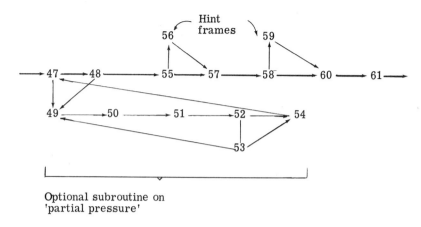

Figure 3

as appropriate; and hence some frames require the students to write down an answer and hand it in for discussion.

It is in the nature of engineering in general, and underwater technology in particular, that it is concerned with real problems and real hardware. At other points in the program, therefore, students are directed to take a diver's aqualung apart to see how it works, or compare the effectiveness of various types of diving suit in an eight-foot cube cold-water tank.

'Man Underwater' is not learned entirely through the medium of a program; appropriateness is all. For example, venturing away from the Polytechnic, students undertake reasoning and psychomotor skills tests in a pressure chamber at simulated depths down to 200 feet. 'Performance decrement due to nitrogen narcosis' thus becomes, not just a technical term, but a memory of an experience. This confluent approach (Dean, 1971) thus combines a variety of relevant experiences, and attempts to harness the motivating effects of some of these experiences.

Other experiences are provided. All students taking the course are encouraged to learn to dive, and most of them do so. When qualified, they join in the monthly field courses to Fort Bovisand, Plymouth, where they experience low visibility, tides, and the problems of organizing working dives in open water.

The classroom, the laboratory and the open sea, as well as film, slide, videotape and the printed word, all provide situations which lead to the attainment of the 'Man Underwater' objectives. And when, in their final examination, the students are required to assess a proposed life support system for a diving chamber, or re-design an item of diving equipment to meet some changed specification, they are usually able to do so.

**A problem-solving approach to 'Structures and Machines Underwater'
and 'Working Underwater'**

We have already said that 'Structures and Machines Underwater' involves the
use of, hopefully, familiar techniques in new situations. The problems are
rather more realistic than they have been in earlier years of the course.
This means that there is more emphasis on identifying the techniques to be
used, or assessing which of the given data are relevant or reliable, or
making an intelligent estimate where data is missing – and being able to
describe what effect such decisions will have on the confidence which can be
placed in the solution.

Students work sometimes alone, sometimes in groups. Problems vary
in length between a few minutes and four hours. They require reference to
data sources, either given to the student or available in the library. However, the learning situations developed for this section of the course have
much in common with those for 'Working Underwater', and we shall devote
the remainder of this description of the course to one 'Working Underwater'
problem.

Two of the component objectives for the course are that the student shall
be able to design simple structures and structural elements for use underwater, and that he shall be able to plan and supervise an underwater operation.
The drilling rig problem below is designed to develop both these skills,
particularly the latter. We give below a log, which records the progress of
one set of students through the problem.

'First hour. The students were given the memorandum (Figure 4).
After initial uncertainty, and some reassurance that the memo means
what it says, they joined in with the 'game'. They decided that more
information was needed. After checking that it was 'allowed', they
decided to 'fly out to the rig to get a first-hand look at things'.
On arrival at the rig, they talked to the superintendent (one of the
authors – BJ). They had three main questions. (i) "Why do you suspect
failure?"; (ii) "Where do you think the failure is?"; (iii) "What have
you done about it?". Answers from BJ (in role of superintendent) were –
(i) "There is a lot more vibration in that cooling water intake pipe, as
well as clanging noises travelling through the pipework"; (ii) "Down
there, about 20 feet below low water springs – you can't see it from the
deck"; (iii) "Dropped drilling speed to half – it's costing us a lot of
drilling time".
The students then prepared a brief for the diver whom they wanted to
go down and look for the damage. They specified the use of CCTV and
a diver communication system, probably a telephone system.
Second hour. Students brief the diver (BJ). He 'goes down', reports
finding the failure, 'a broken cross-member, near which a brass nozzle

63

```
MEMORANDUM
From:        Operations Control, Beppo Petroleum
To:          Underwater Technology Group SA3(b)
Reference:   BJ/7
Date:        January 8 1972

Our offshore drilling platform 'Trident' reports a suspected failure
of a member below water level, after recent storms.  Cause of
failure is at present unknown, but the rig design calculations have
been checked as OK.

Please make a full investigation and recommend action needed to
restore the rig to full operational status.  Also recommend any
work needed at the next refit, due in 10 months.

                                            J. Bloggs
```

Figure 4

on the cooling water intake pipe is flapping about'. (Drawings of the
failure were shown to the students to simulate the TV pictures.) When
satisfied that they have enough data, students started to discuss possible
causes of failure. No firm conclusions.
Third hour. Further discussion among students on cause of failure,
with some reference to lecturer for factual information only. Lecturer's
tendencies to direct the proceedings resisted by exercise of self-control.
With agreement on causes of failure, each student wrote an individual
report on reasons for failure, with his own conclusions on what action
needs to be taken next.
Post-mortem discussions on the reports with the students indicated
general enjoyment of the investigation, and a feeling that the sort of
activity they will carry out during their working life may well be something like this. The students pointed out some ambiguities in the
problem, only some of which had been deliberate. '

Working Underwater includes a variety of other problems, and new ones
are introduced each year to reflect new techniques in underwater operations
as they are reported. Principal data sources are journals, which the
students are encouraged to use in solving the problems.

CONCLUSION

The use of some Educational Technology (Davies, 1972) principles has led
to the development of a very varied course. The design of learning sessions

has not been planned in terms of such questions as: 'How many hours of lecture/seminar/tutorial shall we allocate to this or that topic?' The question has always been: 'What is the most appropriate learning situation which we can devise, economically, which will lead us to the attainment of a given objective?' The next stage, of course, is to abandon the search for one 'best' way of attaining a particular objective, and instead to produce varied routes from which the student will choose the one he prefers.

This course is one evolving answer to one set of problems. The problems will change, and our experience will increase, and for both these reasons the course will continue to evolve. We have used this course in our paper, not because the solution we have produced will necessarily have general applicability, but to demonstrate the process and principles with which we are concerned in action.

Planning and running a course in this way is fascinating, tiring, rewarding. The students respond to our, sometimes clumsy, efforts with enthusiasm. At the worst, we can console ourselves with Mager's observation that, if you tell a student the objectives of his course in detail, you may not need to do much else. On brighter days, the reaction of the students suggests that they find this approach a step forward, and a real help to them in their learning.

ACKNOWLEDGMENTS

George Ackroyd, John Coppage, Ken Hart, Ian Isaac and Jeff Morris, our colleagues in the underwater Technology Group, have helped in the development of the course described in this paper. So have those brave students who have taken the option, little knowing what lay in store for them.

Jim Proctor, Assistant Director of the Polytechnic, and Trevor Wilmore, Head of the Polytechnic's Division of Educational Technology, have helped and encouraged our work, particularly the work on course objectives.

REFERENCES

Baume, A. D. and Jones, B. (1972) Handbook on Aims and Objectives. Internal report NE London Polytechnic
Davies, I. K. (1971) The Management of Learning. McGraw-Hill
Davies, I. K. (1972) Introduction: The Nature of Educational Technology in 'Contributions to an Educational Technology'. (Eds) I. K. Davies and J. Hartley. Butterworth
Dean, T. S. (1971) Learning is Never What One Expects. Paper presented to the American Society for Engineering Education meeting June 21-26, 1971
MacKenzie, N., Erault, M. and Jones, H. C. (1970) Teaching and Learning: an introduction into new methods and resources in higher education. UNESCO
Mager, R. F. (1961) On sequencing of instructional content. Psychological Reports, 9 405-13 reprinted in 'Contributions to an Educational Technology' (Eds) I. K. Davies and J. Hartley (1972) Butterworth
Mager, R. F. (1962) Preparing Instructional Objectives. Fearon Publishers
Popham, W. J. and Baker, E. L. (1970) Establishing Instructional Goals. Prentice Hall

Underwater Technology
Man Underwater
Page 15

Frame Number	
	The next section is concerned with objective b1. We will be concerned with the physiological effects of various important gases involved in diving, and how pressure changes these effects.
47	The effects that gases have on the body usually depend on the partial pressure of the gases. This question will check if you are happy with the concept of partial pressure; if not, some more frames will help to explain the idea. A diver, at a depth of 40m, breathes a gas mixture containing 15% oxygen. What, measured in ATA, is the partial pressure of oxygen in the mixture he is breathing? When you've written down the answer, read Frame 48. If you're not quite sure about this, read Frame 49.
48	The partial pressure of oxygen in the mixture (written as pp O_2) is approx. 0.75 ATA. If you agree, and are quite happy about this, then on to Frame 55. If you don't agree, or would like to go over the idea of partial pressure again, read Frame 49.
49	The Data Sheet tells you what percentage of ordinary air is oxygen. Now, according to a law which may be familiar from your earlier studies of physics, a gas which constitutes x% of a mixture of gases contributes x% of the total pressure exerted by that gas. Thus, what percentage of the pressure of air is contributed by the oxygen it contains? Write down your answer, then read Frame 50.
50	21% of the pressure of air is contributed by the oxygen. This contribution to the total pressure is called the partial pressure. It is measured in appropriate units of pressure – ATA, Nm^{-2}, etc. What is the partial pressure of oxygen in air? Write down your answer, then read Frame 51.
51	The partial pressure of oxygen in ordinary air is 0.21 ATA. What is the partial pressure of nitrogen in ordinary air at 1 ATA? Write down the answer, then read Frame 52.

Frame Number	
52	The partial pressure of nitrogen is .79 ATA (pp N_2 = 0.79 ATA, as it is normally written). What is the partial pressure of oxygen in air at a pressure of 3 ATA? When you have written down the answer, read Frame 54. If you need a hint, read Frame 53.
53	Check back to Frame 49 and Frame 50, where the idea of partial pressure is explained. You know the pp O_2 in air at 1 ATA, and you know how partial pressure is defined. You can thus calculate the pp O_2 in air at 3 ATA. Write down the answer, then read Frame 54.
54	pp O_2 in air at 3 ATA is 3 x 0.21 = 0.63 ATA. Now, back to the question in Frame 47, which shouldn't cause any trouble at all.
55	Before you tackle the next Frames, read the Data Sheet section on respiration physiology. A diver inhales so that he has 5 litres of air in his lungs. He finds that he can hold his breath for 90 seconds. After breathing normally for a few minutes, he inhales a similar amount of air and dives to 20m. a. What will be the volume of free air in his lungs? b. How long will he be able to hold his breath. When you have the answers, read Frame 57. If you need a hint on either section, read Frame 56.
56	a. What is the volume at 20m of a quantity of air which occupies 5 litres at a pressure of 1 ATA? Boyle's Law will tell you. b. Data Sheet 3 describes the physiological factor which stimulates breathing. Does this factor depend on the diver's depth or not? When you've answered both parts, read Frame 57.

Frame Number	
57	a. The pressure at 20m is 3 ATA - so, from Boyle's Law, the answer is $5/3 = 1.67$ litres. b. The pp CO_2 in the lungs triggers off breathing, and so the amount of time for which he can hold his breath is unaffected by depth. It remains – 90 seconds. The next Frames will continue to explore the physiological effects of gases on the body and its functioning. They are leading towards objectives bi and bii.
58	One type of Naval diving equipment involves the diver in breathing pure oxygen. What maximum depth limit would you expect to be imposed on its use? When you've answered, read Frame 60. If you need a hint, read Frame 59.
59	If the breathing gas is pure O_2, then the maximum safe depth will be determined by the depth at which the ambient pressure is the maximum pressure at which the gas can be breathed safely. (Read that sentence again if it wasn't too clear the first time.) And the maximum safe pressure of O_2 is given on Data Sheet 4. When you've written down the answer, read Frame 60.
60	10 metres. (At this depth, the ambient pressure is the same as the maximum pressure at which O_2 can be breathed safely, even for short periods.) In practice, a limit of around 7.5 m is used, to give some margin. The next question is in Frame 61.

The Grounding of the Technologist
M L BRAHAM

INTRODUCTION

The past decades have witnessed the emergence of a hybridization of such diverse fields as electronics (and electrical engineering), information, communication, organization and cybernetic theory, broadcasting (radio and television), psychology, teaching and curriculum theory into what is now roughly designated as Educational Technology.

Two points about this hybridization I believe are clear and can be made almost on a priori grounds: (a) that having competence in technology (as in systems theory and hard- and software) does not imply any necessary competence in education; (b) that having competence in some aspect of what is called education (eg teaching) does signify some competence in certain limited, but hardly generalizable aspects of technology. In other words few professional educationists by virtue of their training can be expected to have very much sophistication, if any, concerning the systems, hardware and software of modern technology, although a certain restricted technology is necessary to the accomplishment of any teaching task.

Hence, with hardly much to go on from the standpoint of common understanding or experience the activities of technologists and educationists are being joined together in some costly but possibly unholy matrimony with a hope for the resolution and integration of differences. It is not clear whether this hope is pious or promising but certainly thoughts about its fulfilment are justified if for no other reason than the social consequences that are involved.

EDUCATION

By education we may understand the process of increasingly intentional self-optimization of individual and social life. It is a matter of natural necessity required by humans because of their particular evolutionary condition. This condition may be stated as follows:

(1) Of all known forms of life, the human is the most deficient in

instinctive adaptive patterns. While infra-human life proceeds essentially according to a programme of unconditioned responses, human life proceeds according to programmes of conditioned responses - or learning.

(2) The function of learning may be briefly considered as providing for the adaption to and participation in the milieu in which the developing human is located.

(3) The lack of an instinctual programme, however, means that there is no end term, or maturational schema to govern the limits of human development, hence the human species is 'open-ended', and from an evolutionary standpoint unfinished, and represents the unfinished, or incomplete nature of human evolution. As a consequence, human life despite its 'highest' attainments is immature, individually and collectively.

(4) Our individual and collective immaturity implies that the direction of human development — and for that matter the direction of evolution at the human or psycho-social phase — is a human affair. That is to say, it depends upon what humans, individually and collectively, intend to and do make of their lives. Thus, human existence calls not only for adaptation to, and participation in, one's milieu, but also for the continual contributions of individuals to their milieu. Since the human milieu is essentially comprised of other humans, the reciprocal contributions of one another results not only in what we call culture, but in cultural evolution.

(5) Cultural evolution, resting as it does on human activity, requires the development of the uniqueness of individuals. This uniqueness is already provided for, not only by their lack of an instinctual or pre-encoded developmental programme beyond the physical level, but by the basically incomplete genetic self-copying that is inherent in all organic reproduction. Further, all life displays a tendency to optimize its developmental potential, to develop its form and fulfil its functions with minimum wastage of energy, ie, with maximum thermodynamic efficiency. The failure of humans to optimize their developmental potential rests on the fact that while the tendency towards optimization exists — hence our language of 'self-realization' and 'self-affirmation' — we must learn not only how to optimize our potentials, but what in each case constitutes optimization.

(6) Self-optimization, and by extension, social-optimization (for the very reciprocity of social life is at once a help and a hindrance) not developing of its own accord, requires the intentional organization of learning — of the acquisition, understanding and utilization of information on two dimensions, the objective and subjective. The objective dimension concerns all that is external to, or perceived by the individual.

70

The subjective dimension concerns the individual's recognition of his own tendencies and possibilities for action, physical, affective and cognitive. Man, to follow a point made by Teilhard, is the only being that we know of, who cannot only know, but also knows that he knows, (Teilhard, 1959) and can develop strategies for knowing.

(7) As young humans are not pre-programmed to intentionally organize their learning, this programming is relegated to adults - those who, due to the complexities of cultural life, are specifically trained for the task. We designate these specialists by the term 'educationist' and the process by which the individual can be assisted in his self-optimization as 'education'. From the perspective of this discussion we can say that education takes up where instinct has either left off in the course of human phylogenesis, or where, due to the evolutionary youthfulness of the species, instinct has thus far failed to become established. Moreover, education thus appears as a necessary agency, not only in the development of individual and social life, but in the evolution of the human species, and by implication, in the continuity of evolution at the human phase. The educationist is thus an agent in the evolution of life at the human phase and finds his sanction not simply in the claims made upon him by the culture in which he works, but in the evolution of nature.

(8) The fact that much of what goes by the name of education, ie, schooling, teaching and learning does not necessarily assist in the optimization of human life, and in fact is often non-, mis-, or even anti-educative, signifies the general inadequacy of the educationists' preparation for, and comprehension of their role.

TECHNOLOGY

At base, technology has a similar naturalistic sanction to that of education. It appears as the organization of activities designed to assist human adaption to, participation in and utilization of the environment. It differs from education in that it does not involve any necessarily normative criteria from the standpoint of its ethical implications. In this it is in company with teaching and learning, in that it may be used for harmful as well as for beneficial ends. The difference between earlier and contemporary technologies lies in the increased complexity and generalizability of the latter – one may think of the evolution of the technology of agriculture or of warfare as examples.

Another feature that distinguishes technology from education, although not from our general concepts of teaching and learning, is its objective character. It concerns the manipulation and use of the 'external world', of the acts, objects and processes in the environment. The development of mining and smelting, of the fabrication of products, of investigative techniques and the accompanying instruments for the study of chemical, physical and biological systems are part and parcel of the development of technology.

The utilizer of a technology, in the sense of one who applies a standardized and repeatable sequence of actions with the appropriate instruments, is designated by the term 'technician'. A 'technologist' however, is one who conceives and develops technological systems for a specific range of tasks or objectives. Hence, an engineer, a systems analyst, a cybernetician, a communications consultant, a computer specialist and an instrument designer are each, technologists.

EDUCATIONAL TECHNOLOGY

This brings us to the more integrative and normative part of the discussion, for it involves the bringing together of two generally differently trained groups of people. On the one hand, we have the educationist whose concern — at least nominally — is with the optimization of human life through the objective and subjective organization of learning. On the other hand, we have the technologists whose concern, based in our day essentially on the study of the 'hard' sciences, is the setting up of viable systems for the attainment of specified goals. Now, while any teacher, in order to bring about learning requires a system — or a technology — of teaching, his work is likely to be based on a rather impressionistic and often highly affective concept of his task and of the nature of the objects of his activity, his students. A contemporary technologist, however, is liable to be a highly disciplined empiricist, far more concerned with the rigour and generalizability of his design. Teaching we are constantly told is a personal activity; technology is reputed to be highly impersonal.

We may, however, suggest that at the point at which we seek to develop an empirically based technology for education, the by now famous distinction between the scientists and the humanists comes into sharp focus. Thus, humanists tend to be generally regarded as being concerned with the optimization of human possibilities, with the expression of man's 'creative potentials', with his freedom, responsibility and right for self-determination. The scientists on the other hand are regarded as being concerned with the analysis and quantification of 'objects of knowledge' whether these objects are human or non-human. Scientists supposedly disdain the subjective and sentimental nature of humanists, and the latter in turn supposedly disdain the cold, hard, value-free attitudes and activities of scientists. While there is probably enough truth in the suppositions to make them common currency, I suspect they are far more of a caricature than all-encompassing truth.

But, the truth is there. Many an educationist grounded in a humanist

72

orientation has little interest in science and its attending technologies. Many a scientist and technologist has little time for the humanistic concerns found in education, and simply demand that particular goals of an objective kind be set and a system be designed and utilized to ensure that students achieve the goals quite apart from what they feel or think about them. From my own standpoint this dualism, is understandable as it is unacceptable; its integration is far more important.

If we return to the point that education implies the optimization of the objective and subjective life of individuals we find it necessary for the educationist to develop a methodology that will provide for this. Socrates, with his particular mode of reflective enquiry; Froebel with his kindergarten that provided for the 'unfolding' of the child; the methods enunciated by Montessori and Dewey are examples of attempts by educationists to develop methods or strategies for teaching.

Now, since optimization involves the developing subjectivity or self-consciousness and self-direction of individuals, either individual strategies need to be developed for each person, (which from the standpoint of mass education is a pedagogical impossibility) or generalized strategies need to be developed that, insofar as is possible, are compatible with each person. With all due regard and concern for individual differences, the question of course arises as to whether there are sufficiently common characteristics about the ways in which humans learn, that general strategies of teaching (or information transmission, if you will) can be interfaced with general patterns of learning (or information acquisition and utilization).

Only through the recognition and generalization of strategies can we go beyond the education of individuals or small groups of people and think in terms of the optimization of humanity-at-large. At the point where our humanistic concern breaks out of the confines of a concern for a few to a concern for the many, technology is required. In fact, we may go so far as to say that there cannot be a thorough going humanism – one that provides for the largest number of people – without a rigorous technological base.

Looked at from the technological side, there is a tendency to simply consider education as a matter of teaching (or requiring the learning of) set items of information based on concepts of physical systems that becomes little more than a sophisticated rote memorization operation with little regard for the subjectivity of the learner, or the way in fact, humans learn. The limited success of programmed instruction other than in discrete job-training type situations can be used as evidence here. Thus, the technologist who is interested in the effective use of his professional competencies in education must turn to a study of human development for his guidelines. Hence, we require of the educational technologist not that he be a pedagogical technician, but rather a comprehensive educational theorist grounded both in

a logically and empirically justifiable concept of man and in technological
methods and systems (Braham, 1972).

THE GROUNDING OF THE TECHNOLOGIST: BACKGROUND TO A COURSE OF STUDY

Our task, then, is to create a new cadre of professionals, the Educational
Technologists: those who are neither simply educationists using audiovisual
or other teaching aids, nor technologists who are mainly concerned with the
development of instructional hard- and software for limited 'behavioural
objectives'. What is called for instead are workers who are both proficient
educationists and proficient technologists.

How is this cadre to be created? Short of entering into a comprehensive
discussion of various types of programs the simplest thing at this point is
for me to refer to the program outline included in the Appendix – others, of
course can be found elsewhere – and to the paper by my colleague P. D.
Mitchell, 'A Curriculum Designed to Produce Educational Technologists'
(1972). I should, however, like to share some thoughts with you about the
philosophical and theoretical grounding of Educational Technologists.

What we may, in general, call 'information technology' refers to the
generation, transmission, reception, storage and retrieval of messages. It
becomes 'educational technology' when the information content of the message,
following R. S. Peters, "implies that something worthwhile is being, or has
been, intentionally transmitted in a morally acceptable manner" (1966).

Immediately questions about what constitutes 'worthwhileness' and
'moral acceptability' arise. They do so both from the standpoint of trying
to establish criteria by which we can judge the educational merit of our
programs and practices, and also because of the nature of educational technology itself. In contrast to the general classroom teacher or university
lecturer the educational technologist is in a position to wield considerably
greater power for good or ill. This power rests on (1) the sophistication of
contemporary communications media which provides for a wider dissemination of messages; and (2) the development of individualized or 'auto-tutorial'
instructional devices which provide for a greater intensity of message
reception, than is possible under general teaching conditions.

Thus, we are thrust into the realm of philosophy as the source of
justification for our programs and practices, and as a fundamental part of
the educational technological training. For obviously, it is the educational
technologists who comprise their own field of activity, and it is the quality
of their thought that shapes the field and in large measure determines its
content and implications. Hence, R. Hooper also argues that "the strength
of educational technology will ultimately depend on the quality of the philosophy and the validity of the science of learning that undergirds it" (1971).

While a philosopher's prejudice might well lead him to wish that educational technologists would be substantially grounded in the fundamentals of philosophy, such an expectation is unrealistic except in the case of those philosophy graduates who turn to educational technology as a profession. Since there are liable to be only a small number of graduates of this kind our task is to provide the most intensive philosophical orientation that is possible within the limited time of what at best may be no more than single course lasting over an academic year.

In my judgement this would not be the sort of course that guides the student through the history of educational thought and the particular 'schools' of educational philosophy, but rather a course that – even in a primitive way – enables the students to learn to deal philosophically with the development of their own educational concepts.

My particular approach, and each will have his own, is to divide a year's course into two main phases, those of analysis and synthesis. Not only do these phases conform to the two major tendencies in philosophy (ie the critical analysis and the constructive synthesis of concepts) but they also conform to the process of conceptual generation generally (Braham, 1972). The course structure provides for a series of 'position' papers on common topics. The research and writing is carried out in three to four week cycles, with no intervening class meetings, followed by intensive meetings for discussion of the structure, content and implications of the main ideas provided in the papers. Little is taken for granted. The papers must conform to the requirements of logical consistency, internal coherence and empirical evidence, along with a recognition of the distinction between knowledge claims and belief claims, and the grounds for their justification. Students are introduced to these basic epistemological areas early in the course and are directed to the relevant literature in philosophy and and philosophy of education.

The first, or analytic, phase of the course concerns the students' 'language of education' (to borrow a title from Scheffler, 1960). A position paper entitled, for example, 'A Concept of Education' allows for consideration of such concepts at 'teaching', 'learning', 'instructing', 'training', as well as the concept of 'education' itself. A second paper, entitled 'The Educationist as Agent' is designed to help the students think through the responsibilities of the educationist. The concept of 'agency', with its implications of action for or on behalf of others, whether they are individuals, groups or institutions is a matter of primary concern. Questions of ethics arise as it becomes necessary for students to consider the effect of program content and method and such criteria as 'good', 'bad', 'right' and 'wrong'.

Following out of an analysis of the enterprise of education and the role

75

or agency of the educationist emerges a concern for the object and subject of education, the human being. What do we know about man? What particular concepts or models of man do we have? What is it about man that calls for education, and what do we anticipate as the effect of our educational activities? While our earlier work has been concerned with the clarification of concepts the second or synthetic phase concerns the integration of information and ideas into theoretical structures for the guidance of programming and practice.

Since any attempt to conceptualize or 'model' man leads into the recognition that man has a place in the total system of events we call the 'Order of Nature', a position paper is devoted to the topic of 'Man's Place in Nature', a topic that is gaining increasing prominence as is indicated by the contemporary concern with the environment. This aspect of our work concerns the education of man from the standpoint of bio-psycho-social evolution (see section on Education above). While it is a hazardous task for even the most accomplished scholar to attempt any sort of generalization about the nature of man, it is something that we do constantly, more often perhaps implicitly than explicitly, and perhaps too often without paying attention to the empirical evidence and its logical implications. The concern in this course is to help the educational technologist seek out information and pay careful attention to its integration and application. Fortunately, we now have an approach that is invaluable, that of General Systems Theory, which concerns locating isomorphic principles that have descriptive and normative applications. Since the idea of systems is particularly applicable to educational technology, this approach, which requires a separate discussion, is particularly valuable.

As the study of man rapidly differentiates into a vast range of topics, the students are asked to select some aspect of human nature that is of particular significance to them for a further paper. Thus, such aspects as the developmental, affective, cognitive, aesthetic scientific, religious and political nature of man (and so forth) and their implications for education are studied by different students. Discussions are used not only to examine the evidence for the ideas presented, but to enable students to contribute to the building up of a larger and more comprehensive picture of human existence than each would normally hold on his or her own.

And finally, since educational technologists are engaged in shaping or directing human life by virtue of the program content and methods that they employ, each student is asked to present a position paper on 'The Nature and Function of Educational Technology', as perhaps their first attempt to develop a systematic basis for their professional activities.

In presenting this course outline, no major claims are made. All that is sought, and all that can be expected within the extent of a single course is to help aspiring educational technologists increase their awareness and be able to approach their professional tasks with openness, a respect for evidence and a concern for grounding their work on a solid base of theory.

REFERENCES

Braham, M. (1972) 'Natural Organization and Education'. In 'Aspects of
Educational Technology VI'. (Ed) K. Austwick and N. D. C. Harris.
Pitman, London
Hooper, R. (1971) 'A Framework for Studying Instructional Technology'.
In 'To Improve Learning: An Evaluation of Educational Technology, Vol.
II. (Ed) S. G. Tickton. R. R. Bowker, New York, page 139
Mitchell, P. D. (1972) 'A Curriculum Designed to Produce Educational
Technologists', presented to the International Conference in Educational
Technology, University of Bath, March 1972
Peters, R. S. (1966) 'Ethics and Education'. George Allen and Unwin,
London, page 25
Scheffler, I. (1960) 'The Language of Education'. Charles C. Thomas,
Springfield, Illinois
Teilhard de Chardin (1959) 'The Phenomenon of Man'. Collins, London

APPENDIX

OUTLINE OF COURSES FOR MASTER OF ARTS PROGRAM IN EDUCATIONAL TECHNOLOGY – SIR GEORGE WILLIAMS UNIVERSITY, MONTREAL

COURSE REQUIREMENTS

All students are expected to complete these courses:

606: Educational Cybernetics

607: Philosophical Aspects of Educational Technology I

613: Learning and Instructional Design

641: Quantitative Methods and Research Design (two term)

Plus one of these

653: Educational Systems Analysis

654: Instructional Systems Analysis

631: Curriculum Development

642: Research and Evaluation in Educational Broadcasting

643: Measurement and Evaluation in Education

Option A

Students who follow curriculum Option A: Research and Development of Educational Technology, take four of the following:

608: Philosophical Aspects of Ed Tech II

611: Psychological Foundations of Ed Tech

614: Seminar and Workshop in Human Communication I

622: Mass Communication Research

651: The Concept of Educational Planning

655: Educational Technology in Developing Nations

661: Educational Simulation & Gaming

662: Computer Based Systems

691: Advanced Readings & Research in Educational Technology I

692: Advanced Readings and Research in Educational Technology II

701: Administration of Educational Technology Units

Option B

Students who follow curriculum Option B: Production and Evaluation of Educational Materials take four of the following:

623: Graphic Communications

632: Curriculum Development

634: Computer Assisted Instruction

661: Educational Simulation & Gaming

681: Seminar on Research and Writing for Media

682: Lab in TV Production and Evaluation I

683: Lab in TV Production and Evaluation II

684: Television Workshop

685: Lab Course in Radio, Audiovision, Tape-Recording and Editing

686: Lab in Motion Picture Production and Evaluation

701: Administration of Educational Technology Units

702: Development and Organization of Educational Broadcasting

The Uses of Educational Technology in Industrial and Educational Establishments

R CLEMENTS

INTRODUCTION

Aims

This paper reports on a survey carried out in June 1972 to discover the extent to which trainers and teachers were using training aids and the techniques of educational technology.

As well as finding out about the techniques that are used, the survey also tried to find answers to these questions:

(a) To what extent are teachers and trainers preparing their own material?

(b) What are the barriers to the wider acceptance of teaching aids?

(c) Which techniques and aids will users (and non-users) want to use more frequently?

(d) How knowledgeable of educational technology are teachers and trainers?

(e) Are there differences between educational and industrial users of the technology?

Method

The survey was conducted by postal questionnaire, because many of the sample were located outside the United Kingdom.

An initial questionnaire was designed and approved by the Scientific and Computing Department of the author's Company. Discussions on the design of this questionnaire were held with leading educational technologists and an amended questionnaire was drawn up and printed (Appendix I). A total of 107 questionnaires were sent out; 98 were completed and returned. This sample of 98 respondents consisted of:

(a) Sales trainers from 13 pharmaceutical companies in the UK   22

(b) Pharmaceutical sales trainers in 24 overseas territories   41

(c) Training instructors from Post Office
   training centres   15
(d) London secondary school teachers   20

For the most part, this paper will consider the total sample, referring to
separate categories only when significant differences occur between them.

FINDINGS

The Person

The overall picture of a trainer/teacher is that of a male (only 11% of the
sample were women) under 40 years of age who has received training in the
techniques of educational technology. Their training had probably been
undertaken two or more years ago (Table I).

Table I. Time elapsed since receiving training in training techniques

Group	6 months	1 year	2 year	2 years+	Total
Pharmaceutical	21	14	17	11	63
Post Office	1	3	2	9	15
Teachers	-	5	-	15	20
Total	22	22	19	35	98

Within the industrial group 86% had been trained by their employers, the
rest received training from outside organizations.

Only one teacher, a headmaster, admitted to having a job title. All the
trainers had titles, although only 47% of these titles contained the words
'trainer' or 'training'.

Respondents were asked what proportion of their working time was spent
teaching or training, including preparation of lectures and training aids
(Table II).

Table II. Percentage of working time spent on training activities

Group	10%	20%	30%	40%	50%	60%	70%	80%	90%	100%	T
Pharmaceutical	16	12	9	4	4	2	6	3	2	5	63
Post Office	–	–	-	1	1	–	–	3	3	7	15
Teachers	–	–	1	-	-	-	-	-	-	19	20
Total	16	12	10	5	5	2	6	6	5	31	98

Not unexpectedly, teachers said they spent all their time in teaching
activities. In contrast, training in the pharmaceutical industry seems to be
very much of a part-time occupation, with more than half the trainers giving
less than 30% of their time to training.

Use of Techniques

When considering educational technology, a fundamental aspect is the specification of the terminal behaviour of the trainee. To quote Mager, "before you choose material, machine, or method, it is important to be able to state clearly what your goals are" (Mager, 1962). Respondents were therefore questioned on their use of objectives (Table III).

Table III. Use of behavioural objectives

	Every session	Some sessions	Never	Total
Trainers	16	40	22	78
Teachers	-	1	19	20
Total	16	41	41	98

In the sample under discussion, the writing of behavioural objectives was widely practised in industry, but virtually non-existent in schools. Of those industrial trainers who 'never' wrote objectives, 64% were working outside the UK.

This initial difference between industrial and educational practitioners set the pattern for almost the whole of this study.

From a list of 15 training techniques and aids, respondents were asked to indicate which items they used and the frequency with which they used them. (Table IV)

Table IV. Frequency of use of training aids

Techniques	Used for all sessions	Used nearly all sessions	Used for only some sessions	Never used
Prepared handouts	22	31	29	16
Overhead projector	12	25	34	27
Cine films	3	3	62	30
Text books	7	19	38	34
Programmed texts	3	9	44	42
Tape/slide presentations	4	10	41	43
Audio-tape recorder	2	3	44	49
Filmstrips	2	3	42	51
Flannel board	3	11	22	62
Videotape recorder	3	-	22	73
Magnetic board	-	4	10	84
TV broadcasts	-	-	10	88
Radio broadcasts	-	-	5	93
Teaching machine	-	-	5	93
Language labs	-	-	1	97

There may be doubts cast on the truthfulness of respondents who claim to have used certain items every time they gave a session. However, remembering that some respondents spent only a small proportion of their time training, it could well be that they did, therefore, 'always' use a particular teaching technique.

The most commonly-used training aids were prepared handouts, the overhead projector and textbooks. Of these, handouts were predominantly used in industry, whilst textbooks were most popular with teachers. Neither of these items could be considered particularly technological, and Table IV shows the fairly infrequent use of the more modern techniques.

It is the final (never used) column in Table IV that emphasizes the lack of use of educational technology. And within the sample, differences occur when each occupational group is considered separately. Table V shows what percentage of each group 'never' used the 15 training aids listed.

Table V. Percentage of each group 'never' using training aids

	Pharmaceutical Trainers	Post Office Trainers	Teachers
Prepared handouts	8%	7%	50%
Textbooks	36%	47%	20%
Tape/slide	30%	53%	80%
Programmed texts	31%	40%	80%
Language laboratory	100%	100%	95%
Videotape recorder	65%	95%	90%
Audio tape recorder	48%	67%	45%
TV broadcasts	97%	100%	60%
Radio broadcasts	98%	100%	80%
Overhead projector	31%	–	35%
Flannel board	48%	80%	100%
Magnetic board	90%	47%	100%
Teaching machines	94%	95%	100%
Filmstrips	44%	60%	70%
Cine films	28%	20%	45%

These percentages were compared for statistical significance at the 5% level with the following results. Teachers used prepared handouts and programmed texts significantly less often than both industrial groups. Overhead projectors and magnetic boards were used by Post Office trainers significantly more often than either pharmaceutical trainers or teachers. Pharmaceutical trainers used videotape recorders and flannel boards significantly more often than either Post Office trainers or teachers. Finally teachers used TV broadcasts significantly more often than both industrial groups. No other techniques were used significantly more or less often by one group. On this evidence, the use of educational technology is more widespread in the pharmaceutical industry than in Post Office training centres or London secondary schools.

Having discovered the extent to which trainers and teachers used the technology at their disposal, the next step was to find out whether or not they prepared their own training aids (Table VI).

Table VI. Frequency with which respondents prepare materials

	Never	Rarely	Often
Write programmed texts	70	17	11
Produce tape/slide presentations	77	14	7
Write teaching machine programs	93	5	-
Prepare o'head projector transparencies	36	23	39
Prepare flannel board materials	63	18	17
Write handout notes	18	27	53
Write VTR productions	85	8	5
Write audio tape productions	69	21	8
Produce slides	78	12	8
Produce wall charts	32	38	28

Apart from wall charts, handouts and overhead transparencies, the groups studied were not greatly involved in preparing their own training aids. If Table VI is compared with Table IV it can be seen that with the exception of teaching machines (which were hardly used anyway), many people using the techniques listed did not prepare them themselves. Pharmaceutical trainers were most likely to prepare their own aids, whilst teachers were least likely to do so.

Barriers to wider use

Respondents were presented with a choice of five possible barriers to the use of educational technology and asked which ones they thought were most appropriate. Lack of both time and money were thought to be the main restricting factors, but with differing emphasis on each between teachers and trainers (Table VII).

Table VII. Barriers to use of educational technology (total percentage exceeds 100%, as respondents often selected more than one answer)

	Trainers	Teachers
Training aids and techniques too expensive	64%	40%
Technology is only for academics	10%	-
Cannot understand theories of ed. tech.	14%	5%
Good lecturers do not need gimmicks	19%	30%
Insufficient time for preparation	45%	70%

Only one-fifth of the total sample felt that the academic nature of educational technology could in some way inhibit its wider use. However, deeper study of other aspects of the survey gives some support to this theory.

Extending the use of training aids

When considering the possibility of extending the use of training techniques that they were currently using, industrial trainers came down heavily in favour of video recording equipment, programmed texts and tape/slide presentations. Teachers made almost no response to this question. Of the techniques they were not using but would like to, trainers again specified video recorders followed by tape/slides and programmed texts. The few teachers who responded favoured video equipment and teaching machines.

Trainers' and teachers' knowledge

Besides the five barriers to the use of training aids covered in Table VII, it was felt that another important barrier might be the lack of knowledge that users had of the techniques of educational technology.

One source of such knowledge is the teachers'/trainers' training course. Others are conferences, journals and books dealing with educational technology and associated subjects.

Everybody in the sample studied had undertaken a training course, but relatively few had been exposed to the other sources of information. Though only 23% of the industrial group had attended a conference on training or educational technology, not one teacher had done so. Nor had even one teacher read a book about educational technology in the three months prior to taking part in this survey. For the industrial trainers, 36% claimed to have read training books recently, and quoted more than 40 titles to back their claim (Appendix II).

This pattern was reversed when journals and regular publications were considered. Eighty per cent of the teachers said they read teaching/training journals either occasionally or every edition. This compared to 37% of trainers. However, although a larger percentage of teachers read journals, their reading was restricted to the Times Educational Supplement, to the exclusion of all other publications.

Besides measuring teachers' and trainers' exposure to sources of knowledge of educational technology, an attempt was made to measure their knowledge of this subject. The questionnaire contained a list of 15 people, 13 of whom had a connection with educational technology (author; educationalist; behavioural scientist etc). Two false names were included as a check on guessing. Respondents were asked to state what significance the names held for them. Of a possible 1,274 correct responses only 85 (7%) right answers were given. Of those 85, pharmaceutical trainers made 68, post office trainers 10 and teachers 7.

Discussion

The facts elicited by this study of 98 trainers and teachers seem to throw up two main areas around which discussion can usefully take place. Firstly, there is the fact that the use of educational technology in industry and schools is fairly limited. And secondly, the figures show a certain lack of 'professionalism' among respondents. This is suggested by their woeful knowledge and the extent to which they do not read the journals and books available to them. There was, in fact, a third major point: that teachers trailed sadly behind their industrial counterparts in every respect. However, there was nothing in the data to suggest why this should be so.

Closer examination of the information regarding the use, and the barriers to the use, of teaching aids shows a certain amount of inconsistency. 'Equipment and aids are too expensive', said the largest percentage of trainers (Table VII) – a reason, one might have felt, that was more likely to come from teachers. However, Table V shows that some trainers are well ahead of teachers in their use of expensive equipment. Teachers too, are making use of the dearer items, as Table VIII shows.

Table VIII. Items which each group uses 'more' or 'less' than other two groups

Teachers		Pharmaceutical		Post Office	
more use	less use	more use	less use	more use	less use
textbooks language lab audio tapes TV b'casts radio b'casts	handouts tape/slides prog. text o'head proj. flannel b. magnet b. teaching mch. film strips cine film	tape/slides prog- text VTR flannel b. teaching mch. film strips		handouts o'head proj magnet b. cine film	textbooks VTR audio tapes TV b'casts radio b'casts

So, even admitting that items such as video recorders, language laboratories and film projectors are expensive, perhaps expense was more of an excuse than a reason for non-use of teaching aids. Flannel boards, magnetic boards, tape recorders and many of the other items on the list could hardly be termed expensive and yet their use was still very limited. And there was one technique that 95% of teachers and 27% of trainers never used that cost no money at all — the setting of behavioural objectives. Something other than money must be inhibiting the growth of educational technology. Insufficient time was cited by 70% of teachers and 45% of trainers as a barrier to the wider use of training aids, and at first glance this seems reasonable.

Half of the industrial group were not even called trainers and spent less than one-third of their working time in that activity. Yet compared with teachers (who spent all their time doing that job), trainers were producing and using more training aids. They were even writing more behavioural objectives, a very time-consuming activity. Finally, and rather oddly, the people who felt time to be a barrier were, between them, producing more training materials than the rest of the sample.

The second main point for discussion was knowledge. It could be argued that trainers and teachers who do not use the available technology demonstrate not a lack of time or money, but a deficiency of knowledge.

Knowledge, in this survey, meant the recognition of the personalities of educational technology. To 71% of the sample, the list of names meant absolutely nothing. The responses made by the remainder showed that those people who read both training journals and books were most knowledgeable.

Despite their apparent lack of knowledge, people who did not read technical books or journals still used several of the training techniques listed in the questionnaire (Table IX).

Table IX. Comparison between reading habits and techniques used

Do you read training literature?	No. of training techniques used													
	0	1	2	3	4	5	6	7	8	9	10	11	12	13-15	T
No	1	2	5	2	8	5	3	7	4	2	1	-	-	-	40
Yes	1	3	3	4	-	3	9	9	10	9	5	2	1	-	58
Total	2	5	8	6	8	8	12	15	14	11	6	2	1	-	98

A Mann-Whitney U-test performed on this data confirmed the impression that trainers who do read training literature use a significantly greater ($P < 1\%$) number of training aids in their work.

Others too have found that teachers and trainers become more knowledgeable and make greater use of educational technology when they read training literature (Davies, 1972). This poses the important question 'Why is it that teachers/trainers do not read publications and books on educational technology and training?' Although this question was not asked of the respondents, some of the responses in Table VII might be interpreted as a possible answer.

One fifth of the sample thought that people could not understand the theories behind educational technology and that its techniques were only for academics. With this attitude it is hardly surprising that so many of the sample have demonstrated avoidance rather than approach responses towards educational technology (Mager, 1968).

Their avoidance of things academic has identified one of the major

barriers to the easy acceptance of new ideas. That barrier is the language
of the communicators. Books, papers and articles describing new theories
and concepts of educational technology (and even old ones) are too often
presented in a style that makes comprehension extremely difficult. Consider
this extract from a paper presented at APLET 1972 (Braham, 1972).

'Overall holism is demonstrated in the articulation of elements, aspects
or parts, that, emerging from minimally differentiated or inchoate beginnings,
become increasingly functionally - specific.'
Or this:
'Thus, unless thought and action is to be dispersive and fragmentary, to be
subject to what Bruner called 'episodic empiricism', the establishment of
functional relationships among and between differentia, and hence the
establishment of a functional structure in cognitive organization, is essential.'

This observation regarding educational communication is not original.
It was made by Rowntree (1966) as long ago as 1966 in the context of the 'fog
index' devised by Gunning (1952). Yet Rowntree's observation that many of
the standard works on educational technology have a high 'fog level' and
therefore are not easily understood, has gone unnoticed. Authors are still
writing non-communicating communications. The fog levels of articles in
APLET Journal are as high as 18 (Gunning says anything above 12 is difficult
to read). Little wonder that readers comment, (Arup, 1972) and teachers
and trainers avoid such publications.

It was not possible to isolate the influence of conferences and therefore
no comment can be made about them.

There remains one other factor for discussion: the training course.
Everybody in the sample indicated that they had received training in teaching/
training techniques.

It is reasonable to assume that the nature and quality of that training
could influence their behaviour and attitudes towards educational technology.
No questions were asked about the depth of training respondents had under-
gone but some comments can still be made.

A survey (Harvey & Romiszowski, 1970) on one aspect of educational
technology (programmed learning) and its use in teacher training concluded:
'A surprising lack of interest is shown by many colleges engaged in such
influential work as training teachers in this relatively new but certainly now
well-established technique..... The techniques are talked about often, discussed sometimes, and practised rarely.' Teachers, it will be remembered,
were shown to be less knowledgeable and less likely to produce or use training aids than the rest of the sample.

Of the 78 industrial trainers, something is known about the training of
50 pharmaceutical trainers. During their training they would have discussed, and seen demonstrated, at least, handouts, tape/slide presentations,

film strips, programmed learning, VTR, overhead projector, ciné films and flannel board. And pharmaceutical trainers knew more, produced more and used more techniques than the remainder of the sample.

SUMMARY OF MAIN FINDINGS

(1) Very few techniques associated with educational technology are used with any regularity by teachers and trainers.

(2) Only a small proportion of teachers and trainers prepare their own training aids.

(3) Time and money were felt to be the main barriers to the wider acceptance of educational technology, but there was nothing in the study to support this view.

(4) Few teachers and trainers read publications related to their professions. Those that did read showed a greater knowledge of educational technology and demonstrated a much wider use of training aids.

(5) Teachers were less well-read, less knowledgeable and less practical regarding educational technology than were industrial trainers, whilst trainers in the pharmaceutical industry seemed best equipped in aspects technological.

REFERENCES

Arup, J. (1972) Letter in 'Programmed Learning and Educational Technology, Vol. 9, No. 3. Sweet & Maxwell

Braham, M. (1972) 'Natural Organization and Education'. In 'Aspects of Educational Technology VI'. (Ed) K. Austwick and N. D. C. Harris. Pitman, London

Davies, I. K. (1972) 'Current Problems of Educational Technology and Training'. European Training, Vol. 1, Spring 1972

Gunning, R. (1952) The Technique of Clear Writing, McGraw-Hill

Harvey, J. M. and Romiszowski, A. J. (1970) A survey of the use of Programmed Learning in Craft and Technical Training. Visual Education, April, National Committee for Audio-Visual Aids in Education

Mager, R. F. (1962) Preparing Instructional Objectives, Fearon

Mager, R. F. (1968) Developing Attitude Toward Learning, Fearon

Rowntree, D. (1966) Basically Branching, Macdonald

EDUCATIONAL TECHNOLOGY SURVEY – QUESTIONNAIRE

1. Are you a:
   (tick appropriate box)

teacher	
trainer	
college lecturer	
other	

1.

2. Do you have a job title? (if yes, please specify)

YES	NO

2.

3. What was your age last birthday?

20-30	31-40	41-50	over 50

(tick appropriate box)

3.

4. Are you:

Male	Female

4.

5. Are you instructing/teaching:

(tick appropriate boxes)

INDUSTRY		EDUCATION	
Operators		Primary	
Craftsmen		Secondary	
Representatives		College	
Supervisors		University	
Managers		Polytechnic	
Others		Others	

5.

6. What percentage of your working time is spent teaching/training? (including preparing lectures and training material)

10	20	30	40	50	60	70	80	90	100

6.

7. Have you received any training in training techniques? (The training referred to here could be Sales Trainers' Courses run by your own company or another organization, teachers training college, etc. Do not include conferences attended)

YES	NO

(If 'yes' give brief details)

7.

BOOKS AND JOURNALS READ BY INDUSTRIAL TRAINERS

(Authors' names are included only when quoted by respondents)

BOOKS

Adults Learning, J. Rogers
Developing Interactive Skills, N. Rackham
Training and Developing the Supervisor, C. M. Bowan
Task Analysis in Training
The Modern Supervisor
Management Training
The Management of Learning, Ivor Davies*
Training by Objectives
Why Children Learn
Discovery Learning
Effective Sales Presentation, Tony Jay
The Human Side of Enterprise, Douglas McGregor
Relaciones Publicas, Neilander-Miller
Lo que Vd. debe saber si mismo, F. Llauge
Lo que Vd. debe saber sobre los demas, F. Llauge
Management Communication through Audio-Visual Aids, Langton Gould-Marks*
New Handbook of Sales Training*
Designing for Visual Aids
Salesmanship- Practices and Problems
Industrial Organisation and Management, Bethel et al
Supervising Salesmen in a Competitive Market, Dartnell
Manual para la Formacion de Vendedores
The Art of Teaching, G. Hignet
L'amination de L'equipe de vente, B. Krief
La formation psychologique a l'entretien de vente, P. Lavand
Showing Off-Display Techniques for the Teacher, R. Leggat
Tecnica de las Conferencias
Direccion de Reuniones de Ventas
Sales Management and Sales Organisation
Modern Psychology in Industry, K. Madsen
Reflex and Soul, Pavlov
The Technology of Teaching, B. F. Skinner
Lernen und Verhalten, Correll
Rationelles Lernen, Naet
Motivation through the Work Itself, A. M. Ford
La Pedagogie de l'adulte, Muchielli
L'animation de groupe, Muchielli
La Conduite de Sessions et de reunions, Muchielli
Techniques of Persuasion, J. A. C. Brown
Up the Organisation, R. Townsend
The Integrity of the Personality
Fundamentals of Psychology, C. J. Alcock

JOURNALS AND PERIODICALS

Industrial and Commercial Training*
Industrial Training International*
Harvard Business Review
Personnel Management*
The Training Officer
Programmed Learning and
  Educational Technology
Sales Management
Canadian Training Methods

Industrial Society
Management Today
C.B.I. Education and Training
  Bulletin
Times Educational Supplement*
Visual Education*
British Journal of Medical
  Education
Audio-Visual*

*Quoted by more than one person

A Model for Systematic Television Research

G O COLDEVIN

The development of television within the more prosperous nations of the world has been both rapid and dramatic. Correspondingly, within the developing nations, television is increasingly viewed as a potentially major component in promoting and disseminating vital developmental campaigns. Yet within the proliferation of terrestrial and satellite networks, it is interesting to note the paucity of deliberately designed evaluation formats which proceed simultaneously with stimulus production. Generally, television research has been conducted in an aloof manner with the researcher confined to his 'laboratory' alien to the practitioner operating in the natural situation (Rao, 1972). Although notable departures from this mode may be found in Sesame Street (Ball, 1970) and to a lesser degree, The Open University (Bates, 1972), for the most part researchers have considered a television programme or series to be a given 'causal' (independent) variable influencing certain outcomes (dependent variables). Within this context, message design is primarily left to producer intuition with the results of (appropriate) research findings left non-applied. The indictments concerning the gulf between research and practice apply equally to mass educational television transmissions and those directed toward formal educational institutions. This paper attempts to set forth a rationale for systematic consideration of the primary elements involved in conducting qualitative television research and the integration of theory and practice.

Broadly speaking, a television communication system should revolve around four main components, which may be diagrammed as shown in Figure 1. In an ideal system, each of the components starting with 'PLANNING' should proceed in an orderly fashion with each component influencing that which follows. Notably, the bulk of the emphasis, with few exceptions within a national/international framework, has been concentrated upon the planning, production and dissemination phases. An overall lack of attention has been accorded to evaluation and its subsequent impact upon the system components. Fortunately, this 'imbalance' has of late received serious international consideration (UNESCO, 1970, 1971).

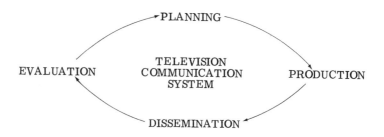

Figure 1. Integral components of a television communication system

For the purposes of discussion, the foregoing model is intended to apply to an 'educational framework', whether it be social, adult or within formal institutions. Correspondingly, the 'EVALUATION' component is to be viewed as one of a qualitative nature, extending from a study of knowledge acquisition to change in behaviour patterns.

Pre-conditions for qualitative television research

Prior to, or in conjunction with the undertaking of any type of qualitative research, the 'physical characteristics' of target audiences should be determined. This type of activity, normally referred to as 'quantitative research' may be characterized by the following terms of references.

Attributes of actual and intended audience

1. Distribution of access to the medium (individual or community set ownership).
2. Demographic and socio-economic, profiles of actual and intended audience (separate and combined). (The term 'demographic' here refers to such factors as age, sex, racial composition, linguistic patterns, religious and/or ideological identification, size, density, growth, distribution, migration and vital statistics. 'Socio-economic' denotes education levels, occupation groupings and income categories.)
3. Viewing habits of actual audience outlined in terms of frequency of exposure, duration of exposure, suitability of timings and choice behaviour in reference to media content (eg, informational, cultural, entertainment, etc).
4. Differential use of other educational and mass media by actual and intended audience.

Having suggested the types of support data requisite to initiating research, consideration may now be directed to each of the components outlined in Figure 1.

ORGANIZATIONAL COMPONENTS OF A QUALITATIVE
RESEARCH SYSTEM

1. PLANNING CONSIDERATIONS

(a) Aim or purpose of programme or series

During the planning stage of the communication system, the broad objectives of a television presentation or series should proceed simultaneously with broad research outlines. The two activities may be regarded as interdependent. The basic presentation theme may also dictate a general production pattern and types of pre and post viewing activities.

More specifically, broad goals may be delineated to concrete behavioural objectives. Two types may be isolated for goal clarification: (1) cognitive or informational; (2) affective or attitudinal. The cognitive objective specifies the information (amount and level) the programme is expected to impart, and the affective objective, the type of attitude modification which may be stimulated through the presentation. A third objective here, which may be more appropriate to developmental, long term research, would involve the combined effect of the cognitive and affective (motivational) elements toward change in behaviour patterns.

(b) Characteristics of target population

Mutually interactive with the specification of behavioural objectives are the characteristics of the target population. Effective, purposive communication must be directed toward a well defined target population. In communication terminology, the 'Field of Experience' or 'Salience Attributes' of the intended audience form the basis for message design. In addition to the considerations outlined earlier (see Pre-conditions for qualitative television research) relevant factors here might include, values, norms and importantly, innovation receptivity.

2. PRODUCTION STRATEGIES

Within the context of 'production', two primary types of variables may be isolated for analysis. For the purposes of discussion these will be termed, Technical and Presentation variables.

(1) Technical variables might include such elements as picture quality, sound effects and background music, special effects such as dissolves, fades, wipes and multiple screen, flat vs key lighting, stage design, camera angle, close-up and zoom shots. The use of the telecine for slide and film inserts may also be included here. Although this listing is far from exhaustive, these factors may be considered as associated 'hardware' variables.

(2) Presentation of 'software' variables on the other hand may include consideration of the following strategies: simple vs complex treatment of

subject; subjective vs objective camera angle; lip sync vs voice over dialogue; overt vs covert audience participation; one-sided vs multisided persuasiveness; efficacy of direct dubbing; use of redundant material vs summary or review segments; utility of graphics to support dialogue. Additionally, speed of presentation, difficulty of spoken material, source credibility (degree to which television source is considered trustworthy) and perceived homopholy of source (degree to which television source is perceived by audience as similar in cultural orientation) merit serious attention. The over-riding concern of production strategies is to tailor behavioural objectives toward the perceptual level of the target population.

3. DISSEMINATION CONSIDERATIONS

Research at the receiving end, whether it be a rural teleclub, classroom, or comfortably furnished living room, is primarily concerned with physical determinants. Factors such as lighting, acoustics, seating arrangements, distance from viewing set, picture quality, and distractions, among others may be considered important variables within this context. (Normally, this type of 'observational activity' would fall under the rubric of quantitative research. Within the context described herein, however, it becomes an integral component in the qualitative research system.) Pre and post telecast discussions as well as related or combined media campaigns may also be considered as relevant components in the dissemination phase of the system.

4. EVALUATION CRITERIA

(a) Construction of performance measures

Performance measures or 'measures of programme effect' should ideally be tailored to original behavioural objectives and production strategies, thus providing a nexus between 'probable' causes and results – between independent and dependent variables. Dissemination variables should also be included, although under ideal conditions these may be difficult to evaluate as independent variables. The case of community and classroom viewing permits a more utilitarian role of inclusion of this measure. Factors which bear relevance to performance measure formulation include instrument construction (closed vs open-end questions, insertion of probe questions, use of scale ratings, etc), interview vs written response administration, check for instrument ambiguities (modification through pre-testing), validity and reliability checks and standardization of data collection procedures.

(b) Research methodology

Associated with performance measure construction is the process of research design, sample selection, randomization strategies and formulation of statistical procedures. Generally, research methodology particularly in developing countries has employed one of two designs, namely, the one group pretest - post test design and the pretest - post test control group design. The former may be designated as quasi-experimental since it does not control for the effects of testing (effects of having taken the pretest on post test results), history (events occuring between the first and second measure in addition to the experimental variable), and instrument decay (familiarity with the instrument and respondents may cause changes in interviewer reactions, in respondent's reactions, or both). The latter, however, because of the control group comparison is not subject to the previously mentioned internal validity violations and accordingly may be termed a true experimental design. Similarly, the post test only, control group design may be given serious consideration because of its ease of administration.

(c) Modes of evaluation

Two basic types of evaluative feedback will be included here as indices of television effectiveness.

1. Action or operational research: This mode of evaluation primarily directed toward the short term 'impact' of television exposure particularly lends itself to a continuous assessment format. The obvious value of this type of research rests in consistent feedback to the system and detection of modification requirements in either the planning, production or dissemination phases (or all of these combined). Generally, this mode of evaluation is confined to the cognitive and affective areas because of the 'time' requirement for behaviour modifications.

2. Developmental research: This mode of evaluation is concerned with the long term influence of television exposure and provides indices of the transfer of cognitive and affective objectives into behaviour patterns. Generally, this type of research is an exhaustive, 'in depth' evaluation designed to complement and extend the value of the operational research. Feedback of this nature may lead to modifications in the broad goals and behavioural objectives of a sustained television series.

With the foregoing discussion in mind, the basic components are incorporated into a systematic television research model (Figure 2). The salient features of the model may now be briefly outlined.

Planning and production components are integrated within the development phase in harmony with the established attributes of a given target population. Additionally, the evaluation criteria is established prior to dissemination. This component has in most television developmental programs been applied after the dissemination phase - in these cases, a 'tack

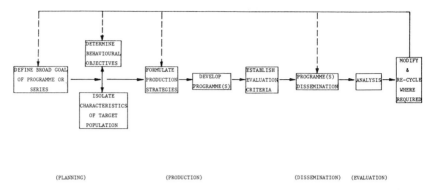

(PLANNING)   (PRODUCTION)   (DISSEMINATION) (EVALUATION)

Figure 2. A model for systematic television research

on' rather than integral component of the system. The analysis task variable
in the present model incorporates evaluation criteria and dissemination
variables, which together form the basis for modification and recycling of
the system.

Significantly, the system may be modified in any (or all) of the key
research components (indicated by dotted lines). The evaluation criteria
and analysis task are assumed to be sensitive indicators (feedback) of the
system's strengths and weaknesses. The modification and re-cycling phase
is further assumed to be proportional to isolation of system error. (As
expressed by Wiener, (1954), "Feedback is a method of controlling a system
by reinserting into it the results of its past performance".) For example,
an error detection in production strategy would involve appropriate modification in program(s) development, evaluation criteria, and analysis, whereas, a weakness in dissemination (eg, faulty functioning of set, over-crowd-
ing) would involve only slight alteration. Error in the broad goal formulation
would invite modification of the entire system.

The foregoing model is intended to apply universally to television research, whether it be a pretest, pilot programme or examination of samples
of ongoing programmes against the criteria they are expected to reach. A
similar rationale may be extended to other educational communication media.

It is significant that research of this nature must be an integral part of
any deliberate communication design and applied on a continuous basis. The
model further attempts to closely integrate the efforts of the researcher and
the producer so that findings may be meaningfully interpreted as feedback
toward effective production design. Similarly, policy and planning decisions
may be based upon practical rather than theoretical guidelines through such
efforts.

PRETESTING

As noted earlier, by substituting the term 'programme(s)' for 'prototype' the model also applies to a pretesting format. The expressed inherent value of pretesting extends to Hovland et al (1949) when they suggest that "....By successive correction and re-evaluation one might achieve a far more effective communication than if the product had been carried through to completion as originally designed". More recently, Sedlik (1971) notes that the probability of feedback being of a major nature is lowest when diagnostic evaluation has been practised at earlier stages. When pretesting is bypassed, the probability of major corrective feedback is higher. In more practical terms, the value of pretesting may be summarized as follows:

1. In terms of efficiency and economy, it is much more practical to test sample formats of a broad theme, than the series itself. Costly mistakes may be prevented. Entrenched programmes are difficult to modify and change.

2. Justification for and validation of applying the medium, in a given situation, to a given audience - a basis for policy and planning decisions is provided.

3. Provides a format for 'continuing' evaluation of a campaign or series and 'continuous' evaluation of samples of new programmes prior to sem-dissemination on a broad scale.

4. Provides an opportunity for the researcher and producer to get to 'know' their audience.

Perhaps the best applied example of the value of pretesting and continuing evaluation to date lies with the researchers and producers of 'Sesame Street'. The 'lessons' from this experience may well serve as an action model for international educational television developments.

In combining the value of pre and post production evaluation, a useful summary is provided by Sedlik (1971):

Preproduction evaluation is important because any check on effectiveness should be based on a clear statement of objectives, definition of target audience and appropriate media selection.

Production pretesting (a) provides producers an additional basis for decision making; (b) allows for revision for maximum effectiveness; (c) acts as a quality check on production; (d) provides management a continuing evaluation of individual performance; and (e) fulfills an organization's evaluative responsibility to assure the cost effectiveness of its products.

Post production validation is the final test of a mediated presentation. It (a) allows for final feedback from the user; (b) validates earlier pretests; (c) determines effects of those presentation which have not been pretested, and (d) supports an effective distribution system by assessing utilization.

It should be noted that the more efficient and economic combination of these activities may be culminated in a well conducted 'pilot project'.

POSTSCRIPT

Communicating effectively through television is a highly complex undertaking which may or may not be satisfied through intuitive reasoning. As Carpenter (1968) notes, the adaptation of the new media for effective learning of students "..... cannot be done by using judgements of a priori reasoning or even by committee decisions, however well qualified the members are. The effective adaptation of media and materials requires the use of empirical methods in the preparation of instructional materials and in the difficult work of improving curriculums". What appears requisite is a thorough grounding in the principles of applied research for the television producer and the techniques of television production for the researcher. The suggestions by Rao (1972) apply equally to educational television. "One looks forward to the day when research in mass communication feeds the practice of mass communication and the lessons learnt in the practice of mass communication feed the researchers..... The essence of the problem is not to bring about agreement but appreciation between the two groups." The model described in this paper attempts to provide a framework for this nexus.

REFERENCES

Ball, S. (1970) 'The First Year of Sesame Street: An Evaluation'.
  Educational Testing Service, Princeton
Bates, A. W. (1972) The Evaluation of Broadcasting at the Open University.
  In 'Aspects of Educational Technology VI' (Ed) K. Austwick and N. D. C.
  Harris. Pitman, London
Carpenter, C. R. (1968) Adapting New Educational Media for Effective
  Learning of Students. In 'Instructional Technology: A Book of Readings'.
  (Ed) F. G. Knirk and J. W. Childs. Holt, Rinehart & Winston, New
  York, p. 237
Hovland, C. A. et al (1949) 'Experiments on Mass Communication'.
  Princeton University Press, Princeton, p. 6
Rao, Y. V. L. (1972) 'The Practice of Mass Communication: Some Lessons
  From Research'. UNESCO, Paris, p. 48
Sedlik, J. M. (1971) 'Systems Techniques for Pretesting Mediated Instruc-
  tional Materials'. Education and Training Consultants Co., Los Angeles,
  p. 80
UNESCO (1970) Proposals for an International Programme of Communication
  Research. UNESCO, Paris
UNESCO (1971) Mass Media in Society: The Need of Research. UNESCO,
  Paris
Wiener, N. (1954) 'The Human Use of Human Beings'. Double Day, New
  York, p. 61

Objective Testing at a Distance
B CONNORS

The Open University has been making extensive use of objective testing ever since its first students began work in January 1971. The size and special nature of the University's operations, with its highly-centralized course-design, correspondence services and student records, made it a very suitable field for the development of some sort of automated scoring system, and very elaborate arrangements for computer-marked assignments (CMAs in our jargon) have now been set up. While these are clearly still some way from being fully developed, the system has already been described by one knowledgeable visitor from the States as the most sophisticated one he had ever encountered. This paper, then, while very much of an interim report, sets out to describe the present situation, to discuss some of the character-istics of an unusual testing system, and to outline some of the problems involved in trying to satisfy a number of conflicting requirements.

There are, of course, several ways in which the automatic scoring of objective tests may be accomplished. The student may, for example, indi-cate his answers by punching or perforating a sheet, and this can be used in one way or another as the input to a punched-card type of data-processing system. This is a pretty slow method, as was the old IBM 805 analogue machine, first developed in 1935, which measured the electrical conductivity of the pencil marks which the student had made. But I suppose that optical scanning, extensively developed by Lindquist and his colleagues from the mid-fifties onward, is the process which holds the field at the moment. There are several machines which can read off pencil blobs (say) which the student has made to indicate his answers, and other machines which can actually recognize letters and figures. Optical scanning machines of this kind can work quite fast, and although there are a few self-contained machines which, within one and the same box, perform both reading and simple marking operations, the system becomes much more flexible if the output from an optical scanner is fed in as the input to a digital computer which can then be programmed to perform almost any desired marking

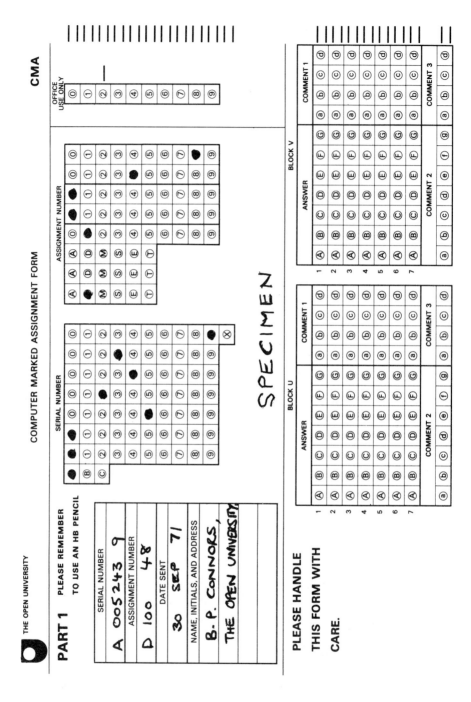

PART 2

BLOCK W

| ANSWER | COMMENT 1 |

1 Ⓐ Ⓑ Ⓒ Ⓓ Ⓔ Ⓕ Ⓖ ⓐ ⓑ ⓒ ⓓ
2 Ⓐ Ⓑ Ⓒ Ⓓ Ⓔ Ⓕ Ⓖ ⓐ ⓑ ⓒ ⓓ
3 Ⓐ Ⓑ Ⓒ Ⓓ Ⓔ Ⓕ Ⓖ ⓐ ⓑ ⓒ ⓓ
4 Ⓐ Ⓑ Ⓒ Ⓓ Ⓔ Ⓕ Ⓖ ⓐ ⓑ ⓒ ⓓ
5 Ⓐ Ⓑ Ⓒ Ⓓ Ⓔ Ⓕ Ⓖ ⓐ ⓑ ⓒ ⓓ
6 Ⓐ Ⓑ Ⓒ Ⓓ Ⓔ Ⓕ Ⓖ ⓐ ⓑ ⓒ ⓓ
7 Ⓐ Ⓑ Ⓒ Ⓓ Ⓔ Ⓕ Ⓖ ⓐ ⓑ ⓒ ⓓ

COMMENT 2 | COMMENT 3
ⓐ ⓑ ⓒ ⓓ ⓔ ⓕ ⓖ ⓐ ⓑ ⓒ ⓓ

BLOCK X

| ANSWER | COMMENT 1 |

1 Ⓐ Ⓑ Ⓒ Ⓓ Ⓔ Ⓕ Ⓖ ⓐ ⓑ ⓒ ⓓ
2 Ⓐ Ⓑ Ⓒ Ⓓ Ⓔ Ⓕ Ⓖ ⓐ ⓑ ⓒ ⓓ
3 Ⓐ Ⓑ Ⓒ Ⓓ Ⓔ Ⓕ Ⓖ ⓐ ⓑ ⓒ ⓓ
4 Ⓐ Ⓑ Ⓒ Ⓓ Ⓔ Ⓕ Ⓖ ⓐ ⓑ ⓒ ⓓ
5 Ⓐ Ⓑ Ⓒ Ⓓ Ⓔ Ⓕ Ⓖ ⓐ ⓑ ⓒ ⓓ
6 Ⓐ Ⓑ Ⓒ Ⓓ Ⓔ Ⓕ Ⓖ ⓐ ⓑ ⓒ ⓓ
7 Ⓐ Ⓑ Ⓒ Ⓓ Ⓔ Ⓕ Ⓖ ⓐ ⓑ ⓒ ⓓ

COMMENT 2 | COMMENT 3
ⓐ ⓑ ⓒ ⓓ ⓔ ⓕ ⓖ ⓐ ⓑ ⓒ ⓓ

BLOCK Y

| ANSWER | COMMENT 1 |

1 Ⓐ Ⓑ Ⓒ Ⓓ Ⓔ Ⓕ Ⓖ ⓐ ⓑ ⓒ ⓓ
2 Ⓐ Ⓑ Ⓒ Ⓓ Ⓔ Ⓕ Ⓖ ⓐ ⓑ ⓒ ⓓ
3 Ⓐ Ⓑ Ⓒ Ⓓ Ⓔ Ⓕ Ⓖ ⓐ ⓑ ⓒ ⓓ
4 Ⓐ Ⓑ Ⓒ Ⓓ Ⓔ Ⓕ Ⓖ ⓐ ⓑ ⓒ ⓓ
5 Ⓐ Ⓑ Ⓒ Ⓓ Ⓔ Ⓕ Ⓖ ⓐ ⓑ ⓒ ⓓ
6 Ⓐ Ⓑ Ⓒ Ⓓ Ⓔ Ⓕ Ⓖ ⓐ ⓑ ⓒ ⓓ
7 Ⓐ Ⓑ Ⓒ Ⓓ Ⓔ Ⓕ Ⓖ ⓐ ⓑ ⓒ ⓓ

COMMENT 2 | COMMENT 3
ⓐ ⓑ ⓒ ⓓ ⓔ ⓕ ⓖ ⓐ ⓑ ⓒ ⓓ

BLOCK Z

| ANSWER | COMMENT 1 |

1 Ⓐ Ⓑ Ⓒ Ⓓ Ⓔ Ⓕ Ⓖ ⓐ ⓑ ⓒ ⓓ
2 Ⓐ Ⓑ Ⓒ Ⓓ Ⓔ Ⓕ Ⓖ ⓐ ⓑ ⓒ ⓓ
3 Ⓐ Ⓑ ● Ⓓ Ⓔ Ⓕ Ⓖ ⓐ ⓑ ⓒ ⓓ
4 Ⓐ Ⓑ Ⓒ Ⓓ Ⓔ Ⓕ Ⓖ ⓐ ⓑ ⓒ ⓓ
5 Ⓐ Ⓑ Ⓒ Ⓓ Ⓔ Ⓕ Ⓖ ⓐ ⓑ ⓒ ⓓ
6 Ⓐ Ⓑ Ⓒ Ⓓ Ⓔ Ⓕ Ⓖ ⓐ ⓑ ⓒ ⓓ
7 Ⓐ Ⓑ Ⓒ Ⓓ Ⓔ Ⓕ Ⓖ ⓐ ⓑ ⓒ ⓓ

COMMENT 2 | COMMENT 3
ⓐ ⓑ ⓒ ⓓ ⓔ ⓕ ⓖ ⓐ ⓑ ⓒ ⓓ

B.P.C. Business Forms Limited D/C11676-11.10.70.

PART 3

VERY DIFF.		VERY EASY
④	③ ② ①	⓪

4 HOW DIFFICULT DID YOU FIND THIS ASSIGNMENT?

VERY INT.		VERY UNINT.
④	③ ② ①	⓪

5 HOW INTERESTING DID YOU FIND THIS ASSIGNMENT?

LESS THAN ½ HR.	½ TO ¾ HR.	¾ TO 1 HR.	1 TO 1½ HR.	1½ TO 2 HR.	OVER 2 HRS.
○	○	○	○	○	○

6 HOW LONG DID YOU SPEND ON THIS ASSIGNMENT?

operation, to record and perhaps notify the results, and to perform the kind of statistical analyses which seek to explore the quality of both individual items and the test as a whole. The Open University's computer-marked assignments are processed in the way I have just described, by the combination of a high capacity mark-sensing device – an optical mark reader, or OMR – and the University computer. For those interested in technicalities, the OMR is an ICL UDR 1900 series and the computer is an ICL 1903A. The latter, of course, performs many other operations besides the scoring of computer-marked assignments, since it carries out most of the University's routine clerical and accounting tasks, some of which, such as the maintenance of the students' records on computer-file, have obvious links with its use as a device for marking objective tests. None the less, for the computer, the marking of thousands of CMAs each week and all the other routines associated with CMA marking, is only a part-time occupation.

To describe only the machine-reading and computerized scoring which takes place, however, is to concentrate on no more than the middle of a long sequence of interrelated operations which in many cases began several years previously in the course-teams which are the creative heart of the University. Most of the objective tests which Social Science foundation course students are currently worrying over, for example, were generated in 1970 as an integral part of the learning materials which were then being designed. Let me use just one of these objective test items to illustrate what the student has to do:

    Z.3.   The von Thünen model of rural land use assumes one of the following in the area being considered:

        A   Soil of variable fertility

        B   A juxtaposition of competing states

        C   Negligible transport costs

        D   Uniformly flat land

Having selected his answer, C let us say, the student indicates this on a standard answer sheet similar to the one shown — you will see that he has entered a pencil blob in the cell marked 'C' on line Z.3, corresponding to the number of the question.

If you now look at the top of the answer sheet, you will see that in the right-hand corner the student has made similar pencil blobs to indicate his student number, A0052439, the number of the course (D100) and the number of the computer-marked assignment (48). This is all the information needed by the computer to identify the correct set of input parameters and to apply them to the student's answers, but just in case the form is rejected for technical reasons, or if it should be queried at some later date, and have to be handled manually, the student writes in his own details, in full, together with details of the CMA. But the computer needs only the coded information in the top right-hand corner, and on the basis of this it scores each item, applies a question weighting factor, adds up the raw score for each block of questions, applies a block weighting factor, works out the percentage of the total marks gained by the student, converts this to a six-point alphabetical scale, prints out a notification to the student and adds the letter-grade he has just gained to his record. This, of course, is a highly simplified account of what takes place, and anyone familiar with data processing of this kind will be able to imagine the quality control routines and validity checks that take place both inside and outside the computer before the student's answer sheet is finally stacked away – in most cases never to be seen again.

The Open University's computer-marked assignment system, then, involves thousands of students, working in their own homes, answering objective tests items, encoding their answers on to a special answer sheet which is posted to Walton Hall, read by an optical scanner and scored by a computer which in due course makes the necessary records and informs all concerned. When set down briefly like that it sounds like a reasonably normal, if somewhat elaborate, machine-scoring system, not too different from others which have been developed over the last few years. But there are, in fact, some quite extraordinary features of the system as a whole, to which I would like to draw your attention.

First of all, the student is in an 'open book' situation in that he is being tested in his own home, under no kind of supervision, with all his learning materials lying around. Indeed, he might better be said to be in an 'open resource' situation, rather than an 'open book' one, since the Open University is, after all, a multi-media institution, and he may, for example, be able to consult a repeat broadcast, or a recording, rather than a book, in order to solve a knotty point. Simple recall-type test items become even more trivial than they normally are in this situation, although they may ensure that students at the very least do have to open their books.

Secondly, the OU student is in a completely open-ended time situation. If he wishes to devote ten, or even twenty hours to a computer-marked assignment, he is at liberty to do so, even if most of that time is spent in worrying over the one or two items he is unable to answer with any certainty, and which would be unlikely to carry his score over the threshold into the next higher grade even if he ultimately got them right. And not only is the student at liberty to spend as long as he likes on his computer-marked assignment; he is not compelled to attempt it on any one fixed day, or indeed in the course of any one week. There is a final date for its submission, to be sure, but this is usually fixed so as to allow some flexibility to the students, whose study habits vary considerably.

If, like me, you have been used to paying as much attention to controlling the test conditions as to designing the test itself, the idea of a totally unsupervised, open-book, open-ended time, test situation may be quite enough to make your flesh creep. If not, here is a further implication of the 'open-book', or 'open resource' situation.

If you believe, as I do, that students often learn as much from each other as they do from their teachers, then you will not object to my classifying a student's friends, particularly those fellow-students who are pursuing the same course, as resources in their own right. To put it simply, perhaps too simply, if a student cannot find the answer in his notes, or his correspondence unit, in his textbooks, or in the broadcasts, there is always a chance that his friend Fred will know, and be able to explain it to him. Or perhaps George knows, or Margaret does. Perhaps, (and this is quite probable), none of them is altogether certain of the correct interpretation of the question, and only after a certain amount of discussion will they be able to home in on some kind of consensus, solve the problem by group consultation, and enter their agreed answer on each of their computer-marked assessment sheets.

What is extraordinary to me is that this kind of very sensible behaviour is called 'cheating' if it takes place inside a conventional examination room, but is saluted in the corridor outside as one of the most important ways in which true education takes place. It seems, to me at least, that it can never be wrong to try to find out something you are supposed to know, and I would like to suggest, just in passing, that the idea of 'cheating' in tests has been invented and used by authority rather like the Official Secrets Act to define as morally wrong any flow of information which happens to be inconvenient to those who are in power and whose lives become just a little more difficult if free interchange is permitted.

This kind of situation, in which the pursuit of wide long-term educational goals demands that the student finds out, while the short-term and rather narrow goals of good testing demand that he remain silent and display his ignorance, is only one of a number of situations in which the requirements of good teaching and the requirements of good testing are diametrically opposed to each other. I hope to suggest others in due course, but let us first consider the OU student and his unsupervised, open-book, no-time-limit, computer-marked tests.

It says something of the way in which the consciences of schoolchildren are manipulated by their teachers that some OU students have been in real doubt as to whether it was at all ethical for students to help each other with their assignments; some even asked that the University forbid such self-help arrangements. The University would clearly be in no position to enforce any such a prohibition even if it were to be made, but I am happy to report that it did not try to adopt a purely negative attitude, or to sit on the fence, but did what all good teachers have to do when forced to make an inescapable choice between good testing and good teaching. The Open University has said publicly to all students:

"We cannot stress too strongly that we think such discussion is highly desirable. It is not 'cheating'. It is a natural expression of students' interest in discussing the course objectives and testing one another's grasp of them – in short of helping one another to learn."

At this point, I suppose, the expert in psychometrics should reach for his hat, install his tongue in this cheek long enough to congratulate the University on its lofty devotion to educational ideals, and go his way in the certain knowledge that a good deal of test reliability has been traded off in order to take advantage of an opportunity to stimulate the self-help practices which are useful in all educational situations and, let us acknowledge, much more than useful, invaluable in fact, in the long-distance student situation. And although the expert in educational measurement will think that we have sold the pass, we still need him, for all is not lost. Many students, through choice rather than necessity, do not take part in self-help groups anyway, for it seems more than possible that the OU has an understandable attraction for the confirmed 'loner'. Furthermore, the scores obtained in computer-marked assignments only carry a proportion of the marks that go towards each student's continuous assessment grade – in other words tutor marked assignments usually have most influence in determining the student's grade for course-work done during the year.

We do have some information on what happens when students attempt computer-marked assignments under controlled conditions, for some courses include computer-marked questions in the final examination which comes at the end of each course. These are answered by the student in the course of an otherwise traditional three hour examination, and are properly invigilated so that what people call 'cheating' does not take place. As far as one can tell from the Social Science courses which have used this kind of examination question there does not seem to be any significant difference between the results that students obtain in the completely open CMA situation and those that they get in the tightly controlled conditions of the examination room. If one wanted to generalize, one might perhaps say that the results of the CMAs provide evidence that a certain amount of study has taken place, while the examinations show that, all other things being equal, some learning seems to have occurred; we assume that students have had to consult their learning materials to answer even the lowest level of CMA question, but that to answer an examination question of similarly low level, they have at the very least remembered something. A pretty low cognitive level for higher education, of course, if the testing reaches no higher than that, but I will come back to this question of the level of CMA items.

The interface between psychometric theory and every day educational practice is often characterized by the friction which occurs whenever a theoretical ideal interacts with highly imperfect reality. When, for example, an expert on testing gently suggests that if all students regularly get 100% marks in Section A of a test it would be easier and cheaper to drop that part of the test altogether, an expert on human nature may well suggest (rather less gently) that if Section A were no longer to be tested, then some teachers would stop teaching it and thus neglect the one part of the curriculum in which they could regularly expect complete success.

Examples like this last, in which good testing practice seems to run counter to the needs of good teaching, are found in many educational situations, but they tend to be accentuated in the OU's long-distance independent-study system. Indeed, it seems to me that one very interesting characteristic of the OU situation is that it throws into high relief many problems that certainly exist in the more usual face-to-face situation, but which are usually less prominent because of the many safety procedures, some of them almost unconscious ones, which operate when teacher and students have more opportunity for personal interaction. If I now go on, therefore, to describe some of the ways in which testing compromises have to be made in order to meet the facts of life in the OU, I hope that this will not merely amount to an account of practices in one rather special institution, but will strike sympathetic echoes in anyone who has to use objective testing in circumstances that are less than ideal, and with students who are on their own, as it were, for all or part of their time.

In Table I which follows, I have tried to assemble some of the often conflicting requirements, and arrange them into some sort of continuum, so that, for example, the quite impersonal, large-scale, and non-educational requirements of the data-processer at one extreme are contrasted with the highly individual, personal, but perhaps equally non-education, emotional requirements of the student at the other extreme. Arranging in this way the many needs which we have to try to satisfy simultaneously, we may be able to illuminate, but not necessarily solve, some of the particularly knotty problems which confront us.

In starting on the left with data-processing requirements, I must emphasize that no data-processing system is the completely flexible and totally obedient servant that the salesman made it out to be. There are always things that you cannot do because you have not got the right equipment, and things that you could do in 1973 if only you had foreseen them and planned for them in 1970 – this latter being a good example of the sort of friction that can occur between data-processing and psychometric theory, in column 2. The test specialist may say, "I need to carry out this kind of analysis by the middle of next month", but this sort of statement usually evokes hollow laughter from programmers and systems analysts whose tidily-planned

Table I. Requirements to be satisfied by a good testing system

1	2	3	4	5	6
Data-processing requirements	Psychometric requirements	Institutional requirements	Educational requirements	Individual study requirements	Emotional requirements
eg adhering to specification, advance notice of modifications, etc	eg discrimination, reliability, validity, etc	eg security, uniformity, appeals system, etc	eg quick feedback, appropriate levels, covering the syllabus, etc	eg time flexibility differing learning styles, problem-solving strategies	eg need for group support need to succeed, reduce uncertainty, etc

world cannot always accommodate the unexpected.

In column 3 I have included certain institutional requirements which are not much concerned with teaching or learning, but which nevertheless affect the student quite closely – such things as fairness, uniformity, security, an appeals system, and so on. Column 4 includes the educational aspects of testing, in which the institutional goal is sound teaching for all students; here we can list such things as the need for issuing prompt feedback on the results of testing, the need to formulate tests at an appropriate cognitive level, the need for testing to be based on the whole curriculum, and so on.

Column 5 contains the individual student's learning requirements, and here we include the many needs thrown up by individual student differences, such as the need for a flexible budgeting of time, the need to cater for different learning styles, and different problem-solving strategies, and so on. Finally, in column 6 we have the affective and emotional needs which complicate the approach of some students (and, indeed, some academics) to the subject of testing.

The range of requirements thus stretches from the mechanical to the human, from reason to emotion, from the general to the particular, and from the modern to the primitive. It is not altogether surprising that it should be difficult to satisfy all these requirements at one and the same time, as one or two actual examples will perhaps show.

I suppose that most of us would agree that once a student has submitted his computer-marked assignment, he should be informed without delay of his results, and should be told which questions he has got wrong. Quick feedback of this kind is calculated to promote learning; it will certainly satisfy the requirements in columns 4 and 5, and, except for the student who has failed miserably, the requirements in column 6 as well.

But, and this is a huge 'but', the CMAs do not all arrive at the same time; if you do this to the first student who submits his CMA, you are, in effect, publishing the correct answers to your tests, and are thus failing to satisfy the need for security and fairness in column 3. Moreover, if the answers are known, your test will lose whatever value it started with as a discriminatory device, and will thus fail to meet the needs of column 2.

At this point someone, probably an administrator, and probably standing not far from column 3 will exclaim, "But that's easy! All we have to do is to insist on a very strict cut-off date, after which no more answers will be accepted, and the correct solutions published."

Unfortunately, it is not as easy as that. In column 5 we include a need for students as far as possible to study at their own pace. Too strict a cut-off date will discourage the laggards who fail to meet it – and these laggards may well be some of the most deserving students of all. On the other hand, too generous a cut-off date will mean that those students who are well ahead with their work will receive CMA feedback at a time when they have long since left that part of the course behind – the feedback will be stale, largely irrelevant and likely to be ignored. I suspect that it would not be altogether impossible to insist on a very tight closing date for receipt of students' efforts (after all, Messrs Littlewoods, Vernons, etc, seem to be able to manage it), but I hope that I have shown that this would be, in a way, penalizing the poor, and rewarding the rich.

But that is not all. One of the psychometric requirements in column 2 is the need to build up a bank of well-tried and validated test items, but, except as a very long-term project, this is not easy if you publish the answers to all your best items. On the other hand, if you do withhold the model answers, you are losing a teaching opportunity. The single-minded tester would not think this a valid objection, of course, since his view would be that you ought not to be trying to test and teach in one and the same operation, but the fact that he is probably right would not prevent academics from complaining that the requirements of column 5 had not been met, nor would some students, operating in an atmosphere of uncertainty, feel that the requirements of column 6 had been met either.

Let us take another example. If you are running an interdisciplinary or multi-disciplinary course, and the OU tries to be an interdisciplinary university, then you have to devise test items to explore several individual subject disciplines within one and the same test paper. The course demands this (column 4) and the student, whose ability is probably not uniformly high over the whole of the subject areas, will certainly expect to find his best subjects fairly represented among the test items presented to him. When the results of a test like this are subjected to item analysis procedures, however, psychometric theory will point out that many of the test items appear to be contributing nothing much to the test as a whole, and indeed that there may be only the slightest correlation between success in some of the items and success in the test as a whole. This very useful idea of individual item/whole test correlation as a measure of the discriminating power of a test item is dependent upon the idea of test 'purity' – in other words, that all the items are trying to measure the same thing. How do you reconcile this psychometric requirement (column 2) with the needs of columns 4, 5, and 6, when the same test has to contain highly quantitative tests of economics and, say, items depending upon the complex verbal language of sociological theory?

As one final example of the conflict between different requirements in a long distance objective-testing system, let us consider the problem of levels. If you are a university you can hardly be satisfied with tests that call for anything less than virtually the full range of cognitive levels laid out in Bloom and elsewhere, and while you may have to rely upon your tutor-marked assignments to explore the higher cognitive levels, you will still seek to make the level of some of your objective test items rather higher than the low-level recall/recognize/paraphrase type. Yet in trying to struggle upwards to higher levels in order to satisfy column 4, you often leave behind the reliable and well-validated territory that alone will satisfy column 2, and find yourself exploring the much less black-and-white territory which is likely to cause trouble to some students in column 6, if not elsewhere. Attempts to raise the cognitive level of objective test items are fortunately made much easier for us by the elaborate range of scoring options planned for the OU by Michael Neil. Examples of various kinds of multiple-choice, graded-preference, confidence-weighted, matching, ordering, and array-based items are shown in the appendix, which in itself will perhaps demonstrate that although much development remains to be done, the system is ambitious, sophisticated, and reasonably flexible.

This paper has outlined the special characteristics of the Open University's computer-marked assignment system, and has mentioned a few of its problems, some of which can be seen to be acute forms of maladies which beset objective testing in other, more traditional, institutions. The University is always seeking to improve its testing practices, and although it is barely humanly possible to reconcile all the conflicting demands that have been demonstrated in this paper, it looks forward to improving its tests without ever forgetting that testing procedures must always be seen to have a pay-off in the Open University's prime activity, which is the promotion of learning. Thus it is that when I hear of our objective tests forming the agenda for student self-help groups meeting all over the country, the tester in me mutters "sabotage!", while the teacher says firmly, "Nonsense – this is education!"

SPECIMEN OBJECTIVE TEST ITEMS IN SOCIAL SCIENCES

1. **Multi-choice 1 from 4, only 1 preferred response**

   According to Hobbes, the government should be obeyed provided it:

   A   keeps within the constitution

   B*   offers security and protection

   C   is democratically chosen

   D   has divine backing

   E   stimulates economic growth

2. **Multi-choice 1 from 7, 2 equally acceptable responses**

   Select one type of climate associated with only one or two traditional ways of life:

   A* polar

   B   sub-polar

   C   temperate

   D   Mediterranean

   E   desert

   F   monsoon

   G* equatorial

3. **Graded-preference 1 from 7, 4 possible responses attracting different scores**

   Which of the following would probably be of most importance in determining the reputation of the leader of a gang like the Nortons:

   A* his past reputation as a fighter

   B* his ability to mix outside the group

   C   his skill in at least some of the gang's activities

   D   his past record of success with the girls

   E   the status of his job

   F* the fairness with which he resolves conflicts

   G* his resourcefulness

4. **Up to 3 from 7**

   Which of these are relatively uncommon among the Kung Bushmen: (select 2)

   A   direct personal criticism

   B   overt aggression

   C   accepting gifts from a disliked person

   D   private property

   E* recounting their myths publicly

   F   public debate of private shortcomings

   G* sexual misdemeanours

5. **Matching**

Match the words and phrases in list 1 with the writers who first used them (list 2):

List 1		List 2	
A	Organic solidarity	A	Runciman
B	Gesellschaft	B	Durkheim
C	Relative deprivation	C	Toennies
D	Generalized other	D	Mead

6. **Ordering**

Using the criteria suggested on pages 27-30 of your correspondence unit, arrange the following in order of importance as urban centres:

A   Newcastle-under-Lyme
B   Burslem
C   Stoke
D   Hanley
E   Tunstall

7. **Array**

From the 49-cell matrix on the following page, select the cells which:

7.1. Indicate political institutions which can be termed informal, and are not part of the formal structure of government.

7.2. Indicate the reasons for the great stability and continuity in the organization of Congress.

8. **Confidence weighting - a note**

Using the comment cells on the CMA answer sheet, it is possible to score simple multi-choice items according to the degree of confidence that the student expresses in his answer:

a   completely confident
b   very confident
c   moderately confident
d   slightly confident

	A	B	C	D	E	F	G
1	The disposition of federal funds	Judicial review	Pressure groups	Bill of Rights	The Executive	Using the media	Seniority
2	Patronage	Veto	Political appointments	Congress	State elections	The Democratic Party	Declaring unconstitutional
3	The Senate	National elections	Organising Congress	Conflict between interest groups	Power through possession of information	Impeachment	Influencing legislation
4	Power to investigate	States' rights	The President	Developing countries	Federal control	The House of Representatives	The Republican Party
5	The Electoral College	Lobbyists	The Chairmen of Committees	Initiating legislation	The Congressional Committee system	The constitution	The Vice-President
6	Professional civil servants	State legislation	Obtaining votes	Outvoting by $\frac{2}{3}$ of each House	Voting federal funds	Power through experience and expertise	The Supreme Court
7	Presidential parties	The safe district system	The central government's rights	Extra constitutional practices	Influencing voters	Congressional parties	A concurrent resolution

The Trend and Extent of Educational Technology in South Africa

P J CONRADIE

BACKGROUND

Although several sorts of technical devices such as projectors, have been applied in South African schools since the Second World War, a general awareness of an educational technology became evident only as late as the previous decade. Since the late fifties a steady flow of news, rumours, scientific data as well as wild speculations in connection with programmed instruction and teaching machines has appeared on the scenes soon to be followed by information in connection with research results concerning other technical aids such as language laboratories, overhead projectors, television education, computers, etc.

By 1963 not only was the source book of A. A. Luinsdaine and R. Glaser, 'Teaching Machines and Programmed Learning' a reasonably well known publication in our country, but our scientific literature was also enriched by our own publications in this field. One of the earliest publications with probably a wide impact was a 1963 monograph of the Johannesburg College of Education, 'Automation in Education', written by W. G. Barnett and L. Proctor.

In 1961 the South African Council for Automation and Computation (SACAC) was founded. The initial impetus came from the International Federation of Automatic Control and was directed to an existing national body suggesting that South Africa should become a member of the International Federation. The objects of the SACAC are to promote the science and art of automation and computation by:

(a) acquiring and disseminating information;

(b) organizing national conferences;

(c) participating in international conferences.

Since its founding this body has arranged nine conferences and symposia. Its 1972 symposium was on 'Automation in Education'.

Since the middle of the sixties the various aspects of educational technology have gradually drawn more and more attention. Computer-assisted instruction, language laboratories, simulation techniques and television instruction have not only been a matter of discussion, but various universities, colleges of education, technical colleges, departments of education, military training institutions, industrial firms, and councils have started research programs, and at least ten dissertations and theses have been completed on various aspects of automation in education.

As was mentioned earlier, the 1972 SACAC symposium dealt with automation in education. From the papers and discussions it was clear that, in general, the different forms of automated education had achieved a high standard. In contrast to previous unjustifiable claims in connection with the significance and possibilities of educational technology, it was also apparent that the various speakers were far less excessive in their views.

SOME RESEARCH RESULTS

Naturally it is not feasible to mention all achievements attained in the total research program. Within the limits of this paper a general overview with the focus on some prominent results would therefore be more relevant.

Results concerning the fundamental theory

From a more formal, fundamental point of view programmed instruction has been criticized as being a too mechanistic way of teaching and learning and as therefore having a dehumanizing influence on the pupils and on education. It has also been pointed out that programmed instruction has resulted from experiments on animals, which do not apply to human beings. In many cases, however, people holding this viewpoint do not take the trouble to implement the method in practice in order to convince themselves of the difference between theory and practice.

Although certain philosophical aspects of educational technology still remain a stumbling block for anthropological-orientated fundamental thinkers, there are other, more pragmatic commitments to which modern cultural structures are bound:

(a) Western society has firmly committed itself to the ideal that education should be available at all levels to all who want it, or can benefit by it. In addition to this democratic commitment, it is increasingly recognized that initial and continuing education is a necessary component of any rapidly developing culture especially in modern times.

(b) It follows therefore, that all education is, or will in future be, mass education. This is a reality long since accepted for the primary and secondary school level, largely accepted for the tertiary level in the USA, and growing in importance elsewhere (Lee, 1972). For universities this entails profound implications in connection with internal organization, training of staff, counselling of students, and above all, methods of teaching. As to this latter, increasing use will have to be made of communication and organization technologies in order both to deal with the rapidly increasing numbers and (in view of the challenge of these growing numbers) to increase educational effectiveness by making learning a more individual process (Lee, 1972; Dieuzeide, 1971).

(c) Not only have the numbers increased vastly, but also the span and the level of knowledge in general, which fact of necessity makes new and big demands on the responsibilities of the various teaching institutions. The fact that the world has learnt more about science during the last 20 years than during the previous 20 centuries has necessitated a new outlook by educators. This knowledge explosion should bring about changing goals in education, for example, that pupils and students should be taught to assimilate, and to apply, relevant knowledge and not merely to memorize facts. Memorization of facts alone is of little value in our present society and the indications are that it will be even less so in future.

(d) Virtually all research evidence (Lee, 1972) indicates that the large-scale use of audiovisual and technological aids is in agreement with the broad humanistic educational aims, but in order to be effective the use of these media must be part of a deliberately planned system of instruction. There is also more clarity on the form of this planning. In a systematically planned course, for example, at least six steps need to be observed: specifying clear and accepted objectives for the course; deciding upon the sequence of achieving these objectives; devising student learning activities that will lead to these objectives; identifying the stimuli required to produce these student activities; deciding upon the appropriate media of instruction in each case; and, finally, preparing the appropriate materials in co-operation with media specialists (Fletcher, 1968).

(e) Media can thus broaden the spectrum of education, but they are not the sum total of education. At times they can be used as a substitute for conventional teaching, but more often they are used to accomplish learning goals never before possible. In other words, these aids are, and always will be, secondary in importance to the teacher. Teaching is an art, and with the revolution in educational technology, the teacher has actually become even more important than before.

Results of research on programmed instruction

In 1964 the National Institute for Personal Research started off with an experimental program in mathematics. It was intended for young adults who had left school without any formal training in the subject and the aim was to give them a working knowledge in mathematics equal to Senior

Certificate level. The teaching program was a linear one with criterion frames which led to limited branching.

A full report and description of the development and validation of this comprehensive course in programmed mathematics was printed in the magazine Psychologia Africana, Vol. 14, 1971. Some of the research results during development of the program were given, as well as research results of the final version of the programs.

The following are the findings and conclusions arrived at:

'Taking into account the results obtained with this programmed mathematics course, the authors are satisfied that results can be improved by using such a course as a teaching aid and/or as a teaching method. However, they agree with Taylor and Williams (1966) that difficulty or inability to adapt existing educational systems and administrative procedures to accommodate a new medium, will certainly detract from its value.

The fact that a program cannot compete with a good teacher is also recognized, but since good teachers are not always available, programmed instruction can fulfil an obvious need and programmed instruction can help the good teacher to do even better.

Research results have indicated that programmed instruction is not rigid, inflexible method as many opponents of the method claim, but that the teacher with imagination and initiative can use it in a variety of ways in order to satisfy students' as well as their own needs. In this connection Skinner's statement that students learn without teaching, but that the teacher arranges conditions under which they learn more rapidly and effectively, clearly assigns to programmed instruction a legitimate place in the teaching situation.' (Skinner, 1965)

In 1964 the State Department of Education, Arts and Science initiated the institution of language laboratories which later on were successfully used in teaching immigrants the two official languages.

It has already been mentioned that various research efforts in programmed instruction have resulted in dissertations on the topic. These research projects include work on the teaching not only of the natural sciences but also languages and the social sciences.

Since the early sixties programmed instruction has also been used in military training on quite an extensive scale and with remarkable success.

Results of research in connection with television instruction

Since there is no national TV broadcasting system in South Africa as yet, the main efforts in this field have so far been directed toward the use of closed-circuit television. During the late sixties the Transvaal Education Department in collaboration with the Council for Scientific Industrial Research (CSIR) initiated two different research studios at the Colleges of

Education in Pretoria and Johannesburg respectively. They are still in operation. At the latter College the emphasis is on teacher training, while television is also used in an integrated way with micro-teaching and team teaching.

Several universities are at present engaged in television instruction research programs and a few dissertations are in the course of production.

At the moment the feeling among some research workers in the field is that the unique qualities of TV should be exploited in the structure of every TV lesson if this aid is not to be misused. It must be stressed that from this viewpoint all types of lessons are not considered fit to be televised; as a matter of fact only a few types of lessons can best be presented by television.

Results of research on computer-assisted instruction

While most of the universities in South Africa make extensive use of computers, these devices are primarily used for administrative purposes. There are, however, at least two universities where the computer is being used as an aid in instruction. The first project of this kind to be applied to university education in South Africa was undertaken by the University of Witwatersrand, Johannesburg, and is called the WITCAT (Witwatersrand Computer-Assisted Teaching) system. Although modest in design and rudimentary in terms of hardware interfaces the system has made possible the assessment of student reaction to computer-assisted instruction. In spite of severe handicaps as to available resources the system has been successfully applied and has been generally accepted by the students in the teaching of pain physiology. An assessment of student reaction has revealed areas of weakness where improvement can be made. Fortunately, the system design is sufficiently open-ended to allow these improvements to be made.

Some of the early findings and inferences of the WITCAT project are:

(a) Students were keenly critical of shortcomings in the system, such as the need for an interrupt mechanism, greater branching possibilities and more extensive diagnostics. In spite of these shortcomings, however, an overwhelming majority felt that the WITCAT system was a better teaching medium than some of their lecturers.

(b) A teletypewriter terminal is not the ideal interface for man-machine communication. When no alternative (such as a CTR terminal) exists, however, it can be applied, particularly in the reinforcement of courses when the lecturer does not have sufficient time to cover the whole field himself.

(c) The teaching of medical subject matter often involves the presentation of coloured visual material. The possibility of using this method to combine desirable but untaught areas of instruction was warmly received by students.

(d) It is generally accepted that the institution of a general learning resource of this nature using the WITCAT system would provide students with the necessary and valuable learning facility. The fact that a sub-system such as WITCAT can be embedded within the already existing and heavily used time sharing system, makes it even more attractive. It is in this area that future applications of WITCAT, embodying the necessary improvements are being planned (Meyer, 1972).

CONCLUSION

In South Africa a keen interest in education technology is at present evident. But most persons concerned are anxiously careful not to repeat the mistakes made elsewhere – we want to make our own mistakes. By which it is conceded that the road ahead is a bumpy one.

REFERENCES

Dieuzeide, H. (1971) 'Educational Technology and the Development of Education'. British Journal of Educational Technology, page 180
Fletcher, L. (1968) 'Preparing for 20th Century lectures'. Audiovisual Instruction
Lee, R. H. (1972) 'Elements of educational theory relating to the use of mediated and automated instruction'. Presentation at 1972 SACAC symposium, pages 4, 5
Meyer, J. H. F. (1972) 'The design, implementation and assessment of a simple computer-assisted teaching system'. Presentation at 1972 SACAC symposium, page 14
Retief, T., Krige, H. L. and Gouws, J. S. (1971) 'The development and validation of a programmed course in Mathematics'. Psychologia Africana, Vol. 14, No. 1
Skinner, B. F. (1965) Reflections on a decade of teaching machines. In 'Teaching Machines and Programmed Learning, II'. (Ed) R. Glaser, Data and Directions, NEA, Washington, DC, page 62
Taylor, C. W. and Williams, F. E. (Eds) (1966) 'Instructional Media and Creativity'. John Wiley, New York, page 109

An Intermediate Assessment of a Developing Learning Unit

J COWAN, J MORTON, E BINGHAM

INTRODUCTION

In situations at either end of the development spectrum an assessment of cost-effectiveness is either meaningless or pointless. Such extreme alternatives occur frequently in the field of teaching, either as short experiments or as major innovations to which a commitment has already been made. It is less common to find an intermediate situation which is still steadily developing from an experimental to an established status. Yet it is in those circumstances that an appreciation of the cost-effectiveness of the development would be most useful. The writers happen to be in just such a position. They have set out here a case history of their decision making during the development period, followed by some information on costs and material production rates which may be of assistance to others entering a similar ad hoc situation.

1. A DESCRIPTION OF THE UNIT

Titles can often be deceptive. It may sound impressive to describe a group of facilities as the 'Learning Unit of the Department of Civil Engineering at Heriot-Watt University'. But it is more realistic to explain that this title describes five teaching rooms of moderate size in a converted school of uncertain age, inconveniently located some distance from the other University buildings. Two members of staff supported by two part-time technicians carry the brunt of the load of preparing syllabi and material; both have other commitments, including participation in the programme of engineering/ research within the Department.

The four year course in the Department is followed by classes of 60 - 96 students. Departmental teaching, tutorials, drawing offices and labs take up 62 class contact hours per week, of which about 20% is centred on the learning unit, where courses are given in each of the first 3 years of study. The instructional material used is almost entirely prerecorded in some form or another, and the teaching staff there are mainly employed in preparation of material or in what is described as 'mop-up'. At the time of writing the library of master cassettes for audio-tutorials, tape/slide presentations and tape/overhead projector presentations amounts to approximately 120 tapes. The current average production rate (in-term) for new teaching materials is shown in Table I.

Table I. Average production rates per week of term
(new material)

	Tapes		Slides or Transparencies		Support Material (Sheets of Originals)
	No.	Running Time (mins)	Sets Av.	No/Set	
Audio-tutorials	3	50			8
Introductions	2	30	2	20	1
Tape/slide sequences	1	30	1	60	
Radio Headphone commentaries	$\frac{1}{4}$	15			$\frac{1}{4}$

All learning sessions are closely linked to printed objective sheets whose use has been described elsewhere (Cowan, 1972). Open-ended work is included in the syllabi in addition to the structured programmed learning: the objectives for these projects are usually published in the same way.

Materials are available to groups of 8 - 12 students during timetabled periods and may thereafter be booked out at any convenient time. Apart from the tape/slide sequences and CCTV recordings, group or self-pacing is the standard procedure and the staff exercise no control over the mode of use of the learning materials, which is known to vary considerably from student to student.

2. A REVIEW OF THE DEVELOPMENT PHASE

When a technical college becomes a university, the rapid change of title is the occasion for much discussion by the staff of the need, if any, for a change of role. Within the writers' department this review led to spasmodic and loosely linked attempts to revise teaching methods and syllabi (Cowan & McConnell, 1967). There were policy changes in the first year syllabus (Cowan, 1972), CCTV was used for certain items of group work (Cowan et al, 1970) and project working was introduced at an early stage of the course (Cowan & McConnell, 1970). Over several years these innovations became part of a trend to ensure closer individual contacts between lecturer and student. It was about this time that loosely programmed documentation was first issued to first year students to give more direction to their use of recommended texts in relation to report writing and laboratory work.

The concept of using pre-recorded instruction to free the lecturer for contact with the students had led to the fabrication of 12 learning booths which were equipped with cassette recorders. In the first short trials the results were not particularly encouraging. The students found the learning method strange. Timetabling was difficult, since only 12 students at a time could use the booths; and the staff found it incredibly difficult to produce an audio track which they would consider acceptable. The new method was demanding that other talents should be exercised by staff and students, and that different attitudes be acquired. Such changes did not happen overnight.

Elsewhere the department was expanding and it became necessary to rehouse the first writer and a colleague in the premises which were described earlier. Here they were to set up laboratories for heavy structural testing. The study booths went with them and were sited in one of several smaller rooms which were unsuitable for use as engineering labs.

By a twist of fate the innovators now found themselves in an ideal situation for the next step in the development (which had eluded them hitherto). The division of accommodation into small rooms lent itself admirably to the adoption of a timetable in which several small group activities were permutated; and the difficulties facing commuters from the main buildings meant that students taking classes at the annexe would **have** to be timetabled in one subject for one long 'block', rather than to have an hour or so each weekday.

The head of department agreed to schedule one class in group activities for one complete day per week, supporting this with prerecorded instruction in place of conventional tutorials. This was really the Rubicon of the development. The revised room allocation now made it impossible for this class to meet together as one, or to follow the same activity at the same time; a change in the complete University timetable would have been needed to permit a revision to the status quo.

The first writer hurriedly began to plan the new style of course, and unfortunately was soon to suffer a severe leg injury in the humorous circumstances which usually surround a middle-aged attempt to learn a young sport. In the term that followed, the venture literally and metaphorically limped along. But the strengths of the new arrangement quickly became apparent in adversity. With prerecorded instruction, the principal lecturer can be called into hospital for a minor operation – but the class can still continue, for even the demonstrators can take their briefing from a tape. With group working, minor flaws in material can be made good before the next group makes use of it; and with carefully defined objectives very much less 'mop-up' is needed.

By the time the writer was fully fit, the experiment was proceeding relatively smoothly and it almost seemed that he was not really needed in a full-time capacity. With subtle presence of mind he disposed of a demonstrator to understaffed conventional tutorials elsewhere, at the same time extending the audio-tutorial scheme to cover remedial tutorials on selected topics in another class altogether.

The increased level of activity began to involve the second writer to an appreciable extent. By the end of the session two members of staff were fully committed to the production of prerecorded instruction, and the reduction in staffing for the self-instructional classes was apparent. The saving was admittedly no more than a book entry, for the surplus staff were simply being switched to other classes. But it was sufficiently encouraging to support the purchase of a high speed cassette copier and the employment of a part-time teaching assistant.

The activity had now become a team approach rather than an individual effort. The title 'Learning Unit' was adopted and the learning method was presented to the students as an established practice rather than as an experiment. The commitment in contact hours quickly escalated to the situation described in the first section of this paper. Preparation of new materials proceeds as rapidly as class contact requirements permit and the capacity of the existing facilities will near the practical limit by the autumn of 1973.

In retrospect it can be seen that the development has been based on several important features:

1. The creation of a course structure centred on behavioural objectives, and on their use by the student during the learning process.
2. The allocation of substantial capital to teaching equipment.
3. The change to prerecorded instruction, to make it possible for staff to have time to make contact with individual students.
4. The provision of self-paced or group-paced learning materials which permit the student to select his own rate and method of study.
5. The use of non-teaching staff for management of resources.

It is easy to look back on any haphazard progress and to present a rational justification of the decisions which were made, although the logic of the sequence may have been less apparent at the time. In this case it is only fair to admit that the Learning Unit developed irregularly, empirically and intuitively, and may not even be the best solution in the given situation. The most significant factor in the growing stage was the tendency to experiment with rather vague ideas and to set up small pilot schemes before attempting to weigh up the pros and cons.

3. COST AND EFFECTIVENESS

The writers were prompted to assemble this data by a Calvinistic reluctance to seek continued support if the venture were to seem unduly costly in their eyes. Tentative cost comparisons were therefore drawn up and the sparse information available on teaching effectiveness has been studied.

Table II. Equipment costs

Location	Equipment	Cost	Totals
Learning Lab	Cassette Copier	£920	
	16 cassette recorders (Phillips)	£352	
	14 headphones	£ 40	
	12 study booths (own make labour included)	£224	
	Storage cabinets	£ 73	£1609
Classroom	Carousel projector	£ 84	
	Mirascreen (occasional use)	£ 11	
	Recorder and pulsing unit	£ 35	
	Amplifier	£ 7	
	Loudspeaker	£ 8	
	Stand	£ 8	£ 153
	Overhead projector	£ 68	
	Screen	£ 9	£ 77
Seminar Room	Recorder and pulsing unit (standby)	£ 37	
	Amplifier	£ 7	
	Loudspeaker	£ 8	
	Overhead projector	£ 75	
	Screen	£ 9	
	Stand	£ 8	£ 144
Laboratories	3 No. radio headphones	£ 41	£ 41
Resources Room	Transparency display units (own make)	£ 16	£ 16
General	Canon Camera, enlarging rings etc	£138	
	Enlarging stand (own make)	£ 4	
	2 No. photofloods	£ 17	
	2 No. Recorders (for master production)	£ 61	£ 220

- Total		£2260
+ capitalisation (say)		£ 440
Total cost		£2700
		= £ 900/year

(a) Relative costs of equipment, materials and staffing

Table II shows the cost of special audiovisual equipment purchased for service use by the unit. The few items which would have been necessary in any case, if the floor area had been united into a single lecture room, have not been included. The costs have been capitalized over a three year period to give an average expenditure per year.

Table III. Costs of class materials

Material used in Unit	Cost of median period	Share of Departmental Budget for materials for conventional teaching
Graphic card	£ 7	
Letraset etc	£15	
Films	£42	
OHP transparencies	£14	£30
C-60 cassettes	£48	
C-120 cassettes	£11	
Carousel magazines	£31	
Miscellaneous	£12	
Totals (six month periods)	Total £180	£30
Annual Costs	£360	£60

The figures for class materials which are set out in Table III are taken from the six month period (September 1972 - February 1973) which will be the mid-period of the first three years of full use. During this half year, new or revised learning materials were being produced for over 85% of the range of timetabled activities. The department contains 320 undergraduate students, 18 members of staff and 5 demonstrators in the department. With 62 formal class contact hours per week, the staff allocations to the Learning Unit have been compared with the average proportion of departmental staff resources. Both staff members in the Unit have teaching commitments in the conventional program of the main department. However, two other members of staff do some teaching or tutorial work within the Unit's program (although they do not prepare self-instructional packages). After making allowance for this cross-accounting, Table IV has been prepared, and shows a comparison of staffing costs.

A final net cost difference has been established in Table V, which includes no allowance for overheads. (There is no reason to suspect that the proportionate increase in costing for overheads would be any greater under the revised system.) Having arrived at the summary in Table V, the writers were satisfied that the Unit is financially viable at present and that consolidation of the experiment is defensible on an economic basis.

Table **IV**. Net cost of staffing

Category	Equivalent full-time member of staff (aggregating teaching commitment in Unit)			Normal Proportion of Departmental Resources (based on class contact hours)		
	No.	Rate	Cost p.a.	No.	Rate	Cost p.a.
Senior Lecturer	1	£4500	£4500	1	£4500	£4500
Lecturer	$1^1/_6$	£3000	£3500	$2\frac{1}{2}$	£3000	£7500
Part-time Assistant	1	£ 900	£ 900	$1/_5$	£ 900	£ 180
Demonstrator	$1\frac{1}{3}$	£ 180	£ 240	1	£ 180	£ 180
Technician	$3/_5$	£1100	£ 660	$2/_5$	£1300	£ 520
Totals			£9800			£12880

Table **V**. Summary of comparative costs

Item	Unit Cost	Norm Cost
Equipment	£ 900	–
Materials	£ 360	£ 60
Staffing	£9800	£12880
Totals	£11060	£12940

Hence **Net saving** = £1880 (which is almost 15% of the budget for the norm)

(b) Effectiveness of teaching

The conditions in a normal university will never permit a rigorous large scale experiment to compare a complete year of teaching by two alternative methods. The steady-state situation cannot therefore be studied properly. Experiments of short duration can admittedly be examined more thoroughly, but the extrapolation of the results to the general case is of questionable validity. With these important reservations, the following comparisons are offered as the most complete information available.

(i) Several short tests of 2 - 3 hour duration have been made. Groups of 12 students have received prerecorded instruction, structured to a common objectives list prepared by one lecturer, but slightly modified in form to suit the media and the order of presentation. No significant differences in immediate learning resulted from any of these variations, and a controlled comparison with unstructured live tuition was not thought possible. The audiovisual presentations were somewhat more effective than the programmed text, but the sample sizes made it difficult to show any significance in this. (A very marked reduction in students learning time was noted through the use of student paced pre-recorded materials.)

From these tests it was concluded subjectively that the structuring of the material was more critical than the detailed choice of media or order of content.

(ii) The sudden change in the third year course made it possible to attempt some comparison with classes in previous years which had been taken by the same lecturer with the same objectives and standard of examination (Table VI). The sudden reduction in failure rate is encouraging. (Unfortunately it will not be possible to continue this comparison as the method of examination in the course concerned has now been modified to provide a complete provision for continuous assessment.)

Table VI. Third year failures (first examination)

Session	Subject in Question F_1	First Control Subject F_2	Second Control Subject F_3	Ratios		
				F_1/F_2	F_1/F_3	F_2/F_3 (control)
68 - 69	12	6	12	2	1.0	0.5
69 - 70	13	7	14	1.9	0.92	0.5
70 - 71	18	9	17	2	1.06	0.53
71 - 72	15	11	24	1.35	0.63	0.46

(iii) During the three sessions in which the first year class was gradually revised to include a fair proportion of prerecorded instruction, the failure rate in this subject was steadily reduced from 30% of the class to less than 10%. But it would be foolish to draw any conclusions from a situation in which so many other variables were involved.

(iv) The most striking improvement in student performances has been observed in the drawing offices. The use of prerecorded introductions, closely related to the specified objectives for the exercise, has increased student productivity by a factor of more than two. At the same time the standard of the drawings has improved almost as much as the work rate.

Recently it has been necessary on two separate occasions for the lecturer who had prepared the prerecorded instruction to give the same introduction **live** to one student group. On each occasion the work rate of the group has diminished by approximately 30% compared with the self-instructed groups, and the standard of draughting has been below the new norm.

From a subjective review of all of these observations, the writers are satisfied that the present overall standard of work is **at least** as high as it has been previously in the courses taken within the Unit.

(c) Summary

It has been suggested that the cost of the Unit is less than that of the conventional teaching arrangement which it replaced and that the teaching effectiveness is comparable. The analysis of costing was quite strict, insofar as no allowance whatsoever was made for the extra cost and effort being put into a development stage. The assessment of teaching effectiveness, though subjective, made use of the only criteria which are used to assess the capability of individual students from year to year. The writers therefore believe that the teaching method they have described is a viable economic proposition, but would not make or infer any higher claim at present.

4. PLANS FOR THE IMMEDIATE FUTURE

The remainder of the present 3-year growth period will be devoted mainly to consolidation rather than to expansion. For it is easy to see where worthwhile improvements can still be made; but it is difficult to forecast the overall effect of the new system on a student who will now become acclimatized (or even blasé) during the first three years of his course.

The curriculum must now be integrated more thoroughly to form a completely cohesive sequence, inter-related throughout in objectives and strategies and offering a variety of media and types of activity. This will entail a new review of objectives in the three main courses, and a more thoughtful integration of project working within the syllabus. Learning material is already being prepared to offer the student alternative routes through the syllabus, but this facility must be extended to include further remedial and revision loops. An increasing administrative load will therefore develop shortly which will divert one of the writers from his present function.

Although copy cassettes are available to borrowers, if requested, the emphasis on learning centred on the Unit will be retained and the provision of adequate 'mop-up' staff at all appropriate times will be emphasized. The formal lectures which still remain in the courses will not be substantially reduced in number, since an attitude survey has revealed that the students would prefer them to be retained with the audio presentation reserved for summarizing and revision as at present.

A number of pilot schemes in other curriculum subjects are under discussion at present, but a priority in the near future is a limited programme of controlled experiments. In the situation which the students now regard as normal, it should soon be possible to study alternative uses of self-instructional material and to obtain worthwhile results which will influence future planning.

Timetabling for individual needs and rates of progress presents problems, and the fact that students must make a special journey to reach the Unit aggravates these problems considerably. A completely satisfactory solution has still to be found, since there are conflicting priorities involved: complete self-pacing for the individual student may not be achieved without creating an even greater administrative load and lowering the overall utilization of materials and equipment. Certainly it will have to be supported by limited printing or copying facilities, since the distance to the main printing department is now constraining the mobility of the Unit to meet unexpected demands for resource materials.

Cataloguing, storage and issue of materials are problems of a different nature and magnitude from those foreseen a mere six months previously. The student must be offered a simple way to find materials to suit his immediate need. At present he can only do this by scanning over a catalogue list which grows longer each month, although most students following the 'main-line' sequence find that the Organizer has their materials ready at hand, and advises them of the next step to follow. At the same time there is a need for immediate access by students or staff to an advice sheet, giving full details of how the material should be used. It is very easy for a lecturer to forget some of the important subtleties of presentation in a production made four months previously, even if it was he who supplied the material originally.

5. CONCLUDING COMMENTS

The writers have been very fortunate in having had the sympathetic support of a liberal head of department, who has tolerantly permitted them to take incredible liberties with his timetables, curricula and staffing. In this favourable climate the process of change has still to be gradual, because a department with an adverse staff/student ratio cannot afford to make changes until they have been successfully demonstrated on a small scale: expenditure and capital and effort cannot be permitted to run far ahead of an equivalent return or saving. It has always been an intuitive process, because all the important early decisions have been made subjectively in the almost complete absence of objective information. It has only been an adaptive development, in the sense that each new idea has only been an adaptation of something which has been used or discussed elsewhere.

The Unit is simply an in-service effort to improve university teaching at the grass roots. The writers hope that the description and figures they have given will be of use to other lecturers who are similarly inclined to experiment with new teaching methods.

REFERENCES

Cowan, J. (1972) 'Student reaction to the use of detailed objectives'. In 'Aspects of Educational Technology VI' (Ed) K. Austwick and N. D. C. Harris. Pitman, London

Cowan, J. (1972) 'Two Case Histories of Curriculum Development'. Paper presented at Lehrsystem 72, Berlin

Cowan, J. and McConnell, S. G. (1967) 'An Experiment in the Teaching of Materials Science'. Metals and Materials, July

Cowan, J. and McConnell, S. G. (1970) Project Work for Undergraduate Civil Engineers. University Quarterly

Cowan, J., McConnell, S. G. and Bolton, A. B. (1970) Learner Directed Group Work for large Classes. In 'Aspects of Educational Technology IV'. (Ed) A. C. Bajpai and J. F. Leedham. Pitman, London

AMOS: A Material Organization Scheme for School and Teacher Centre Resources Areas

W J K DAVIES, F L McKENZIE

INTRODUCTION

This paper describes a material organization system for school and teachers centre resource areas. We call it a material organization system rather than a 'retrieval system' because it is designed to undertake a variety of functions: 'retrieval' in the physical sense is only one of them, and material classification is only a part of that. The system design is based not on pure theory but on the problems encountered in practice by a group of non-librarian teachers who were confronted with the problem of organizing an existing growing resource bank so that individuals could use it quickly and easily. It is thus based on continual evolution over a period of years combined with a systematic analysis of the problem.

SCOPE

The organization system to be described is intended specifically for use up to about the level of a County or Borough authority's area (ie a fair range of schools and colleges served by a unified library service and one or more teachers centres or similar organizations). We do not claim that it would be suitable for large scale libraries and its application to regional resource centres, if they arise, appears irrelevant; 'inter-authority' interchange of materials would not normally involve pre-classification. For practical purposes a local education authority, we feel, is likely to be the largest unit with a centralized internal loan service and therefore the largest unit to which a unified organization system needs to be applied. We accept, too, that the system is likely to be used mainly for non-book materials and therefore must be linkable to the Dewey system used in the average school book library. None the less provision for including books is built-in for those schools who might want to use a unified system.

AIMS AND OBJECTIVES

The overall goal of the system is fourfold: First, a growing collection of

130

varied materials – henceforth called a resources bank – must be able to be classified easily without the teacher/classifier having to agonize over how to do it; second it must be able to be stored in such a manner that the physical location of items can be changed without disrupting the whole system; third, at the same time it must be organized so that a user can see clearly what any given resource item covers, and so that he can get hold of it without trouble; fourth, the user must be given clear indications of problems that may arise in using any complicated resource item (eg a slide/tape presentation) and must be given what help is required to use that item.

Specifically these requirements impose the following constraints on the design of any system:

i.   Once the initial resource bank has been set up, extensions, alterations (eg changes in physical storage areas etc), even excisions of complete parts should require an absolute minimum of clerical indexing and cataloguing work: this is unproductive and can rapidly lead to a build-up of errors, for example in cross-referencing.

ii. The resource stock must be able to be moved around as learning circumstances require (eg it must be easy to create specialized sub-stocks for specific projects, or to have separate small resource banks in subject departments but still linked to the central resource bank; it must be easy to incorporate, and to separate out for return, loan items from other places). Typically these might be internal - from central stock to a specialist stock; or external - teachers centre to individual school or vice versa. **The system must serve its users not just its organizers.**

iii. The final set-up must be easy for an individual customer to use. In this context, we suspect the motives of those who argue that complicated retrieval systems are a good discipline for the learner; it sounds too much like a justification for making the best of a bad job. We would argue that once the novelty of 'working' a system has worn off, anything that interposes problems between a learner and what he wants to learn is an interference to learning and not an aid.

Sub-system 1. Retrieval

The retrieval element is a true system based on several pre-requisites, and customer oriented rather than classifier oriented as is, for example, the libraries' Dewey system. It is based on the major premise that when dealing with resources the user (customer) is likely to know at least roughly what he wants, (eg 'Vectors' rather than 'Maths'). He then needs to be able to see quickly:

(i)   if there is anything available on that topic

(ii) if the level of difficulty is likely to be right for him - or for his class.

(iii) if the resource item is an information source or a learning instrument.

(iv) if its use requires any special equipment, etc.

The two minor premises are:

(i) that having found the material is available, and likely to be of use, he must be able to locate it physically without too much trouble.

(ii) that, if the resource item is for individual study he must be able to get to an appropriate study point or 'student station'- or if it is for external use he must be able to acquire any equipment needed, compatible with the resource item. Some resource areas may always have supervisory staff on duty but the system should be designed so far as possible so that their presence is not vital.

To meet these requirements, the basis of the overall system is as outlined below:

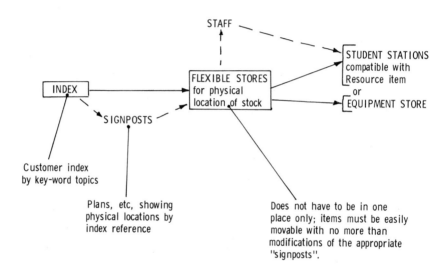

Figure 1. AMOS overall system model

The retrieval sub-system is based on two major elements:

1. The index or catalogue which consists basically of cards bearing the information shown in Figure 2. (There is no reason why other catalogues should not be generated if a school needs them but they are not vital. Most useful is the descriptive title catalogue described in Appendix IV).

2. The item reference combination which consists of a group of symbols capable of a variety of tasks

eg   31/Ms/5

This is designed to:

(a) tell a student what **type** of resource (eg cassette-tape/slide) is involved

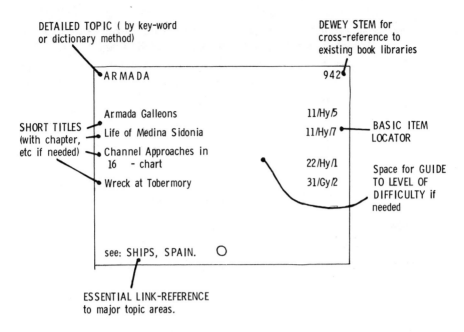

DETAILED TOPIC (by key-word or dictionary method)

DEWEY STEM for cross-reference to existing book libraries

ARMADA   942

SHORT TITLES (with chapter, etc if needed)

Armada Galleons   11/Hy/5
Life of Medina Sidonia   11/Hy/7
Channel Approaches in 16 - chart   22/Hy/1
Wreck at Tobermory   31/Gy/2

BASIC ITEM LOCATOR

Space for GUIDE TO LEVEL OF DIFFICULTY if needed

see: SHIPS, SPAIN.   O

ESSENTIAL LINK-REFERENCE to major topic areas.

Figure 2

(b) enable a student to locate the item physically in the store

(c) if required, to enable a user or the resource supervisor to find equipment that is compatible with the resource item (in the case of a book this may well just be a table!).

The reference combination has three major parts; its allocation may cause problems to the classifier but for the student it has the advantage that, once he has obtained it, he need never concentrate on more than 3 or 4 characters at a time.

The parts are: eg   31/Ms/5

31 a two-bit control cipher. This is not a conventional number 'thirty one' but 3 + 1: the first figure indicates the overall type of resource item, classified by its most complex element (eg here 3 is the code for audio-based items). The second figure clarifies the type more exactly (eg 3 (1) indicates compact cassette).

This cipher is used for locating the overall physical area in which the item is stored (Place labelled '3'). It can also be used to guide the user to a student station or an equipment store: any such place bearing the cipher 31 will accept his resource item, or provide compatible equipment.

Ms Indicates 'broad area of knowledge' or subject. While important to the classifier (qv), to the user it simply locates a smaller area within the major area described above: items are filed alphabetically by 'subjects'

133

within each item type. (eg Item labelled 31/Ms user goes to area 3 and looks through it until he reaches the part devoted to 'Ms').

5   Indicates a section or 'pigeonhole' within the subject section: here the student having reached 3/Ms looks along Ms 1, 2, 3, 4 and reaches five. Each 'pigeonhole' can accommodate one or more items according to storage problems but should not have more than 10 or 12. The student can then simply look through that section and pick out his item by its title.

Note that the system is based on 'coarse filing' principles. The reason is that if an area of search is narrowed down to about 12 items – or less for awkward ones – a user has little trouble in finding what he wants; at the same time it is easier to replace an item and there is less risk of misfiling.

Sub-system 2 – Classification

A practical guide for classifiers is beyond the scope of the present paper. Briefly, the rationale is that classification and indexing must be user-oriented. It is therefore:

(a)   based on key-word topics, which are as detailed as possible (for example see Figure 4). This minimizes one anomaly of the Dewey system – the facts that Dewey subject headings are quite irrational in some cases and

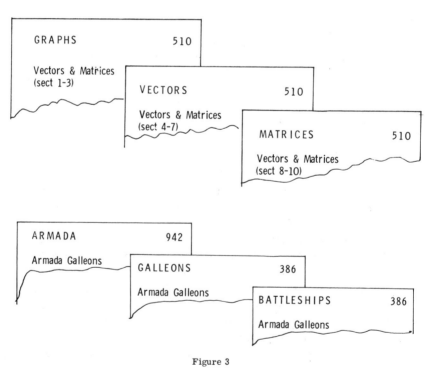

Figure 3

134

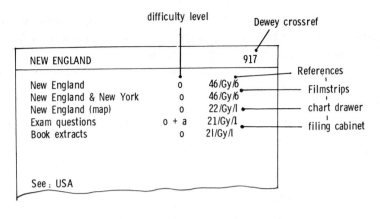

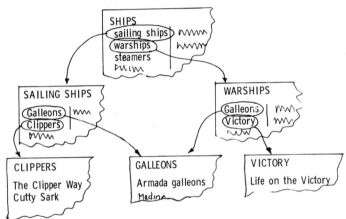

Figure 4

that their 'magnitude' varies far too widely.

(b) referenced 'up' and 'down' (ie from broad to detailed topics) rather than across. (Figure 4)

(c) linked to Dewey via a subject list using only the Dewey stem number for simplicity. This enables a cross reference to existing book collections.

(d) designed to incorporate active anti-squirrelling measures: Squirrel's Disease (the tendency to acquire and store items willy-nilly, regardless of their effectiveness) is one of the most worrying aspects of resource organization and prevention is better than cure.

Sub-system 3 – Storage and Organization

Storage is flexible because it depends on: (i) the reference system, (ii) coarse-filing principles.

The first allows use of the idea of 'notional location' – ie there is no invariant sequencing so that a complete collection does not need to be stored in a particular order round the room or rooms.

Specifically since the major location area is by item complexity, all tape-based items (3) can be put together, all charts (22) can be filed together. The availability of two figures in the cipher means that as the collection grows areas can be narrowed down. For example, we classify teaching machine programs (8) by their individual equipment (eg 83 – Bristol Tutor) because the equipments are incompatible the program storage problems are different and there are sufficient programs on each subject area for each machine to make it worthwhile. On the other hand all '1.' series (book based) are classified together for user convenience.

The 'pigeonhole' system used in coarse filing also allows flexibility. Thus all the big oversize items in, say, 11/Me can be grouped together as 11/Me/5 although in a Dewey system they might have individual entries 610; 611.12; 612:3 which would prevent this; moreover if one acquires a number of similar items – say cassette tapes – one can create an appropriate pigeonhole.

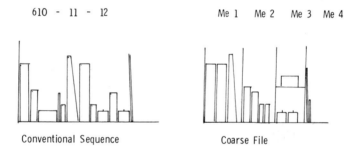

610 - 11 - 12   Me 1   Me 2   Me 3   Me 4

Conventional Sequence   Coarse File

Figure 5. Advantage of coarse filing in multi media collection

The reference number also allows student-flow to be organized so that the user can not only find his item physically but also locate a suitable place in which to use it, or a store from which he can draw compatible equipment.

It is also possible to make up mini-resource banks by simply coarsening the system further.

For a geography project, say, a collection of assorted items from the main collection is taken to a classroom; the teacher can use the main catalogue to select what she wants but its complexity is not needed for a small group of, say, 50 items. She can therefore ignore one element (eg file by subject area/pigeonhole number, ignoring the initial cipher) and tell the children what to do (Figure 6).

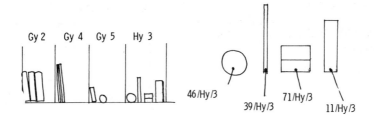

Figure 6. Small collection filing by subject area

The children will then locate the item by 'subject' and only then use the initial cipher to find compatible equipment if required.

Alternatively, of course if conditions dictate, the teacher could file by the initial cipher with individual items sequenced alphabetically within that.

Indeed the number of items is not likely to get so great that individual items cannot be located by browsing. If as suggested in Appendix IV, a copy of the 'descriptive title index' entry is posted to each item, the job is made even easier.

The essential advantage of the index/storage combination, however, is that the master catalogue rarely needs amendment. Most movements simply require a modification to the drawing or plan that shows the current physical location of storage areas.

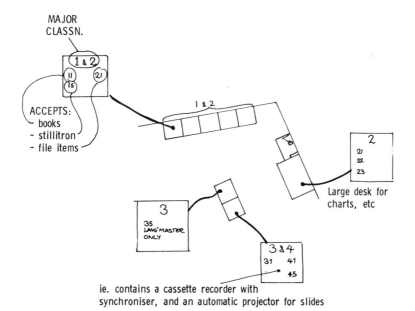

Figure 7. Using a cipher to direct student to a study place

137

EITHER: A NOTICE   OR: A PLAN

Equipment Store in	Holds
Room 4	31, 41, 52
Room 8	49
Hall	53, 49

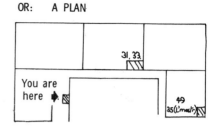

Using cipher to: locate equipment via staff   to: label equipment

31?   " Ah yes, You want a
                 cassette recorder. Here
                 you are. "

Figure 8. Using cipher to direct teacher to equipment

Lastly, all this means that it is simple both to incorporate and separate out items on loan from an external source using the same system — say, the local teachers centre. The teachers centre simply uses a different coloured index card, issuing one with the item. The card takes its appropriate place in the school topic index where it is easily spotted because of its distinctive colour; the item goes into the appropriate pigeonhole (eg loan item: 11/Ms/9 into school location 11/Ms/9. If the school only has, say, 7 Ms locations, an Ms 9 one is created next in sequence — if you feel a user may be puzzled, call it '8 and 9' !)

APPENDIX I

For reference purposes, the following 'broad areas' of knowledge appear
sufficient to cope with the Dewey list of subjects and their sub-divisions.
They must not be too few, or the number of 'pigeonholes' per subject area
becomes too great, nor too many for in that case the 'subject area' part of
the reference becomes too fine – it often nullifies the pigeonhole cipher but
at the expense of great complexity in the generation of similar letter-groups.

Ae	Architectural Studies
Ag	Agriculture (cultivated natural resources, ind. marine)
As	Arts (mainly in the recreational sense)
Ay	Archaeological studies
By	Biological/botanical studies
Ch	Chemical studies
Ds	Domestic studies - to include food and clothing
*Eh	English studies
En	Educational studies (theory and practice)
Gy	Geographical/geological/meteorological/astronomical studies
Hy	Historical studies (but note: all 'countries' - general topics under Gy)
Ll	Language and literature (not English)
Me	Medicine and health
Ms	Mathematical studies
*My	Military studies
Ps	Physics
*Rg	Reading
Rn	Religious (philosophical studies)
Sc	General Science (pure)
St	Sports
Sy	Sociological studies
*Tt	Transport
Ty	Technology (applied science)

*There are several anomalies (eg Eh) but these are largely owing to subject
specialisms in schools and are intended to conform to the reality of the
situation. There is a certain amount of flexibility for individual compilers
since for the user the letter-group is simply an alphabetical locator with
familiar overtones: if a book is classed 11/Se he will look for Se...., if it
is classed 11/Ps - for Physics - he will look for Ps....   Interestingly,
different coding by different classifiers does not entirely invalidate the
system: loan material goes in the alphabetical area to which is has been
classified.

APPENDIX II

SUGGESTED CONTROL CIPHER CLASSIFICATION:

NB   A 2-bit cipher has been found to be the best compromise between too much simplicity and too much complication, having regard to the various uses to which the cipher must be put. Its use would not stop large permanent collections inserting a third cipher to provide fine distinctions within categories but for ordinary resource area use this appears unnecessary.

1.   Broad classification: - by maximum complexity
    1X   paper based, book form
    2X   paper based, file form (sheet) - eg charts
    3X   tape based
  * 4X   still visual (projected)
    5X   moving visual (projected) closed (film loop etc)
    6X   moving visual (projected) open-end (film, video-tape, etc)
    7X   awkward (boxed) items - games, etc
    8X   teaching machine programs
    9X   miscellaneous

* To avoid complications over student station locations it is suggested that combined sound/still visual be incorporated here. Alternatively it could be indicated in 7X (3+4), all 7 stations automatically accepting '3' or '4' items with a compatible second cipher. In that case 8 would be for boxed items.

    Examples of the proposed detail classifications are given below. Note that coarse filing demands that, to avoid undue proliferation, non-standard items be grouped together and identified additionally by name. (eg 35 = tape on card:)there are currently two incompatible systems Languagemaster and Audio Page. This is simply covered by marking both on the resource item and on the student station or equipment store '35 LANGUAGEMASTER' or 35 AUDIO PAGE as the case may be. The user consulting an index does not need this technical information until he arrives at one of those places.

    3X   Audio-based
    31   Cassette-compact
    32   cassette-other
    33   reel/reel 4 track
    34   reel/reel 2 track
    35   tape on card
    36
    37
    38
    39   gramophone records

APPENDIX III

Specimen page of Dewey subject list with 'broad areas of knowledge' classification.

Wales	914	Gy
Wasps	595	By
Watches	529	Ty
Water		
- Transport	386	Tt
- Science	532	Se
- Supply	628	Ty
Waterways	386	Tt
Weapons	623	My
- Armies	355	My
- Armour	391	My
Weather	551	Gy
Weaving	677	As
- at home	746	As
Weeds	585	By
- gardening	635	Ag
Welding	669	Ty
West Indies	917	Gy
Whales	639	By
- study of	599	By
Wheat	633	By
Wild Flowers	582	By
Windmills	621	Gy
Winds	551	Gy
Winter		
- nature study	574	By
Wireless	521	Ty
Wood		
- Timbergrowing	634	By or Ag
- Trees	582	By
Woods		
- nature study	574	By
Woodwork	684	As

Suggested 'Descriptive Title' Index

It may be useful to have each item described in a manner similar to that
shown below and accessible from the master topic index by its short title.
Should this be thought desirable, we suggest it be on paper, filed rather than
in index drawers, and created in triplicate: one master copy, one user's
copy (which can be renewed by photocopying the master) and one copy affixed
to the actual resource item.

The British Village   43/Gy/12
                                                   Dewey   910

Slides with taped commentary, showing changes in typical village
structure from medieval times to 1920's. Concentrates on
architecture and farming patterns.
No arrangements for student response but slide changes marked by
audio tone.
Work cards available to cover following topics, with tests:
    (a) define the changes in agricultural use and relate them
        to changes in the social pattern.
    (b) how village housing has changed and why.

TOPICS: Houses: farming:

User's comments:

British and American Intelligibility for Non-native Students of English: A language laboratory experiment

S EL-ARABY

In many parts of Asia, Africa and Europe students have been exposed to different varieties of English. For the last hundred and seventy years British educators have worked in the fields of teaching English and training native teachers to teach the language. These non-native speaking teachers seem to have acquired identifiable pronunciation habits that may be labelled Indian British, Arab British or African British, etc. Each of these labels suggests the language of origin of the teachers and their native linguistic habits. However foreign their accent may remain, it is always an attempt at some British English accent or other. Most of their students believe that they have learned a near-to-authentic British pronunciation.

During and shortly after the Second World War, American educators started to cooperate, and sometimes compete, with the British in teaching English to non-native speakers. Teacher training programs were arranged for scholars from South East Asia, South America, Africa, the Middle East and other parts of the world. Peace Corps volunteers and other American teachers joined institutions where most of the students had been exposed to British English or to any of its hybrid sub-categories. Students in those parts of the world were again faced with another variety of English, namely American English, together with a host of other subvarieties: Indian American, African American, Arab American, etc. While textbooks largely remained British in orientation, the students had to make adjustments to a few different features of pronunciation and vocabulary used by American or American-trained teachers.

Students of English in the Arab Republic of Egypt have passed through all the above stages. American missionary schools were established in many small towns in Egypt towards the end of the nineteenth century. At the same time the British were in control of the system of education in the country. British English became the medium of instruction in all stages of education. Later, in 1923, Arabic replaced English in teaching almost all school subjects as a result of strong national feelings against the use of a foreign tongue in education. English continued to be taught as a subject, chiefly by British educators or by Egyptians speaking the Egyptian British hybrid variety. Prior to admission to the American University in Cairo, the majority of students have never had any systematic contact with American English. Many have seen American films and television programs. Very few have had American or American trained instructors teaching them English in preparatory or secondary schools. Although experience has shown that the change to American English does not result in any appreciable intelligibility problems, many of the students believe that it is largely to blame for incidences of failures and lower grades.

Accordingly, the following experiment was designed to find out if a change to American English would result in any significant comprehension difficulties on the part of British trained multinational students.

PROCEDURE

Two multinational groups of non-native speakers were chosen. They numbered 20 students each who were used to British pronunciation and had not had any systematic exposure to American English. The two groups were comparable in aural comprehension proficiency as measured by the English Department, University of Leeds entrance examination as well as tutors' evaluation on a six points scale that measures their ability to understand spoken English.

Two passages by the same author, from the same book, were selected for testing aural comprehension of British and American English. Written multiple choice questions identical in number and similar in types were set for each passage. Two varieties of English, British and American were used for voicing each passage. Group I was given the first passage recorded on tape in American English. Scores on the tests for each group, as well as scores of both groups on each test were statistically analysed.

THE SUBJECTS

Forty subjects were chosen, twenty in each group, from the Overseas Group, the Institute of Education, the University of Leeds, UK. They were all graduate students teaching English in their respective countries in Asia, Africa and other continents. They presented 15 different countries. Sudan, Nigeria, Hong Kong, Bahrain, Sierra Leone, Kenya, Uganda, Dahomey, Fiji, Thailand, India, Seychelle, Singapore, Botswana and Malaysia.

A questionnaire was given to each student to find out if any of them had been taught by Americans or American trained teachers throughout their school life. In all but two cases the respondents indicated that they had only been taught by either British or British-trained non-native speakers. The two other subjects said that they were taught by American teachers for no more than two years. By coincidence rather than deliberate design, each one of these two students happened to be in each one of the groups selected for the experiment.

CRITERIA FOR GROUPING

The two groups were matched according to two basic criteria: the scores they received on the aural comprehension test administered by the University of Leeds to all foreign students and the rating of their aural comprehension ability by their individual tutors (see Table I).

The test of auditory comprehension, constructed by J B Heaton of the University of Leeds, took the form of a 15 minute lecture recorded on video-tape. The lecture, as explained by the designer of the test, consisted of the biography of a fictitious Yorkshire novelist and was kept neutral as far as possible in language, content and background so that no particular students would have an advantage. The videotape recording took the form of a straight-forward lecture with a single television camera presenting a medium close-up view of the speaker in order to simulate a realistic lecture situation. Students were allowed to take notes during the lecture after which they received 25 multiple choice written questions to test their understanding. Although no formal validation of this test has been carried out, the consensus of opinion of the instructors and its high correlation with other written sub-tests suggest confirmation of its validity.

The second basic criterion was requested of the tutors of individual students in each group. They were asked to rate the ability of each subject to understand spoken English according to a six point continuum scale where 1 stands for 'Almost impossible for him to understand spoken English' and 6 shows that the subject is 'on a par with native speakers of English following the course'. None of the subjects was rated either (1) or (6). As expected, most of them were rated either 3 or 4.

It was felt that a combination of the objective and controlled scores on the auditory comprehension test and the evaluation of the tutors based on their experience with the students would result in a fairly accurate indication of each subject's ability to understand spoken English. Admittedly, the subjects were different on every other count, nationality, age, background knowledge, previous experience. However, it was felt that since auditory comprehension was the only variable tested, matching the subjects according to their ability in this respect was the most relevant procedure.

THE TEST

Two passages were chosen from Bronowski's 'Common Sense of Science'. They were almost of equal length (the second passage had five words more than the first) and almost the same in difficulty. According to the Dale and

Chall system the first passage was rated at 12.7 and the second at 13 indicating that both are appropriate for college freshmen. The Fog Index rated the first passage at 12 and the second at 12.8 indicating roughly the same difficulty level. The scientific and logical content of both passages was considered neutral to language teachers giving no one subject a clear advantage over the other. It is assumed here that these indices would have corresponding values when the passages are voiced for auditory comprehension although the formulas are designed to measure reading difficulty.

Two professors at the University of Leeds were requested to voice each passage. The American professor's accent was considered clear and intelligible by his British students. The British professor's accent was judged as the 'characteristic English accent' by his colleagues. He spoke RP (received pronunciation) which is looked upon as non-regional in character and accepted in the best society according to Abercrombie (1970). The two professors were asked to listen to each other's voicing of the passages. They generally agreed on the ideas to be emphasized, the breath group segmentation of the sentences and the approximate speed of reading.

The recording of each of the two passages started with the following instructions. 'First: read the questions on the sheet given to you. If you need help on any of them, please ask. Second: You are going to hear a passage about science. Listen carefully to all the main ideas in it. If you do not understand the meaning of some words, don't let this worry you. Keep listening until the end and try to remember all the facts. You will then be allowed 20 minutes to answer the questions on the sheet handed to you. If you need help ask for it now. No questions will be allowed later.' The purpose of the length instructions was to familiarize the subjects with the voice of the speaker and his personal style of enunciation. Before the tape was played, the subjects had been thoroughly briefed on what they were supposed to do by their classroom instructor.

The recorded and written test was administered to each group in a separate language laboratory at the University of Leeds. The subjects were told that the tests were for experimental purposes and would have no direct bearing on their course grades. However, it was mentioned that their tutors would see the results of these tests later and explain the full purpose of the experiment.

DISCUSSION OF RESULTS

The raw scores for the 20 subjects in each group are presented in Table I. These have been converted to mean scores for the pretest and the two dialects as shown in Table II. Standard deviations have also been included. Group I responded significantly better to British than American English ($t = 2.692$ d.f. $= 19$ $p = <.01$). There seems to be two possible explanations

for this. One is that they are better used to British than American dialects.
The second is that they gained more experience in the author's style and way
of presentation as well as in taking multiple choice tests.

Table I. Raw score on aural comprehension pretest,
British and American dialects

	AC	Amer	Brit		AC	Brit	Amer
Group ., Amer-Brit	18	5	7	Group 2, Brit-Amer	34	8	7
Group 1, Amer-Brit	26	6	8	Group 2, Brit-Amer	16	5	2
Group 1, Amer-Brit	36	6	6	Group 2, Brit-Amer	28	4	7
Group 1, Amer-Brit	48	7	12	Group 2, Brit-Amer	40	7	10
Group 1, Amer-Brit	38	8	8	Group 2, Brit-Amer	40	6	11
Group 1, Amer-Brit	42	6	8	Group 2, Brit-Amer	34	5	8
Group 1, Amer-Brit	24	5	5	Group 2, Brit-Amer	34	7	6
Group 1, Amer-Brit	30	4	4	Group 2, Brit-Amer	36	10	8
Group 1, Amer-Brit	24	4	5	Group 2, Brit-Amer	34	5	6
Group 1, Amer-Brit	28	7	9	Group 2, Brit-Amer	22	5	4
Group 1, Amer-Brit	40	9	9	Group 2, Brit-Amer	34	3	6
Group 1, Amer-Brit	40	5	10	Group 2, Brit-Amer	30	5	9
Group 1, Amer-Brit	32	5	7	Group 2, Brit-Amer	42	11	9
Group 1, Amer-Brit	40	8	5	Group 2, Brit-Amer	33	7	9
Group 1, Amer-Brit	18	2	7	Group 2, Brit-Amer	32	8	6
Group 1, Amer-Brit	32	4	2	Group 2, Brit-Amer	40	8	10
Group 1, Amer-Brit	30	4	8	Group 2, Brit-Amer	44	7	10
Group 1, Amer-Brit	12	3	3	Group 2, Brit-Amer	34	6	6
Group 1, Amer-Brit	36	3	7	Group 2, Brit-Amer	32	7	4
Group 1, Amer-Brit	36	9	8	Group 2, Brit-Amer	34	7	7

Table II. Mean scores and standard deviations of
the two groups on 3 tests

	Group I Mean	SD	Group II Mean	SD
Pretest	31.500	9.197	33.650	6.499
American dialect	5.500	2.013	7.250	2.337
British dialect	6.900	2.404	6.550	1.932

Students in Group II, who were exposed to British dialect first, did
better on the American part of the test, but not enough to make a statistically
significant difference. They seemed to have improved enough with practice
on the author's presentation and the testing situation to counterbalance any
possible intelligibility problems resulting from the change in dialects. But
it is difficult to separate the effect of dialect change and the effect of order
presentation. The order of presentation of the passages seems to have inter-
fered in the results. It is a variable that should have been eliminated by

having additional groups (two more) take the tests in different order. Another limitation of the experiment is the number of subjects and their different backgrounds. An additional complication was that they varied in their interest and enthusiasm when taking the test. Some of them thought of it as an additional burden on an already busy schedule. Others indicated that they would have felt better if the purpose of the experiment was clearly explained to them before taking the tests. When privately interviewed later, two of them even admitted that they could not tell the American from the British dialect.

On the basis of this study student responses to the two dialects do not seem to be radically different. They consistently scored better on the test that was presented last. While the analysis showed that Group I did better on the British English recording selection, the difference does not seem to justify planning a program for facilitating transition from British to American teaching dialects. Although results of this experiment appear to be inconclusive, they do suggest that more and better controlled research should be conducted to explore American intelligibility problems that British-trained students are likely to face.

ACKNOWLEDGMENTS

I am deeply indebted to Professors Brian Heaton, Brian Page, John Swales and Steven Whitley of the University of Leeds for help in administering the experiment and choosing the subjects. Sincere thanks are also due to Professors Evelyn Hatch, Lois McIntosh, John Oller, and Earl Rand of UCLA for their guidance and effort in analysing the results. All mistakes in the study are, of course, my own responsibility.

I am also grateful to the British Council, the Ford Foundation and the American University in Cairo for their financial support during my sabbatical year that made this study, and others possible.

REFERENCES

Abercrombie, D. (1970) Problems and Principles in Language Study. Longman Group Ltd., London. Page 48

Bronowski, J. (1953) The Common Sense of Science. Harvard University Press, Cambridge

Dale, E. and Chall, J. S. (1948) A Formula for Predicting Readability. Educational Research Bulletin, 27, 11-20, 37-54

Gunming, R. (1952) The Technique of Clear Writing. McGraw-Hill Book Co. New York, pages 36-38

Typographical Aspects of Instructional Design

J HARTLEY, P BURNHILL, S FRASER

INTRODUCTION

The aim of this paper is to describe briefly the work carried out so far in our research project which has been sponsored by the Social Science Research Council for a period of three years (January 1972 - December 1974). The work is carried out by Peter Burnhill from Stafford College of Further Education in collaboration with James Hartley and Susan Fraser from the Department of Psychology at the University of Keele.

Our research can be divided into three areas, although of course, in practice, these areas overlap. We are concerned (i) with theoretical work (ii) with evaluating the practical outcomes of this theoretical work, and (iii) with the instructional implications of our research.

THEORETICAL BACKGROUND

Our concern here is with the need to develop a rational approach to the design of the material to be evaluated.

Much typographical research to date has been concerned with the many variables which printed work exhibits such as type-size, line-length, the use of capital and lower case letters, the 'boldness' of type faces and the style in the printed characters (Spencer, 1969; Poulton, 1972). Our principal interest (in contrast with previous work in typographic research) lies in the organization of space in relation to an overall page dimension. A necessary feature of all printed work is that it exists on a surface (usually a page) of known dimensions and this is the area within which the reader expects to be able to move about without being unduly confused, be he reading a menu, a text of the proceedings of this Conference, or a pocket dictionary. Figure 1 for instance shows material that can be grouped in various ways: some ways may be easier to comprehend than others: some may be more economical to print (Burnhill, 1970).

The reader, in addition to being able to scan the field of view and to discover meaningful relationships, also has the natural ability of focusing

How to tie the Epankylotos Brokhos.

Read the instructions carefully before commencing

Place the cord across the palm of the left hand
between the thumb and forefinger.

Allow at least twelve inches to hang over the back of the hand.

Wrap the other part of the cord around the back of the hand,
over the thumb and across the palm.

Grip it firmly between the little finger and the adjacent finger.

Holding the left hand flat and, using the right hand,
pass the loop nearest the wrist under the other loop.

Holding the first loop tightly, pull both loops off the hand.

The two loops should then form·
one will be in the left hand,
the other in the right hand.

These loops should have a running knot between them
so that when the ends of the cord are pulled
the loops decrease in size.

Figure 1. (by courtesy E. Brown)

down from an overall view of parts of the page to that of noting the unique
arrangement of the marks which form a letter of the alphabet. We wish to
argue that structural clarity at all levels is a function of space as the primary
dimensional variable.

Progress in the systematic study of the spatial problems of textual
matter such as conference proceedings, technical literature, programmed
textbooks and educational material generally, must rest upon the use of
accepted norms for the overall dimensions of the field of view. These are
provided by the recommendations for paper sizes made by the International
Organization for Standardization (ISO). For our research purposes, we have
chosen the size A4 (210 mm x 297 mm) as this is now well established as an
appropriate size for housing the kinds of information we are interested in
working with.

THE PRACTICAL WORK

Our practical work so far has been carried out in three main areas. We
have (i) started to examine some of the preliminary details, which it is
necessary to do, before making any large scale study of implications drawn
from our theoretical orientation: (ii) we have made a comparison study of
the effectiveness of a journal article set in two different typographical
formats: and (iii) we have examined more closely the reliability of several

of the measures used in evaluative work of this kind.

In the first area, we have conducted a pilot study using 10-11 year old children with widely differing reading abilities. In this study we asked them to read aloud stories set in different type sizes and with different interline spaces but all with the same line-length (42 ems) in order to see (i) if it was possible for children to read material of this length and (ii) to see (with this line-length) if there were any clear advantages or disadvantages for any of our typographical settings. (NB previous studies of interline-space and type sizes have not been related to an overall page dimension, nor have they used a line-length as long as ours.)

Our typographical variables were line-lengths of 42 ems (the longest possible on an A4 page) with (a) 10 point type on 12 point body, (b) 12 point type on 12 point body, and (c) 12 point type on 15 point body. In effect the X-height/interline-space ratio is common on (a) and (c) but (a) is more economical: (b) was included to see if it was more difficult than either (a) or (c). (Examples of these settings will be demonstrated at the Conference.)

In this experiment, each child (N=36) read an extract from a story set in each of the three ways described above. (Reading aloud has the advantage that reading is slowed down and that errors can be recorded and measured, but it has the disadvantage that as it is not silent reading, it is slower and less natural than is the more common reading situation.) The order of the stories and of the settings were counter-balanced. The errors made and the times taken were recorded. Errors were computed according to the categories used by Zachrisson (1965). These include the wrong pronunciation of a word, unsatisfactory reading (shown by the insertion of an unwarranted pause, or by jerky reading), the exchange of one word in the text for another word, skipping a word, inserting a word not included in the text, repeating a word, transpositions (eg 'are we' instead of 'we are'), skipping a line, and inability to read a word.

Analysis showed that no significant differences resulted from the three presentation methods (either in terms of time or errors). Examination of the ten most able and the ten least able readers was similarly unrevealing. Very few of the children in fact made line-skipping errors, a finding we think surprising in view of the recommended type-sizes and line-lengths for materials for children of this age. (Burt et al, 1955, for example, recommend 14 point type on a 15-16 point body for 9-10 year olds, 12 point type on a 14 point body for 10-12 year olds, and a much shorter line-length – 4 inches.)

To follow up this study we shall now take the 10/12 setting and present the page as (a) a single column structure of 42 ems as before, and (b) as a two column structure of approximately 20 ems. (Unjustified type settings are being used, ie equal interword spacing causing a ragged right-hand margin, because this is more rational than justified typesetting: research on unjustified typesetting is reviewed by Hartley & Burnhill, 1971 and Hartley & Mills, 1973.) We aim to work with children of the same age and ability as before to examine whether or not a two column structure with this line-length helps (or hinders) readers of this age and ability. In this study we may introduce yet another measure – that of reading a text upside down – which is a further effective device for slowing down reading speed (Kolers, 1972). (Preliminary studies carried out with university students using this measure suggest that a narrower column structure might help speed up the reading of difficult material but that it might slow down the reading of easy material – but this suggestion has yet to be tested rigorously.)

By chance, a journal article set in proof form for 'Programmed Learning and Educational Technology' became available to the writers in (i) the 'old style' of the journal, and (ii) the 'new style' (adopted in January 1972). The major differences between the styles were that the 'old style' used a two-column structure (justified columns 16 ems) with an 11 point type set on a 12 point body. Headings and tables were centred over the text. The 'new style' had headings ranging from the left, a single-column structure of 33 ems, and used 10 point type on a 12 point body. (These differences will be demonstrated at the Conference.) Some of these changes might have been advocated by typographers on the basis of typographical research, but certainly not all of them would have been. (For those interested, typographic research relevant to journal design is concisely summarized by Poulton et al, 1970.)

In our study 26 university students read the passage in the form of xeroxed copies of the 'old style', and a further 26 students read the same article in the form of xeroxed copies of the 'new style'. The measures taken were reading speed, comprehension, and scanning. (Scanning is a measure devised by Poulton (1967): it involves presenting the student with a list of phrases selected in order at approximately equal intervals from the passage, with a word missing from each phrase: the student has to scan the passage, find the phrase, and write in the missing word as quickly as he can.)

In this study the major finding (apart from the fact that few students understood the article in question) was that there were no significant differences between the effects of the two layouts on the performance of the students on any of the three measures used.

However, in an Open Day display at the University of Keele visitors were asked to state their preferences for (i) the 'old/new style' journal cover, and (ii) the 'old/new style' article layout. The new cover (red with black and white lettering) was significantly preferred to the old (mustard yellow with green lettering), but particularly so by men. The men (N=56) also preferred the 'new style' article layout much more than did the women,

(N=50), who seem ambivalent in this respect.

In the experiment described above, because a large number of variables were altered by the change in format, it was not possible for us to assess properly the 'two column versus single column' issue. In fact, in reviewing the related research in this area, we were struck by how so few studies had controlled all the necessary variables – indeed we could only find one study which did so (Foster, 1970). Foster found in favour of a two column structure (17 ems justified) as opposed to a 36 ems single column structure (with 9 point type on a 10 point body) but he used the method of scanning as his measure. We are not confident, however, that this is a very reliable measure to use for testing for differences between the typographical layouts of prose materials.

The reliability of measures

A number of different measures have been used in order to assess if different typographical layouts have differing effects. Our experience in the research described above indicated to us that these measures might differ in their reliability, and also, that there might be sex differences in this respect.

To test the reliability of the measures commonly used in typographical research we are taking groups of university students and/or eleven - twelve year old secondary comprehensive school children of mixed ability and getting them to do a series of tests twice. We shall then correlate the results of the first with the second testing. We shall also examine the results for sex differences.

The measures we are currently hoping to examine in this way are:
(1) silent reading speed
(2) silent reading speed under knowledge of a forthcoming test
(3) reading aloud
(4) reading aloud when the text is upside down
(5) comprehension
(6) scanning with technical materials
(7) scanning with prose materials - phrases close together
                                                  - phrases wider apart
(8) cloze procedures (filling in missing words appropriately)
     - number attempted
     - number 'correct' (ie same as original author)
     - number 'correct' (allowing for synonyms)

At present we may report that we have done experiments in all eight areas but we have not yet worked out the full results. At the time of writing (January, 1973) we have found the correlations shown in Table I.

These results indicate that reading speed, and the cloze procedure seem to be at about the same level of reliability, but that scanning with technical

Table I. Reliability coefficients for some different measures used in typographical research

	Reading Speed (without test)	Scanning (technical material)	Cloze (No. attempted)		Cloze (No. correct)		Cloze (No. correct with synonyms)	
University	0.78	0.88	0.83	0.64	0.76	0.71	0.81	0.68
Students	(N=45)	(N=45)	(N=21)	(N=24)	(N=21)	(N=24)	(N=21)	(N=24)
Males	0.97	0.86	0.78	0.46	0.66	0.68	0.73	0.59
	(N=26)	(N=26)	(N=13)	(N=13)	(N=13)	(N=13)	(N=13)	(N=13)
Females	0.45	0.91	0.88	0.68	0.92	0.70	0.95	0.71
	(N=19)	(N=19)	(N=8)	(N=11)	(N=8)	(N=11)	(N=8)	(N=11)

material (in this case locating 'phone numbers from a page of the telephone directory) may be more reliable.

At the Conference we should be in a position to present a much fuller picture of the results.

We predict from some of our earlier studies that scanning with prose materials will be less reliable than scanning with technical material, as students tend to get lost in looking for phrases: we also anticipate, likewise, that scanning for phrases which are widely spaced (eg approximately 12-15 lines of text apart) will be less reliable than will scanning for phrases which are closer together (eg 6-8 lines apart).

The data shown in Table I have yet to be supplemented with the data from the mixed ability schoolchildren. In brief, we are not optimistic that the measures used in typographic research will turn out to be very reliable, and certainly, too, we question their validity – ie whether they measure what it is that they are supposed to measure. Tests which are not reliable are, by definition, not valid. Tests, however, may be reliable, but not valid. How far, for instance, reading speed in an experimental situation is a valid measure of reading in a normal situation is, of course, an open question.

Instructional implications

The present and the previous work in typographical research is of clear relevance to the educational technology (although, until recently, it has been largely neglected here). In this area of our research we have examined one issue, which is an extension of work carried out previously by Hartley et al (1970). This work examined the effects of giving a test before instruction on test results obtained after instruction. The design of these studies generally requires the after or post-test to be split into two halves of equal difficulty (a) and (b). One group of subjects does one half (a) before instruction as a pre-test and one group does the other half (b), and a third (control) group does not do a pre-test at all: all three groups are then post-tested after instruction on the combined tests (a) and (b). The results typically obtained are either (i) no significant effects; or (ii) specific effects (eg subjects doing pre-test (a) do better on (a) in the post-test than do the control subjects); and (sometimes) (iii) generalizing effects (ie subjects who do pre-test (a) do better on (a) in the post-test but they also do better on (b) on the post-test than do the control subjects).

In our study we did not divide the post-test into two halves of equal difficulty: we varied the difficulty of the pre-test. Group 1 (N=30 14-15 year old children) studied an easy pre-test on their knowledge of traffic signs: Group 2 (N=33) studied a difficult pre-test, and Group 3 (N=30) did not do a pre-test. All groups then studied the Highway Code section on traffic signs for ten minutes, and they were then post-tested with the combined easy and difficult pre-test. The results were as shown in Table II. There were specific pre-test effects from both pre-tests, but as the tests were marked according to their difficulty, doing the difficult pre-test led to the best post-test performance.

Table II. The effects of pre-test difficulty on post-test performance

		Pre-test A	Pre-test B	Post-test A	Post-test B	Post-test Total
Group 1	Median	5.75	-	7.0	9.5	16.25
N=30	(Range)	(1.5-8.0)	-	(6.0-8.0)	(1.0-16.0)	(7.0-23.0)
Group 2	Median	-	2.0	6.5	13.0	19.0
N=33	(Range)	-	(0.0-11.0)	(2.5-8.0)	(7.0-17.0)	(10.0-25.0)
Group 3	Median	-	-	6.5	9.0	16.0
N=30	(Range)	-	-	(4.0-8.0)	(0.0-15.0)	(6.5-22.0)

Pre-test A (Easy) marked out of 8
Pre-test B (Difficult) marked out of 18
Median rather than averages presented because the data are not normally distributed

These results suggest other areas of typographical research. We need to know what the effects of doing a pre-test are, and how, for example, these might interact with the typographical design of the instructional materials in question. There is much related work here which is of interest to the typographer and the educational research worker. The kinds of thing that have been studied are the effects of questions in passages; the position of questions; the rate of questioning; the kind of question (eg specific vs general); the order of sentences, information, paragraphs etc; and the use of headings, subheadings, underlining and other typographic cues. Much of this research has been summarized by Frase (1970) and more recently by Glaser and Resnick (1972). The spatial organization of the text – to return, in conclusion, to our theoretical orientation – may well be crucial in such instructional materials as, for example, algorithms and, more generally, programmed instruction (Davies, 1972).

Concluding remarks

Rules for the organization of space are now beginning to appear in for example Civil Service report and letter writing. Experimental tests demonstrating their superiority (in terms of speed to type) have been and are in process of being carried out (for example by Fowler). We are interested in applying this logic to the presentation of tabular materials and we are at present working on a taxonomy of table design in this respect. In all of these theoretical emphases we insist that the procedures should be rational, not ad hoc, and that they should be subject to experimental test. Valuable initial work on the presentation and understanding of tables has been done by Wright (1968).

In conclusion, at this point, we may mention that we are much interested in how language and, in particular, how the structure of a communication affects and can be affected by the spatial organization used to convey its meaning. When we come to redesign something (eg a college prospectus) we also often want to change the wording. We are also interested in how the writer's skills are affected by the typist's skills, and how in turn the type-written document is interpreted by typographical designers and finally by printers. We suspect that each person is little aware of how his/her skills affect those of the person who precedes or follows and we hope to be able to present at the Conference the results of an investigation designed to examine this experimentally. All these ideas indicate that there is a strong case for interdisciplinary work in this area.

ACKNOWLEDGMENTS

We are indebted to the Social Science Research Council who financed this research, to the headmasters, teachers, pupils and students who have assisted so generously with our experiments, and to the Road Research Laboratory, who provided some of the experimental materials.

REFERENCES

Burnhill, P. (1970) Typographic education: headings in text. Journal of
    Typographic Research IV, **4**, 353-365
Burt, C., Cooper, W. F. and Martin, J. L. (1955) A psychological study
    of typography. British Journal of Statistical Psychology VIII, **1**, 29-57
Davies, I. K. (1972) Presentation strategies. In 'Strategies for Program-
    med Instruction'. (Ed) J. Hartley. Butterworths, London
Fowler, G. H. E. (undated) Typing topics - towards a simpler letter layout.
    O & M Bulletin, **24**, No. 3

Fowler, G. H. E. (undated) Typing topics II - producing impressive reports. (Paper available from the Civil Service)

Frase, L. T. (1970) Boundary conditions for mathemagenic behaviours. Review Educational Research, **46**, 3, 337-348

Foster, J. J. (1970) A study of the legibility of one and two column layouts for BPS publications. Bulletin of the British Psychological Society, **23**, 113-114

Glaser, R. and Resnick, L. B. (1972) Instructional psychology. Annual Review of Psychology, **23**, 207-276

Hartley, J. and Burnhill, P. (1971) Experiments with unjustified text. Visible Language V, 3, 265-277

Hartley, J. and Mills, R. L. (1973) Unjustified experiments in typographical research and instructional design. British Journal of Educational Technology. (in press)

Hartley, J., Holt, J. and Swain, F. (1970) The effects of pre-test, interim tests and age on post-test performance following programmed instruction. Programmed Learning and Educational Technology, **7**, 4, 250-256

Kolers, P. (1972) Experiments in reading. Scientific American, **227**, 1, 84-91

Poulton, E. C. (1967) Skimming (scanning) news items printed in 8 point and 9 point letters. Ergonomics, **10**, 6, 713-716

Poulton, E. C. (1972) How efficient is print? In 'Contributions to an Educational Technology. (Ed) I. K. Davies and J. Hartley. Butterworths, London

Poulton, E. C., Warren, T. R. and Bond, J. (1970) Ergonomics in journal design. Applied Ergonomics, **1**, 4, 207-209

Spencer, H. (1969) The Visible Word. Lund Humphries, London

Wright, P. (1968) Using tabulated information. Ergonomics, **11**, 4, 331-343

Zacchrisson, B. (1965) Legibility of Printed Text. Stockholm. Almquist & Wiksell

The Application of the Systems Approach to Training in the Royal Naval Supply School

P F HAWKINS, R E HAWKINS

The Royal Naval Supply School, a shore establishment, is situated in HMS PEMBROKE, Her Majesty's Naval Base, Chatham, Kent. The School's primary task is to train commissioned and non-commissioned personnel of the Royal Navy, Royal Marines and Womens Royal Naval Service to manage Supply and Secretariat departments and, at the lower level, to be cooks, stewards, caterers, stores accountants and writers (clerks). The School runs 70 different types of courses, a total of 350 courses per year and has a throughput of approximately 2,500 trainees per year. The bulk of the courses provide training to fit officers and ratings for each stage of their career — New Entry, Leading Rate, Petty Officer, rating to Officer and Officers at basic and advanced level.

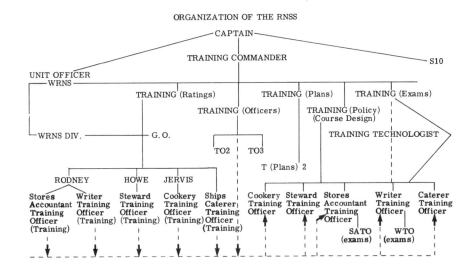

Figure 1

One hundred officers (25) and ratings (75) are available to run the school and in 1970 it was decided to reorganize the staff into a management structure that would cope with the new systems approach to training that was then about to be introduced.

The main constraint imposed at this stage was that, with one exception, no increase in staff was allowed. Accepting this, the management structure shown in Figure 1 was introduced in late 1970. The structure is headed by a Commander who controls four main training sections — Training Design, Training Execution, Training Assessment and Course Planning. These sections are shown in Figure 1. It should be noted that there are in fact two Training Execution sections, one for officers and one for ratings. Each of the sections is headed by a Lieutenant Commander.

The one addition to the staff was the Training Technologist, T(T), whose main task is to functionally control the work of the Training Analysts in the Training Design Section but who also acts as a methods consultant for all training design, exectuion and assessment.

The training model used for the system was that which had been adopted by the Commander-in-Chief, Naval Home Command, as a guide for all training establishments and the complete model is shown in Figure 2. It shows the processes and activities involved in the system and the documents which result from those activities: (a) Job Description; (b) Operational Performance Standard; (c) Trainee Specification; (d) Training Performance Standard; (e) Instructional Specification; (f) Lesson Plan; (g) Course Plan; (h) Training Criterion Test; (i) Training Assessment Results; (j) Operational Criterion Test; (k) External Assessment Results.

The model covers the five basic areas of (a) Job Analysis; (b) Training Analysis; (c) Course Design; (d) Course Execution; (e) Assessment, each of which will be dealt with in turn in this paper. It was decided to follow the model without deviation and, in spite of the large time delays involved, to accept the discipline of starting with the Job Analysis and working steadily through the system for each of the 70 courses run at the School.

The first course to be tackled was that of the Stewards' New Entry training. It was thought that as more ratings are trained at this level, than at the higher levels, the payoff from the design work would be all the greater. In practice this starting point has been justified as it has been easier to state what should be included in the higher courses having established a firm basic level. This paper concentrates on the Stewards' course but incorporates the developments that have been included in subsequent work.

JOB ANALYSIS
The Job Analysis was carried out by a team of three Work Study Analysts

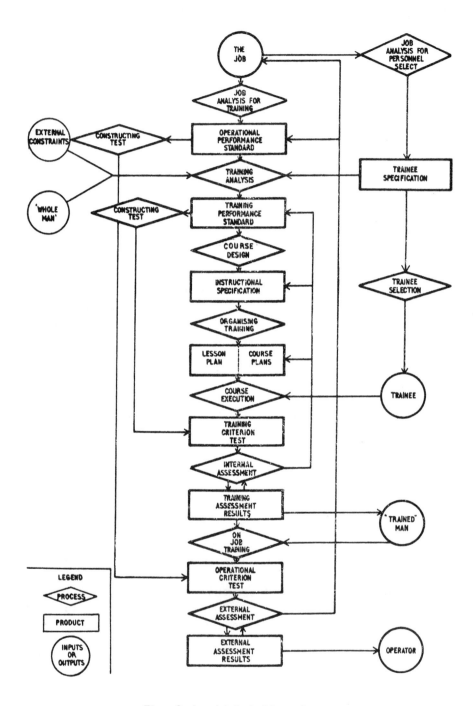

Figure 2. A model of a training system

from the Naval Manpower Utilization Unit. The NMUU is an independent
organization not connected with the Royal Naval Supply School. They visited
ships and shore establishments to determine exactly what tasks the steward
carried out. The investigation was carried out by interviewing a minimum of
10% of all the ratings in the branch in as many different ships and establishments as possible. Each interviewee was invited to complete a 250 question
questionnaire which was compiled to cover every aspect of his job. The analysis of the questionnaire was produced in the form of a histogram, as shown
in Figure 3. Each question was listed and against it was plotted the percentage number of times a task was performed in a given period of time; this

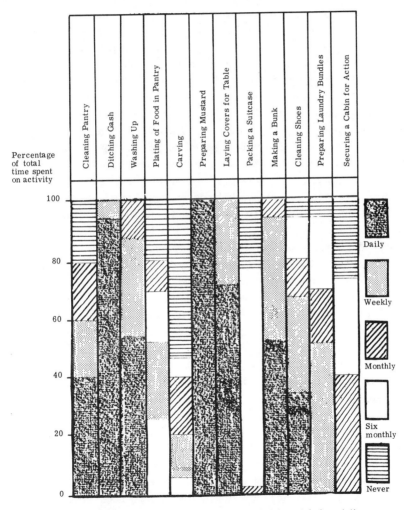

Figure 3. Sample extract from histogram compiled from job description

period has been reduced from two years to three months for later surveys. The histogram was coloured to bracket the times: eg never (black), weekly (red), daily (blue) etc. The final report was passed to the Captain, HMS PEMBROKE and was used as the basis for the production of the Job Description.

TRAINING ANALYSIS

Under the Training Technologist a team of two analysts was set up; both were seconded from instructional duties to work full time on the project. The Senior analyst, a Chief Petty Officer Writer, was attached to the Training Technologist in order to build up an expertise in techniques. The second analyst was taken from the Steward Training Execution Section to follow the system through the analysis and design stages and then to implement the course and validate it. Both these ratings were trained in the analysis techniques by the Royal Naval School of Educational Training and Technology.

The initial work involved analysing the job down from the tasks shown in the NMUU report in order to compile a Job Description (and to break each task down to the elements and key points). The technique used was that described in the paper by the author (1972). The Job Description is a list of the actual tasks that a steward can be expected to carry out and it was evolved with much assistance and advice from the subject matter experts, the course design and policy officers. A critical examination of the report was made to determine those tasks which should be carried out by a steward as a regular part of his job, because the Job Description is intended as a guide to the employment of the rating, but not as a final limit. The description also helps to identify the difference between those tasks carried out by the Steward and the Leading Steward. The final Job Description was submitted to the Commander-in-Chief for approval and distribution.

Having completed the Job Description, the analysts then wrote the Operational Performance Standard (OPS). This is the collective name given to the Operational Objectives, written in precise behavioural terms and gives in greater detail than the Job Description the definition of a Master Performer. The major discipline of the analysis was to define what the steward actually does, not what he is thought to do. The production of this document caused much heart searching among the professional experts and the destruction of some traditional beliefs, eg the young steward does not now press an Admiral's Cocked Hat, nor does he mix drinks such as a Dog's Nose! In some cases, tasks were also omitted even though some stewards did carry them out at certain intervals; this may have been because they were tasks for a higher rate, eg packing a suitcase for a senior officer is a Leading Steward's task.

The analysts' next move was to define what tasks could be trained in HMS PEMBROKE. In itself this involved two separate stages: (a) an analysis of the initial ability of the trainee, and (b) the definition of constraints to be imposed on the training.

As far as the constraints in (b) are concerned these also fell into two lists: (a) physical constraints — the fact that HMS PEMBROKE is a shore establishment and that training would have to be carried out in a school with limited live sea-going resources, and (b) this specialist professional training is only part of the training of the 'Whole Man'. Naval training is not only directly related to the future employment of personnel, but it also considers the development of the rating's character and his spiritual, naval and physical welfare. This part of the training involves periods of Physical Education, Religious Instruction, Current Affairs, Expedition Training, etc. Training for City and Guilds of London Institute qualifications was also considered, but it was decided to delay this until the Leading Stewards course.

When all these factors had been taken into account a document was produced entitled 'Training Performance Standard' (TPS). This was the collection of all the Training Objectives which would be achieved within HMS PEMBROKE. This is a management document which states exactly what the steward has been trained to do. There is a gap between the OPS and the TPS and this is the training that has to be carried out on the job. Both the OPS and the TPS were forwarded to the Commander-in-Chief Naval Home Command for approval.

COURSE DESIGN

The third stage for the analysis led into course design; at this point some of the Steward Training Execution Staff were brought into the discussion. The aim of the design work was to produce a document entitled the Instructional Specification (IS) which would be handed to the Instructor for him to use as a guide when making out his lesson plans. The Instructional Specification takes each training objective and breaks it down into the component enabling objectives, all written in student performance terms with conditions and standards. The whole was scheduled into a teaching sequence so that certain enabling objectives from several training objectives were grouped together into a lesson. From the Instructional Specification an estimation of the time to achieve each enabling objective was made and these were used to build up the course timetable. The specification also listed the visual aids available, where the training was to be carried out, the key points to be covered in the lesson and the method of testing. This document has a dual purpose, as it (a) acts as a guide to the Instructor, and (b) provides a control over him, ensuring that each and only the points laid down are covered. In this way it is hoped to get a uniform course from all instructors and uniform training for all ratings.

COURSE EXECUTION

The selection of the best method of training was the next vital step and the discipline of the system led to the introduction of a vast amount of practical training in simulated cabins, pantries and wardroom. The steward now never sits at a desk but takes his lessons around a wardroom table or in other simulators. In fact the course has become almost 90% practical. This gives the rating the feeling that he is really being trained to do a job and that his course is not an extension of his school life. Where wholly practical work is not possible then paper exercises, films and visits to ships have been incorporated.

The final stage was to establish the assessment procedures to be employed. Each objective was analysed to determine whether it required the testing of facts interpretation, application or practical work. This led to testing at four different levels: (a) factual knowledge — tested with multi-choice questions using the Cosford Cube Responder. Every question is put on an overhead transparency and the student's response recorded on the instructor's mark sheet; (b) practical testing — carried out by the Senior Instructor using a standard check off list; (c) interpretation and application — tested by written answers to questions from a question bank, at weekly, mid-course and end-of-course tests.

With all this continuous assessment it is possible to get a profile of the student's progress, and also of the instructor, and it enables defects to be easily identified and rectified. It also ensures that the student is given every corrective assistance during the course.

External assessment as yet has not been precisely established. Reports of the students' development after the training has been sought by questionnaire and to date these are most favourable, and confirm that the training being given is correct. However, the reports do indicate that due to particular circumstances in establishments there are difficulties in giving the on-the-job training. This final step in the training cycle is vital as it completes the gap between the Training Performance Standard and the Operational Performance Standard. Because of the problems encountered here, the problem is being given further detailed consideration.

OTHER COURSES

The process explained above is now being applied to the career courses for Leading Steward, New Entry Stores Accountants and Cooks, and Petty Officer Caterers. For each project an instructor has been seconded to the design team to work for the Professional Designers but functionally controlled by the Training Technologist. Time is the major factor and it has been found that to redesign a new entry course of eleven weeks takes about nine months, from the receipt of the Naval Manpower Utilisation Unit's report.

However, the results achieved are proving to be worthwhile:

a)   The efficiency of the course is improved; all that is taught is related to job or civilian examination, and this motivates the student.

b) Instructors like the fact that the course is designed to relate to the job, provided they are kept in the picture throughout the development, because they realise that in their next appointment they will have to employ the trainees they are instructing.

c) The teaching material is considered in much greater detail so that it is tailored to suit the ability of the student. The larger amount of practical work involved gets the student away from the classroom atmosphere. Also, because of the control of the material taught, the instructors are given more guidance on what to teach.

d) As a side effect to the redesign, a large slice of the superfluous 'Nice to Know' material has been removed. In some cases this has led to a shortening of course time by as much as 20%. However, in certain courses it has been realised that the course was too short, and with the added practical work extra time had to be added.

It would be wrong to leave the reader of this paper with the idea that the system has no particular danger points. Experience has shown the following main problems must be considered:

a) When converting the results of the Job Analysis into a Job Description it must be borne in mind that by the time the trained rating reaches his first job some 12 months or more will have elapsed. Training Analysts must be aware of, and inject into the system, any known future changes in the employment of the ratings/officers concerned.

b) We are dealing with individuals. The fact that we are training a 'Whole Man' cannot be over-emphasized. An individual has many other require-ments to be satisfied in addition to that of being able to make a bunk, lay a table, or serve a gin and tonic (see page 163). To forget this may produce a man lacking motivation.

c) The more practical training becomes the more difficult it is for the instructor to give personal attention to students. This can be over-come by increasing the amount of assistance given to the instructor in the form of ready made vu-graph transparencies etc. If necessary the number of students per class must be reduced.

REFERENCES

Drinkall, B. W. (1971) Visual Education, November 1971, page 27
Hawkins, R. E. (1972) What, How, and Key Points for Training Analysis. Paper presented to APLET Conference 1972

Media Taxonomies and Media Selection
D G HAWKRIDGE

INTRODUCTION

One of the questions I am frequently asked by visitors to the Open University is, "How do you choose which media to use for different parts of your multi-media courses?"

I feel that I am expected, in answer, to point to a beautifully constructed algorithm and explain how a carefully balanced analysis of pedagogical factors leads to the best choice. In fact, I have to admit that no such algorithm or analysis exists, and that the University's selections of media are controlled by logistical, financial and internal political factors rather than by soundly based and clearly specified psychological and pedagogical considerations.

I do not like admitting this: it seems as though it is not to the credit of the University, a leader in the multi-media field. But I do not feel too defensive about it. The fact is that instructional researchers and designers have not provided even the foundations for constructing strong practical procedures for selecting media appropriate to given learning tasks. If there has been British work in this area, I have been unable to discover it. In West Germany, the Deutsches Instituut fur Fernstudien has recently turned its attention to the problem (Dohmen, 1972). In the United States, over 2,000 media studies have not yielded the answers we need.

In this paper I shall summarize some of the approaches made to this problem and will comment upon them before telling you of a recent study financed by the Council of Europe. I shall then examine in detail the advice on media selection in the principal published handbook on instructional design procedures. Having cleared the ground, as it were, I shall try to explain how the Open University deals with this problem at present. Finally, I should like to indicate the directions the media research in the Institute of Educational Technology is likely to take in the light of these findings and the University's needs.

THE PROBLEM APPROACHED

In an article published in 1968, Saettler (1968), an authority on media, stated bluntly that instructional design was still an 'unexplored theoretical and research frontier, with no texts or guidelines for designing instructional media messages'. He said that the media research of over 50 years had had little relevance to the problems of instructional design. In particular, he noted that, "What we need are criteria and procedures whereby we may match a medium to the requirements of a learner. An urgent need exists for a taxonomy of instructional media which can provide a systematic approach to the selection and use of media for educational purposes."

Briggs (1967) wrote how he was constructing a programmed text one day in 1964 when he suddenly began to wonder why programming had to be the best medium for that particular instructional message. He undertook a literature survey, and concluded that, "there hadn't been any research on how to choose the best medium of instruction for particular teaching objectives".

Twyford (1969) wrote a review article for the fourth edition of the Encyclopaedia of Educational Research, but in it he has little to say on media selection or media taxonomies. He notes the large number of studies comparing one medium with another, and claims that the research shows that a medium's effectiveness is more dependent upon the nature of the message than upon the characteristics of the medium. He refers to selecting media on the basis of their relative efficiency and makes vague allusions to the use of systems analysis and behavioural objectives. I looked in vain for solid advice on media selection.

As I dug deeper into the work done up to about 1968, I realized that there had been one or two attempts to identify the theoretical bases on which instructional design should proceed. Glaser (1966), for example, suggested some psychological considerations; some would not agree with his behavioural approach, and I shall note a few of its practical weaknesses in dealing with Briggs' work later.

Meredith (1965) put forward suggestions for a taxonomy of educational media. He envisaged a four-fold classification of variables:

(a) physical variables in the material, and the form of the physical medium providing the stimulus;

(b) the neuro-anatomical variables in the sensory-motor structures involved in the responsive behaviour of the learner;

(c) ecological variables which take account of architectural and other environmental factors responsible for the context of media;

(d) a collective set of variables which embody the time dimension, factors of memory, learning, growth, history of the student, attention, purpose, expectation, imagination and anticipation.

This very comprehensive classification indicates emphatically that we are dealing with a multi-variate design problem, in which simplistic analyses will have no place. It makes the work of Fleming (1967) on the classification and analysis of instructional illustrations seem elementary and merely preliminary. Fleming provided a taxonomy of illustrations which included physical types, verbal modifier (captions, etc) types, educational objective types, and subject matter types. More recently, Jamieson (1973) has attempted to relate visual media to different categories of learning tasks, but he offers little guidance for multi-media system designers.

Edling (1968), in a review of educational objectives and educational media, added nothing that would help me, although he touched on a large number of studies of different learning modes and media.

Sometime in the 1960s, perhaps arising from the work of Glaser, Briggs and others in America, people writing about the systems approach to education and what an ideal educational system would look like began to insert in their flow-diagrams a box that said 'Select media' or something equivalent. Silvern (1964), Schagin and Poorman (1967), Kaufman (1968), Lechmann (1968), Haney, Lange and Barson (1968), and Gerlach and Ely (1971) are among those I noted using this approach. In fact, I myself have written in these terms (Hawkridge, 1970), and in Germany Schmidbauer (1970) has done the same. I am not suggesting that we were all wrong, but I do think we underestimated the contents of the box. That leads me to tell you about the Council of Europe study.

THE COUNCIL OF EUROPE STUDY

Some $2\frac{1}{2}$ years ago I proposed to a technical committee of the Council of Europe that an attempt should be made to produce a media taxonomy. I told them that what was needed was a practical guide to instructional designers working in multi-media systems for teaching adults at a distance, like the Open University. The work plan envisaged the possibility of selecting appropriate media for given learning tasks, having regard to the characteristics of the learners. My idea was not original; I worked in the same Institute as Briggs in California. I hoped that the Council could go beyond what Briggs and his colleagues had reported in 1967 in their classic monograph on instructional media design (Briggs, Campeau, Gagné & May, 1967).

As a first step, the Council commissioned an updating of part of that monograph. Campeau, who did the original literature review, was asked to prepare a selective review of the results of research on the use of audiovisual media to teacn adults (Campeau, 1972). At the same time, Kaye prepared a set of learning tasks in the natural sciences (Kaye, 1972), following Gagné's (1970) suggestion that the most important single criterion for a choice of medium is often the nature of the learning task.

I had some hopes that Campeau would be able to find some guiding principles in the research since 1965, the date of the original review. In fact, in spite of an extremely thorough search, she found little. This is not the place to explain why: her report does so, very well. She concludes that the research is yet to be done that may yield principles for media selection, and makes some suggestions about how this research might be designed. She foresees, for example, that multi-variate analysis will be required to detect not only main treatment effects but also interactions between variables. I shall come back to that point later.

When Kaye had prepared his set of learning tasks or objectives, it was at once clear that there would be fundamental problems in using it as a basis for media selection. The set itself is well compiled. The problems arise chiefly from levels of specificity and from the inadequacy of language for conveying full intentions. These, of course, are the problems that plague anyone trying to use Mager or Glaser-type behavioural objectives in instructional situations. A comprehensive paper by Macdonald-Ross (in press) deals with these and other difficulties in formulating and using objectives, and I will not go into them here. It is enough to say that one of the most fundamental obstacles in the way of preparing algorithms for media selection is that tasks cannot easily be specified at an appropriate level. If we examine three of the tasks listed in Kaye's paper, this point will be clear.

1. Describe how the relativistic mass of an object changes as the speed of the object increases towards that of the speed of light.

2. Demonstrate how Avogadro's Law and Dalton's Law of partial pressures may be derived from the gas law and simple kinetic theory.

3. Compare and contrast igneous and metamorphic rocks in terms of their differing mineral content.

Each of these tasks or objectives has to be broken down, and decisions have to be taken about how much of their intellectual context is to be taught, before media can be chosen. Is 1. to be undertaken simply through writing the right formula? To teach the right formula then becomes the task for which media must be selected, but even that task must still be broken down into what Briggs calls instructional events. More likely, however, 1. includes far more. The same remarks apply to 2. In 3. we might reasonably expect more than a bookish understanding of the differences between the kinds of rocks. Students might handle them, or look at microscope slides of rock-sections, and so on. None of these tasks is actually specified.

My comments are not an attack upon Kaye's list. They are intended to emphasize the difficulty of selecting appropriate media before a very detailed analysis has been carried out. Such an analysis may be feasible, but not as a routine practice, to be employed by relatively untrained personnel, as I had originally proposed. The question of whether such reductionism is desirable also remains to be answered.

This conclusion is an important one for educational technologists, and needs to be examined in the light of the principal published prescription for instructional systems design, Briggs' 1970 Handbook.

BRIGGS' PRESCRIPTION

If we are looking for a systems model for the design of instruction, with the idea of governing media decisions with specific kinds of learners in mind, then Briggs' (1970) handbook deserves to be studied closely. This volume, entitled Handbook of procedures for the design of instruction, is the culmination of years of work in the field (Briggs, 1967, 1968). Its theoretical foundations appear to rest partly in Glaser's behavioural approach and partly in Gagné's (1965) book, The conditions of learning. Certainly the handbook is the most comprehensive existing treatment of the topic. It was tried out in Briggs' classes at Florida State University.

Briggs claims that in his handbook the entire process of instructional design is described, in an orderly series of steps to be taken. He says too that in this process 'media are deliberately and carefully chosen to comprise a certain strategy of instruction, ...the objective being to employ the most effective media for each (instructional) event'.

What is the process of instructional design that Briggs describes? He lists the three main components as:
(a) specification of instructional objectives;
(b) development of tests measuring attainment of those objectives;
(c) selection of media and design of instructional materials.

For the third component, the one that interests us now, Briggs offers this behavioural objective for readers of his handbook:

For each instructional event .... you choose a medium of instruction and defend your choice on the basis of one or more of the following:
(a) a systematic model for the design of instruction;
(b) other theoretical or logical analysis models;
(c) research findings in this subject-matter area;
(d) other documented evidence (not intuition).

It seems quite clear from these excerpts, especially from the warning about not using intuition, that Briggs is about to put forward in the handbook what I am looking for, a logical way of selecting media for instruction. His flow-chart has a box labelled 'Select media'.

In the chapter on media selection, however, we find we are little better off than before we started. The reasons are much the same as those I encountered in the Council of Europe study. The complete summary of Briggs' instructional design steps (see Appendix) is too long to discuss here, so I shall concentrate on those steps relating directly to media selection.

Briggs wants us to choose a medium of instruction to match each instructional event. He expects the designer trying to select media to start off by turning what is to be learned into what Briggs calls 'competencies'. For each competency the designer thinks up one or more instructional events. When the designer has accomplished this arduous analysis, in which he is called upon to make a large number of judgments without adequate supporting criteria, he will have a long list of instructional events. The next step is to analyse for each event what stimuli would be most appropriate, considering somehow both learner and task characteristics. Only after all this has been completed does the designer list the media alternatives available and appropriate for presenting the stimuli. Then he makes a tentative selection of one medium.

Figure 1 summarizes the stages:

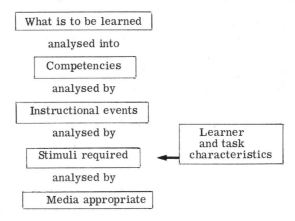

Figure 1. Selected steps from Briggs' (1970) procedure for instructional design

At this point we hear a sharp note of reality. Briggs sees that the learner cannot easily switch from one medium to another at very frequent intervals during a complex learning task, and he suggests in an anti-climactic way that final decisions about selecting media are made in practical terms of what makes a good 'package'.

Briggs provides some examples of how his own graduate students have followed the routine. Perhaps it is again a matter of words being inadequate to convey full intentions, but I am not impressed by the examples he has chosen. The problems of using the routine show up in the analysis he provides. I am afraid it would take too long to provide a detailed critique of even one example, say that for the objective: 'Given any circle, the student will be able to compute the degrees in any segment of the circle.' From studying this example, however, I would say that a number of media could have been used quite easily to the same ends.

What Briggs offers the designer is a series of difficult analyses ending in some commonsense decisions. I do not doubt that the commonsense decisions are usually better informed after such analyses, but I do doubt whether it is practical to propose this routine for everyday use. Even if it were practical, is the routine likely to take into account the interactions between variables assumed in Meredith's taxonomy and referred to by Campeau? I think not.

At this stage you are probably hoping that somebody will come up with a better idea. I certainly am. But I do not think we have one at the Open University, yet.

MEDIA ALLOCATION VERSUS MEDIA SELECTION IN THE OPEN UNIVERSITY

How has the Open University tried to deal with the problem of media selection? Its staff certainly have not indulged in Gagné or Briggs analyses.

To some extent, the problem of media selection has been dodged by resorting to media allocation. By media allocation, I mean the process by which courses receive quotas of each medium. The course team chairman knows near the start of the course development cycle how much he will have of various media available in the system. For example, he will be told how many broadcasts on television and radio he has, how much printed material can be produced, whether he can send out tape recordings, and so on. Most of these items are allocated according to rules of thumb, well in advance.

Once the chairman knows his budgets and quotas, the problem is how best to use them. The people who have a say in what goes into which medium include the academic subject-matter specialists, the BBC producers, and the educational technologists. They tend to fix first what should go into the printed material, but it is very hard to generalize about the ways in which media decisions are taken within the framework of the budgets and the quotas. What can be said is that once a certain amount of, say, television time is secured, this has an influence on course design, encouraging course producers to change their objectives to take advantage of television. Of course, they only have that television time because they put up a pedagogical case of some kind in the first place. For instance, science course teams will claim a larger quota of television on the grounds that they need to demonstrate scientific principles, while a course on the history of music will ask for extra radio.

In the early days of the University's growth there was less competition for resources than there is now. The fact that course producers quite often want now more than they eventually get is a stimulus towards more rigorous thinking out of what is needed. Where demand exceeds supply, argument is fiercest about how best to use what is available. Over the next few years

the debates should rise in standard, with producers being increasingly careful
in their media selection.

As yet, however, the University has not codified or made explicit the
criteria for its internal media selection. Nor has it tackled on a broad front
the problem of integrating the media. Briggs clearly assumes in his
examples that there is to be integration of media, with one medium being
used for one learning task within a series, then another for another. True,
he is working on the microscopic level, as we have seen. Integration at that
level is fairly rare in the University's courses, although it occurs generally
at the macroscopic level.

MEDIA RESEARCH IN THE OPEN UNIVERSITY

It seems very unlikely that Briggs' analyses will ever be used in the Open
University, except perhaps experimentally, and then on a small scale.
Media allocation, based mainly on logistical, financial and internal political
considerations, is likely to continue to provide the operating framework for
the University's vast production. The influence of psychological and pedagogical factors on this allocation system, and on the detailed selection of
media content, can grow, however, if two of the research programs in the
Institute of Educational Technology are successful. One, directed by Dr
Bates, concerns the broadcast media; the other, under Mr Macdonald-Ross,
concerns textual communications. Both are in their infancy at present, but
it is worth noting their aims.

Among the objectives of the broadcast media project are the following:

(a) to draw up and test a list of the most appropriate functions for
television and radio on a multi-media system;

(b) to produce design models for multi-media teaching systems,
including:

(i) models ensuring the full integration of broadcasting with
other components;

(ii) criteria for deciding on the allocation of broadcast resources;

(iii) criteria for deciding on the kind and extent of broadcasting
resources needed.

This partial listing indicates the inter-relatedness of problems of media
selection and allocation. It also indicates that we expect to go on working
at the macroscopic level.

One of the principal research tools we hope to use is content analysis
(Gerbner et al, 1969). By analysing in various ways the content of what the
University has already made, we hope to be able to start compiling the list
of functions. These analyses in retrospect, as it were, will probably lack
the detail of Briggs' but they should enable us to make generalizations about
how the media are being used in various courses or for various purposes.

The generalizations, in turn, should have some influence on how new courses are produced and on how the media are allocated to and used in them.

In much the same way, the textual communication project is searching for design principles that can be used in new course production. Content analyses will be necessary here too to find out what different subject-matters require in textual communication, and how the effectiveness of the texts can be enhanced.

As course teams are offered better ways of designing course material, both broadcast and textual, they may decide to alter their media mix, using more or less text or radio or television than is the custom now for the same type of course, depending on what shifts they make to other media.

In other words, the Institute of Educational Technology is relying on a cyclic evolution of design principles, based on careful analyses of experience, rather than Briggs' prescriptive approach. To be fair to Briggs, he does expect the media choices arrived at through his routine to be tested out, and revised on the basis of their effectiveness. That proposal takes us to another question being approached not only by Dr Bates but also by an Institute team working under Professor Lewis, with a Ford Foundation grant: How do we measure the effectiveness of various media?

Allen (1971), who has worked in media research for several decades, recently declared, "The time is far off .... when we can identify an instructional problem, then faultlessly select the proper instructional mix to solve it". It will take some years to evolve design principles for the University, but I believe it needs them, and should use these principles, 'NOT INTUITION" (to quote Briggs for the last time).

SUMMARY

In this paper I began by posing the question of how the Open University, or any multi-media system, should choose media for various learning tasks. I have described and commented upon some of the approaches made to this problem, mostly by American researchers. In my view, these approaches have not been successful in providing useful answers. I have explained how the Council of Europe agreed to finance a further study. I have told you what was done by Campeau and Kaye, and what difficulties the study came up against.

I have shown you how my hopes that Briggs might offer a suitable design procedure were not fulfilled, on account of the need for such complex analyses before media selection. I have described in a general way how the Open University allocation of the various media, made on rules of thumb, determines to some extent the expectations of course teams and results in a kind of media selection.

I have said that I believe that the University and other multi-media systems really need guiding principles for media selection, based on research, and I have told you a little about the research beginning in the Institute of Educational Technology that may hasten the evolution of these principles.

There must be others present who have thought about the problem to which this paper has been addressed. I shall welcome discussion.

REFERENCES

Allen, W. H. (1971) Instructional media research. Audiovisual Communication Review, **19**, 5-18

Briggs, L. J. (1967) Multi-media instruction: a true story. Audiovisual Instruction, March

Briggs, L. J. (1967) A structure for the design of multi-media programmes. Audiovisual Instruction, March

Briggs, L. J. (1968) Learner variables and educational media. Review of Educational Research, **38**, 160-176

Briggs, L. J. (1970) Handbook of Procedures for the Design of Instruction. Pittsburgh, American Institutes for Research

Briggs, L. J., Campeau, P. L., Gagne, R. M. and May, M. A. (1967) Instructional Media: a procedure for the design of multi-media instruction, a critical review of research and suggestions for further research. Pittsburgh, American Institutes for Research

Campeau, P. L. (1972) Selective Review of the Results of Research on the use of Audiovisual Media to Teach Adults. Strasbourg, Council of Europe

Dohman, G. (1972) Mediendidaktik. Paper presented at a Council of Europe symposium at Bad Godesberg, September 1972

Edling, J. V. (1968) Educational objectives and educational media. Audiovisual Communication Review, **18**, 177-194

Fleming, M. (1967) Classification and analysis of instructional illustrations. Audiovisual Communication Review, **15**, 246-258

Gagné, R. M. (1965) The Conditions of Learning. Holt, Rinehart and Winston, New York

Gagné, R. M. (1970) Learning theory, educational media and individualised instruction. In 'Commission on Instructional Technology'. To improve learning: a Report to the President and the Congress of the United States. Government Printing Office, Washington DC, USA

Gerbner, G., Holsti, O. R., Krippendorff, K., Paisley, W. J. and Stone, P. J. (Eds) (1969) The Analysis of Communication Content: Developments in Scientific Theories and Computer Techniques. Wiley, New York

Gerlach, V. S. and Ely, D. P. (1971) Teaching and Media in a Systematic Approach. Prentice-Hall, Englewood Cliffs, NJ

Glaser, R. (1966) Psychological bases for instructional design. Audiovisual Communication Review, **14**, 433-449

Haney, J. B., Lange, P. C. and Barson, J. (1968) The heuristic dimension of instructional development. Audiovisual Communication Review, **16**, 358-371

Hawkridge, D. G. (1970) Long-term prospects for educational technology in Southern Africa. Symposium

Jamieson, G. H. (1973) Visual media in a conceptual framework for the acquisition of knowledge. Programmed Learning and Educational Technology, **10**, 32-39

Kaufman, R. A. (1968) A system approach to education: derivation and definition. Audiovisual Communication Review, **16**, 415-425

Kaye, A. R. (1972) A Set of Learning Tasks in the Natural Sciences. Strasbourg, Council of Europe

Lehmann, H. (1968) The systems approach to education. Audiovisual Instruction, **13**, 144-148

Macdonald-Ross, M. (in press) Behavioural objectives - a critical review. Instructional Science

Meredith, O. (1965) Towards a taxonomy of educational media. Audiovisual Communications Review, 13, 374-84

Saettler, P. (1968) Design and selection factors. Review of Educational Research, 38, 115-128

Schmidbauer, M. (1970) The Application of Combined Teaching Systems and the New Aspects and Functions of Education Which Depend on them. Strasbourg, Council of Europe

Silvern, L. C. (1964) Designing Instructional Systems. University of California, Los Angeles

Smith, M. D., Schagin, M. and Poorman, L. E. (1967) Multi-media systems: a review and report of a pilot project. Audiovisual Communication Review, 15, 345-69

Twyford, L. C. (1969) Educational communications media. In Encyclopedia of Educational Research' 4th edition. (Ed) R. L. Ebel. Macmillan, New York

A SUMMARY OF BRIGGS' PROCEDURES FOR THE
DESIGN OF INSTRUCTION

1. Define the boundary conditions. Note any limiting conditions for both development and implementation in terms of time, costs, skills, and resources available.
2. Decide between individual and group instruction. This affects the media choices, as well as how the finished instructional materials are used. Two analyses of the same objectives and competencies could be made, one for individual, and one for group instruction. Or, different competencies could be planned for the two methods, for use with a single group of learners.
3. Identify the characteristics of the learners.
4. Identify a competency to be analysed. Note carefully the significant verbs (behaviours) and objects (content reference).
5. List the general instructional events to be used.
6. List the special instructional events for the type of learning the competency represents.
7. Arrange the entire list of events in the desired order, and consider whether more than one application of each event is needed.
8. List the type of stimuli for each event, considering both learner and task characteristics.
9. List the alternate media from which a choice is to be made for each event.
10. Make a tentative media selection for each event from among the alternates recorded. Note a rationale of advantages and disadvantages for group of individual use.
11. Review an entire series of tentative media choices, seeking optimum 'packaging'.
12. Make final media choices for package units.
13. Write a prescription to the specialist for each package unit, or one continuous, uninterrupted use of a medium.
14. Write a prescription for the teacher for instructional events not provided by the other media.

(From Briggs (1970), page 114)

The Introduction and Development of an Integrated Self-Paced Company Training System

K B HORNER

In common with many types of large organizations covering a range of activities our Company has training problems to be overcome. As a large multi-national organization with basically commercial interests, these problems are ultimately concerned with the improvement and maintenance of standards of an Engineer force which represents the Company's interests and investment into the world of business equipment. In an attempt to ensure that these interests and investments were effectively developed and protected Company training staff are currently engaged in a 'quiet revolution' in training techniques, attempting to devise a form of training which will not only help the Company in its commercial interests but will enable the individual employee to realize his full potential and to utilize his abilities to his own satisfaction.

We would like to show how we are meeting these requirements. First, by describing the nature of training problems within the multi-national structure of our Company. Secondly by comparing an existing training philosophy, based on conventional training methods, with a developing new philosophy, based on integrated self-pacing training. Thirdly, by describing the construction and implementation of integrated self-paced training courses to meet Company training needs. And lastly, by providing a basis for discussion of an attempt by a commercial organization to produce a totally self-paced approach to training.

THE NATURE OF THE TRAINING PROBLEMS

The Company has a brief history. Established in 1956 with a minimal working capital and only one product to market, it has developed into an international organization employing people with a wide span of skills, to produce, sell and service a range of products of varying degrees of complexity and sophistication. In simple terms the main activity is to provide industry and commerce with machines which produce copies of documents. Unlike many competitors the machines are rented to the users who pay for each copy made on the machine. This is the basis of revenue. It is also the basis of the Company's training requirement. Since the machines belong to the Company it has the responsibility for repair and maintenance, and machines which cannot produce copies because of a fault lose revenue because customers cannot use them, thus downtime must be kept to a minimum. In order to gain the greatest possible output from the machines, and hence the greatest revenue from copies, it is essential that a highly efficient service engineering force be trained and maintained.

This problem is not confined to the Company's activities within the United Kingdom, but international growth which has taken place means that the same kind of commercial activity is carried out throughout the major countries of the world, and many of the smaller nations. In Europe, Australia and parts of Africa and Asia, these multi-national activities are coordinated by an International Headquarters based in London, who work with the various Operating Companies established in each country. But, although the activities are of a similar nature their range depends upon the stage of growth an Operating Company has reached, since each one began business and developed independently of the others. Thus, according to individual national needs the range of products and servicing required varies considerably.

The establishment of Operating Companies has one prime objective: to develop internationally the original concept of commercial activity by installing products designed primarily in the USA and UK. In other words, there exists an international usage of the same Company products whilst there are differences both in language and in technical requirements. There is also the recognition that the original need for a highly efficient engineer force is now expressed in the form of a need for highly efficient individual **national** service engineer forces. Without central coordination individual Operating Companies would develop their own approaches to providing the necessary training. This would mean that different levels and standards would be adopted and that there would be a considerable duplication of work and errors. Considerable effort would have to be exerted to mount courses for small numbers of students and there would be the serious problem of the availability of new machines for training purposes. Even with direction, the differences in training are clear — and this is an important problem when an international standard of training is needed — mainly due to different standards for recruitment and selection of new engineers. There is also a noticeable difference in the products of the various educational systems. Engineers in Italy begin training with the Italian Operating Company with a very different educational background to that of new engineers in, say, Sweden or the United Kingdom.

In order to establish an overall standard of training the various training organizations and the parent Company must be in a position where training needs, problems and solutions are established on a common basis. Thus, a rapport brought about by a continuing dialogue between the two bodies is of vital importance for successful training. In this situation a mutually agreed common approach to training must be concerned with: (a) the establishment of common overall training objectives; (b) the interpretation of these objectives on a similar basis; (c) the use of the same training information; (d) the use of training methods selected from those mutually accepted as suitable; (e) the implementation of the same evaluation techniques for validation purposes; (f) the establishment of a common training approach flexible enough to cope with individual differences. These problems together point towards the major requirement: the need to produce service engineers able to deal with servicing to an internationally accepted standard.

COMPARING CONVENTIONAL AND SELF-PACED TRAINING METHODS

Our Company is a young one, but its growth has been quite extraordinary even by today's standards of big business. In 1963 the Company made a pre-tax profit of £1 million and by 1972, this had increased to £105 million. As more machines are installed so the need for service engineers increases and, consequently, the training organizations have had to implement training under extreme pressure.

In the early years there was a natural tendency to use well-tried conventional group training techniques. There was no reason at this time to try a new, unproved method, particularly as specialists in such a method would have to be found. Training personnel recruited into the Company had considerable experience of working with trainees in a fairly formal 'classroom' learning environment and engineers who later became training officers tended to accept these techniques because, as trainees, they had become familiar with them. The explosive growth of the Company allowed no time to experiment or put new sophisticated techniques into operation, even though training staff had begun to consider them. So, the training problems were met by well-tried methods and success was indicated by the continuing increase in the popularity of the Company's products and service. But the expansion of the range of products and their greater technical complexity have created an urgent need for the development of more effective training.

The International Headquarters Training Department was concerned with the weaknesses of the group learning system in dealing with the training needs of the labour force. Whilst the advantages of the system had satisfied the first urgent training requirements, these weaknesses had become apparent as the Company expanded. It was felt that learning which coped with the needs of the individual rather than of the group would eventually make more efficient use of the abilities of service engineers. At the same time the Company had decided to adopt a policy of Specialization and to introduce Basic Knowledge Modules in training new engineers. Each machine is placed within a 'family' of machines which reflects the common elements in their design. Consequently engineers would be restricted to working within one particular family of products. The implication was that it would no longer be possible to train a New Intake Engineer on simpler machines and then progress him to the more complex. There was a need for basic knowledge of the products, eg the Xerographic Principle, Optics, and Mechanics, which could be developed quickly to enable inexperienced manpower to cope with a family which would include machines of a high degree of technical sophistication. Thus, Specialization and Basic Knowledge modules indicated that a restructured training approach needed to be closely related to the job and highly effective in teaching individuals to the required standards. Three alternative approaches were available: (1) The development of conventional group training; (2) An improved Training Officer to Student ratio; (3) A switch to a training approach customized to individual learning requirements.

Developing existing group training techniques, perhaps by improving facilities and instructional standards, would not overcome the weaknesses of such a system. Weaknesses expressed in terms of rigid time-tabling, availability of training machines, and the impossibility of ensuring maximum individual performances.

At the same time, an improvement in the TO/Student ratio, within the group learning system, would be an expensive way of only slightly improving individual performances and, in any case, would not solve time-tabling or machine availability problems.

The answer seemed to be to choose a training approach customized to individual learning requirements. Thus a training philosophy is being constructed based on 'Integrated Self-Paced Training'. We define this concept as follows:

"Integrated Self-Paced Training is the integration of selected learning methods to form a course of study enabling the student to learn at his own speed and to satisfy his individual learning requirements, so that he is capable of performing the job satisfactorily."

The enormous task of producing a total training programme in self-paced form is being met by pooling the training resources of both the parent Company and the various national training organizations. But the adoption of this approach is enabling the Company to cope with the need to produce trained service engineers to an accepted international standard, ie a labour force capable of dealing with a job becoming more complex. This approach to the training problems works in several ways:

1. The unity and involvement ensures a common approach to training and the establishment of an international standard of service engineer performance.

2. The implementation of a fresh training philosophy presents an opportunity to unite and involve the international training organizations.

3. The rigorous approach to the development of self-paced courses identifies priorities in teaching material more effectively.

4. The use of integrated self-paced training methods provides better organizational flexibility in training, effective individual learning, and requires that the training officer is utilized most effectively in a tutorial role rather than as a presenter.

THE CONSTRUCTION AND IMPLEMENTATION OF
AN INTEGRATED SELF-PACED COURSE FOR A SIMPLE PRODUCT

Having defined a fresh approach the next task was to construct a training pattern which would, in its various parts, reflect the philosophy of integrated self-paced training. Because the concept was new and untried within the Company the initial moves to implement training were accepted as experimental but from the outset three vital aims were established:

1. The structure of the training organizations of the parent Company and the Operating Companies would have to change to accommodate the new training approach.
2. Integrated self-paced training specialists within the training organizations must form the linchpin of the new system.
3. Management must be familiarized with the new training approach.

Less than two years ago work began on the design of the first integrated self-paced training course. Whilst this was being developed the first specialist courses were held to train selected training officers from the Operating Companies in self-paced learning techniques, each specialist becoming the Project Leader for his own training organization. One of their responsibilities is to ensure that their own management are familiar with the new training approach.

The first course was designed for the new Rank Xerox 400 Telecopier, a facsimile transmission unit which can send or receive documents over ordinary telephone lines. This is a new product for which engineers had to be trained to service without any previous knowledge of facsimile devices to assist them. The choice of this machine for the first course was based on two factors. First, the product was a stable one from a design point of view. Secondly, the product was not too complex in its design and construction.

As the training had to be designed before the machine went into the field there was a complete lack of field experience. Thus, there was virtually no information available concerning the actual servicing requirements of the machine. However, a number of pre-production models were examined and the design team experimented with the machine to identify possible weaknesses. Overall training objectives were agreed and a breakdown of the information into modules was undertaken. It was found that there were three broad categories of information reflected by the objectives:

THEORY CIRCUIT FUNCTION	OPERATION TO PRODUCE A COPY	SKILLS FAULT ANALYSIS & SERVICING

General discussion had indicated several acceptable means by which learning material could be presented in a self-paced format. By examining the characteristics of the information to be taught and the nature of the methods it was possible to match each category with a first choice of method and one or two alternatives.

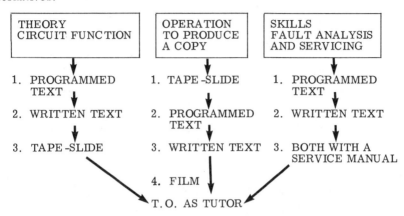

THEORY CIRCUIT FUNCTION	OPERATION TO PRODUCE A COPY	SKILLS FAULT ANALYSIS AND SERVICING

1. PROGRAMMED TEXT
2. WRITTEN TEXT
3. TAPE-SLIDE

1. TAPE-SLIDE
2. PROGRAMMED TEXT
3. WRITTEN TEXT
4. FILM

1. PROGRAMMED TEXT
2. WRITTEN TEXT
3. BOTH WITH A SERVICE MANUAL

T.O. AS TUTOR

Using this approach each of the modules was prepared and a picture of the complete course began to emerge. A short film introduced the product to the student and served as the motivating element. This was followed by a key-operation sequence talking the engineer through the operation of the machine to produce a copy, and then an audio-visual parts location preceded the first of the theoretical areas in a linear programmed text. Finally, faults were placed on the machine to be dealt with by each student.

The initial courses run for validation purposes demonstrated two serious problems. The student in a self-paced situation relies very heavily upon his service manual information, but if this information is not reliable his faith in the learning method can be badly shaken. The second problem was that the theoretical areas dealt with by programmed text needed to be broken up as they could last for about $2\frac{1}{2}$ days. The answer to this was to introduce tape-slide summaries after each module.

After amendments had been made to the training materials and a special self-paced training area established, courses were run on a regular basis. To date 90 engineers have been trained using this integrated self-paced learning course taking from $2\frac{1}{2}$ - 10 days to complete training. A period of six months was given to allow for field experience and then a questionnaire was prepared and sent to 60 engineers, 49 being completed and returned, of which 47 were used for evaluation purposes. The resulting information has not been used in statistical form as no form of controlled research on the course's training effectiveness had been established. Nonetheless the answers to the questions revealed a general satisfaction with the nature of the training and its relevance to the job situation and confirmed that the chief difficulty lay in the reliability of the servicing documentation.

The amended course documentation has now been issued to those Operating Companies who will be conducting Telecopier 400 training and it is anticipated that further useful feedback will be received as other courses get under way.

DESIGNING AN INTEGRATED SELF-PACED TRAINING COURSE FOR A MAJOR BUSINESS PRODUCT

Having designed, run and evaluated an integrated self-paced course for a relatively simple product the next step was to utilize the experience gained in designing an effective course for a major business product. The machine selected had to be an established product since its design had to be stable. It is considered that it is just not cost-effective to design sophisticated training materials for a new product subject to considerable design changes during its early life in the field. The machine chosen was the 3600, a large, high-speed copier/duplicator which was launched five years ago and is the basis of a family of products. In selecting this machine three important points were realized:

1. The machine was stable in its design and had been in the field long enough for considerable job experience to have built up.

2. As the basis of a product family derivatives of the original self-paced training materials could be fairly easily produced to cope with related products.

3. The new service documentation system, being introduced on other products, could be prepared for the 3600 in conjunction with the preparation of the training course. Thus, control over the main problem area, which had occurred in the first experimental course, could be exercised.

The design team consisted of two 'self-paced learning' specialists, and two subject matter experts, all being training officers. This proved to be an ideal combination of knowledge and skills, not only because of the interaction of training skills but also because experienced training officers exerted a considerable influence on the design of the service manual as the training course development work proceeded.

The first task undertaken was to examine the job of the 3600 Service Engineer and to tap the pool of experience accumulated during the five years the machine had been in service. There was insufficient time to complete a full job analysis but since the procedural aspects were already well-known and documented, the job was examined in two ways. First, by each member of the team spending approximately one week in the field, observing the engineer and work and discussing the job with both him and his managers. The objectives of the field visit were: (1) to define the tasks which the engineers found most difficult either because of the inherent difficulties or because of a lack of knowledge or skills; (2) to define areas in which the engineer's performance was less than satisfactory.

The second method was to process data, resulting from reporting forms completed by the engineer after each service. This information enabled analysis of a very large number of service calls to be made. Using the two sources of information it was possible to specify the major tasks involved in the actual job on an objective basis.

A comparison of the existing conventional training material with the job study information revealed that the course did not reflect the job. For example, only 4% of the engineer's time is spent dealing with electrical faults and yet the existing course deals almost exclusively with these faults.

From the job study it was possible to estimate training weights and to conclude that a redesigned course would place the emphasis on resolving mechanical faults, diagnosing copy quality problems, and dealing with customers. At this stage a decision was taken to structure the course so that the student could progress from the resolution of simple electrical faults to the diagnosis of any type of fault in a simulated customer relations environment. A modular structure was then defined and specific behavioural objectives prepared. Post-tests, designed to show the student's success in achieving each objective, were prepared and inserted at frequent intervals. Experience on the first integrated course had shown that a good distribution of tests was vital if the course tutor was to be fully effective since they could indicate individual problems.

The objectives were categorized in a similar way to that of the first self-paced course. Due to the greater complexity of the 3600 machine, six instead of three categories were defined:

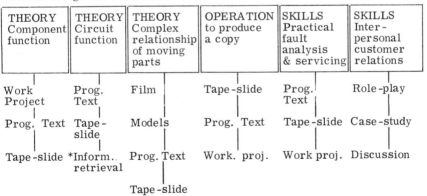

THEORY Component function	THEORY Circuit function	THEORY Complex relationship of moving parts	OPERATION to produce a copy	SKILLS Practical fault analysis & servicing	SKILLS Inter-personal customer relations
Work Project	Prog. Text	Film	Tape-slide	Prog. Text	Role-play
Prog. Text	Tape-slide	Models	Prog. Text	Tape-slide	Case-study
Tape-slide	*Inform. retrieval	Prog. Text	Work. proj.	Work proj.	Discussion
		Tape-slide			

*Information retrieval is a term used to describe a learning situation in which the student extracts information from the service manual guided by answering multi-choice questions.

The characteristics of the objectives, the need to give practical men as much work on the machine as possible and the requirement for a variety of presentation methods were taken into account. Of course, an essential element in each of these learning methods is the tutor. Experience of the Telecopier Course had shown quite clearly that he is the linchpin of the system, acting as a modifier of information and diagnosing and remedying student's problems.

Although the course is self-paced, a means has been found by which the use of role-play and group discussion techniques can be applied to teach the skills of customer relations. These skills are then reinforced later when the student is working as an individual on the machine. Although it is realized that there will be administrative problems in incorporating these techniques into a self-paced course the Customer Relations module is independent of the technical training material and it is considered that the use of the most appropriate learning method for the area of interpersonal skills means that organizational difficulties must be overcome.

At this time the development of training materials is almost complete and the first validation course is being arranged. It is estimated that students will complete the course in 3-4 weeks and that there will be feedback at a later stage from the field.

CONCLUSION

The development of a sophisticated training system such as this has required considerable forethought and planning and the full cooperation of training staff on an international basis. Already, the Company has had to commit itself to the retraining of training officers to enable them to fit into the new system, and has invested much time and money in preparation and experimentation. It is considered that the approach is already proving to be more effective in achieving good training than previous methods would have been. After the 3600 course has been validated other major products are due to be self-paced and the training of New Intake Engineers will take place utilizing self-paced Basic Knowledge Modules.

The participation of training organizations in the Operating Companies is already having a healthy effect. The interchange of information and regular meetings to discuss progress have promoted a respect and understanding which can only lead to a greater mutual understanding of what is required of training within the Company.

The Video Cassette; some experiences and an estimate of its potential for education

J F LEEDHAM

WHAT IS A VIDEO CASSETTE ?

The audio visual press of the 1970s has been agog with rumour, claim and counter claim about the video cassette since new methods of electronic re- cording enabled the production of the cheap helical scan video recorder. It has been the customary ploy to link all development under one label and to regard whatever could be put in a cassette and play a picture, a video cas- sette. For many years we have had such situations; the 8mm and super 8mm film loop cartridges, with and without sound track, have been with us a long time and it is important at the outset to establish that this is definitely not what is referred to.

For the purpose of clarity, and to conform to what is now emerging as a definition, the video cassette is regarded as any packaged system which en- ables a programme of vision and sound to be played and replayed on a tele- vision screen. The system must be technically simple so far as the viewer is concerned, so that play and replay is positive and easy.

The justification for this definition is included in the rationale given later; the reason that one is required is that the video cassette as defined could well become the most important carrier of communication since the book. Where there is a television set, then there is the subsidized and endorsed outlet for the video cassette. It is this implication which needs to be grasped by educa- tionalists at the outset. The home, the institution, the business are all accessible, wherever they may be; it is a commendatory reflection that even the shanty towns of South America are first remarked by their television aerials. The potential is enormous.

A BRIEF HISTORY OF THE PRESENT SITUATION

Recording sound on magnetic tape and replaying the material when appropriate has been a regular practice for only eight or nine years with many education authorities. Perhaps this claim appears absurd when the scheduled recording of BBC broadcasts by Primary schools is a regular procedure; but a little enquiry amongst suppliers justifies the statement. The fact that many educational institutions still do not employ any recording method, but alter their timetable to suit the broadcast may be a truism, but it is disappearing. The point to note is that the practice of making audio recordings has become so widespread in such a short time. It is now, for example, quite possible for the BBC to contemplate not making broadcasts, but supplying special tapes and booklets direct to the contributing schools and using the air time for support experiences. Such an example would be any of the excellent Radio Vision series where tape, filmstrip and printed commentary make a package.

This, then, is the endorsement of the practice of making and using audio cassettes. The addition of vision to the cassette introduces not just another range of perception, but a far vaster field of representation. It also introduces some extra problems. For example, audio tape will bear the imprint of imagination more readily than the video cassette, because it is easier to make a sound recording of adequate quality. Indeed, it was only within the limited sphere of broadcast work that video recording of any sort was used up to ten years ago. From that time on very considerable advances have been made. The first developments were in terms of large video tape recorders making their programmes on 2" wide tape. They were costly, used black and white, and were usually concerned with programmes made by the BBC or ITV or at the larger Universities and Colleges. Around 1965 the first reliable 1" recorders appeared in this country and this enabled much more experimentation to go ahead. But even as late as 1968 the cost of the equipment precluded the use of the video recorder on a wide scale and it was not until the introduction, around 1968, of the cheap $\frac{1}{2}$" helical scan video tape recorder that wide use of video recording came about. Even at that stage such institutions as the BBC were particularly cautious about its use, and even more doubtful about how widespread it would be likely to be. Whereas, even today, it would be the expected thing that a school would obtain a 16mm film projector, the case for video recording 'off-air' programmes has made itself clear to many schools, and already the priority list is switching from those who would require a projector first to those who would want a video recorder first. But at this stage we have not reached the video cassette. Essentially we are still talking about the use of a video tape recorder of an open reel variety; that is one which requires lacing and some manipulation. Even the most simple and lightest are cumbersome and require special provision to transport. Nevertheless, the establishment of the economically priced black and white $\frac{1}{2}$" helical scan video tape recorder can be regarded as the true precursor of the video cassette recorder. Indeed, many who read or listen to this paper will probably be planning to acquire such a machine for the purpose of making recorded or original programmes so that they may free a timetable or equip a resources area. It is true that the newer, more versatile video cassette recorder is in very limited use at the moment and the function of this paper is to place it in context with other modes of communication on the basis of acquired experience.

Broadly speaking one can summarize the video cassette as existing under three headings: those using magnetic tape technology, those using disc technology, those using laser technology. At Loughborough we have been concerned with the development over the past two years of the systems employing magnetic tape and have experimented with laser holography. It is with systems of magnetic tape with which this paper is concerned, since these appear, at the moment, to be the most practical and operational; but some explanation of the other systems is included later. Considering the systems using magnetic tape we can cite three particular types at the moment. In Europe Philips have established a consortium of all the major manufacturers to turn out their NM 1500 video cassette recorder using $\frac{1}{2}$" tape and illustrated in this article. The producer at this date in the UK is the Thorn

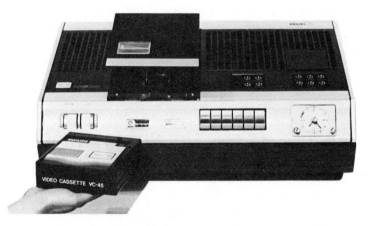

Figure 1. NM 1500 VCR and cassette

Group. Any machine, wherever produced, will play the cassette of any other similar machine. This is most important and is one of the particular features that commends the machine. Currently there is one version available capable of recording off-air programmes, either automatically or by manipulation, and of playing any cassette appropriately recorded elsewhere. Modification to the device makes possible the creation of locally produced black and white programmes. Other models capable of playback only or incorporating locally recorded features will be produced.

A similar machine is the Sony 'Umatic'. Japanese produced it is at the moment used in the USA and employs $\frac{3}{4}''$ tape. It will doubtless appear on the British market at some time, but at the moment it is not a serious contender, its price is far higher and only a very few are available which receive PAL signals on 625 lines. Nevertheless the technology of the system is the same and early accounts make it clear that its use is being widely and rapidly endorsed now that its teething problems are over. Other systems in Japan are under way and are referred to generally as conforming to the EIAJ standard. This indicates that a measure of compatibility is built into the Japanese sets, from whichever firm it emanates.

Film devices which employ super 8mm film in a closed box, inspected by a weak laser or corresponding system are also serious contenders to produce video cassettes and the trade name 'Cartrivision' has established itself to some degree in this respect. Essentially, however, any device which uses film demands a remote processing function. This is true of the EVR which some of the audience may have seen in exhibitions. Essentially this is a film medium accepting electronic signals and, after processing, playing back onto a television set. It is this feature, that film needs processing, which most particularly distinguishes the video cassette which employs magnetic tape. Usually tape is capable of local or remote recording and replication. It is this feature which places it most advantageously within the field of education.

The case is equally true when video discs are considered. Whilst demonstrations of these have been made over the last three years it is not possible

Figure 2. VCR adapted for camera work

to use or purchase one to my knowledge.
The reason is quoted as being the difficulty in making the discs (essentially
high quality gramophone records revolv-
ing at very fast speeds) last long enough.
However true that might be, and making
allowance for the reputed lower cost of
such systems, their lack of local record
facility is almost sure to be a severe
limitation.

There remains the use of holography.
This indicates that three dimensional
colour cassetting is possible. It may be;
but it will undoubtedly be some time
ahead. In such work as is quoted, mainly
the RCA's 'Selectravision' it does not
appear to have been possible to do much
more than produce a two dimensional
representation of 3D. We have also succeeded in doing this experimentally, but
it is a closed laboratory system using
laser technology and as such is not
likely to be of more than interest at the
moment. It will, undoubtedly, make a
case in the future. For now, therefore,
we appear to be concerned with systems

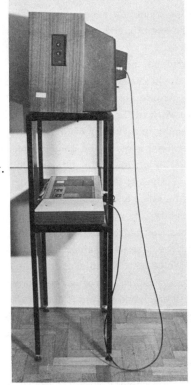

Figure 3. VCR with adapted TV

employing magnetic tape and this we have found to be the case in practice.

Before we demonstrate the use of cassettes insofar as we have experimented with them, it is apposite to quote the reason or rationale which determined our approach. We are shortly to implement the large scale use of the
colour video cassette, and we ought to have other arguments than the expedi-
tious to justify the very considerable outlay involved.

THE RATIONALE

Marshall McLuhan's argument that life is experienced at the interface of
television screen and audience may incur argument, but it is significant that
such an argument can be stated and widely perceived. The existence of a
method of communication capable of constructing its own culture is not a
particularly new idea. It is probably more difficult to perceive it happening
when one is the produce of a literate society used to examining argument
and communication in print. Perhaps a brief reflection on the place of the
transistor radio as the major prime news giver of today's scene can indicate

some of the areas likely to be covered by electronic display in the future. Most of us now receive our information by transistor rather than from print. The use of computer-stored material retrieved from disc or magnetic tape is already a condition of our day by day life if we use banks, libraries, health services, post office facilities, courts of justice, mail order catalogues, motoring associations, holiday arrangements, air travel. In particular cases electronic signals give access to research features associated with fundamental work in the sciences and medicine. Much of this material is available for display in a variety of forms; frequently the cathode ray tube is the medium chosen for speed and convenience.

Thus without considering the particular feature of the video cassette we have already the milieu into which a system of electronically stored visual material is acceptable. This acceptability is endorsed enormously when we consider the availability of the outlets. The case has already been stated that wherever there is already a television set there is an outlet. There is a particular case to consider here: it is one of significance to all who intend to use video cassettes and concerns the use of colour TV receivers. There has been some research already concerning the use of colour television as compared with black and white. It appears to be the case that if one uses a particularly motivated group with a programme which is prepared in colour, but is presented to a control group in black and white, that the amount of learning achieved does not appear to be significantly different. It is not the object of the paper to examine the somewhat slight research in any depth, but it is essential to take notice of the trend and emphasis, at the moment, towards colour provision. Certainly we can say at Loughborough that over a period of two years, working colour by the side of black and white representation, the colour presentation always gains the attention. It is true that if emphasis were to be placed upon pre- and post-test situations it could well be that there would not be a very considerable gain as yet. This is largely because broadcasts for education have only produced programmes in colour, not used colour for educational programmes. Once this is done there is little doubt that colour will show an appreciable gain over black and white. In any case, pupils or students used to seeing colour in other circumstances refer to black and white as Chaplinesque and it is likely that this feature has caused the BBC to advance the date of their colour broadcasts in education. Whereas a period of some five years transition was forecast, the next two years will see a total conversion.

Thus, in considering the video cassette recorder, we have to acknowledge its particular ability, at a comparatively low cost, to record and play back colour. This compares with the limited ability of a low priced video tape machine which uses black and white only. Nevertheless, to pursue the rationale, we have in the video cassette machine a system of recording, storage and playback which is contemporary in terms of communication media, apposite in terms of its relevance to students and logical in that its outlets are a millionfold already subscribed and located.

The point regarding the ability to process magnetic tape immediately and locally as against other systems of recording needs re-stressing. The existence of thousands of excellent programmes made for education and broadcast each year is the compelling reason, at the moment, for the employment of the video cassette machine. In the future it could be that pre-recorded or hired cassettes will be the major feature, but a brief survey of video recording carried out in some twenty schools during 1971-1972 in Leicestershire showed that the recorders were used for 85% of their time recording or playing back off-air programmes and the remainder was occupied with the cameras in local circumstances or playing back other schools' tapes.

It is this feature of record and play back which is particularly significant at the time of curriculum change upon which we are embarked. The new techniques and procedures involve the type of organization loosely described as 'resource-centred'. It is quite customary now to find that at all ranges of primary, secondary and tertiary education, classroom procedures have in part been superseded by the provision of an open area where reference material is available for individual or small group study. The provision of this material often leads to a degree of attrition; local enterprise and regional endeavour can often stimulate an enquiry which requires a national resource to satisfy the need. The broadcast programmes arranged on cassette with relevance to the course of study customarily contain so much material that the acquisition of colour cassette recordings could well be the major provision for many educational resource centres of the future. The provision of the programmes by the Open University require, at the moment, special recording permission and payment, but there is little doubt that the acquisiton of more broadcasting channels will open up the recording facility in this respect.

The probability of cassettes being employed in conjunction with satellite broadcast is confirmable. Several projects, for example the SIRIO satellite project initiated by Italy, will use satellites for broadcasting to remote populations in South America. These can receive the programmes at regionally located centres and the facility of storage and replay must be implicit in any plan for mass education via satellite.

To sum up. The argument for the video cassette, especially using magnetic tape, is that it is educationally opportune, that it is correctly orientated technologically so far as communication is concerned, that it already has access to all locations where a television set or station operates and that it is capable of sustaining future growth, especially in the field of curriculum change and mass education.

CURRENT USAGE

It proves somewhat difficult to quote at this moment a reliable account of sustained usage because video cassettes are very new, not in intention or demonstration but in actual operation at field level. The two cases we quote from America are authenticated and our own experiences will be demonstrated on the sets available at Conference.

THE USA

Videocassettes in Action. John D Hershberger
Quoted from: Educational and Industrial Television, 607 Main Street, Ridgefield, Conn, USA

Videocassettes form the basis for training medical auxiliaries concerned with nutritional problems in the State of New York. Previously, eight video tapes produced in a series "One Strong Link" were produced as training material. With the advent of the video cassettes opportunity was taken to use the cassettes in some areas in preference to the tapes.

Hershberger states "On the basis of comparison two of the manufacturers promises, low cost and ease of operation, seem to be realised. With the video cassettes no engineer's time was needed and no operational difficulties were met. The initial cost of each unit is hundreds of dollars lower than the 1" machine and the saving in engineering time was significant. "

In order to get the videocassette machines operational the playback units, video cassettes and a manual were supplied together with a telephone number to ring if necessary. This compares with the essential training needed to operate and sustain the video tape recorders. The agents who used the video cassettes all report the system as highly successful and the Nutrition Education tion Program will rely upon it as a delivery system in future. The video cassettes used are the Sony Umatic.

Also of Video Cassette in Training Programmes

VidNews (Billboard Publications) February, April, December, 1972 report the progress of the Pepsi Cola Corporation in building up a communication training programme for area managers and bottling operatives. Initiated by Real Time Communications the programmes are so organized that "The cassette and tape combined to do several things. When the message is expired in value then the tape cassette is used over and over again, the savings are unbelievable. You have a capability for the use of tape in cassettes which was never possible with open reel. "

The October 1972 issue quotes John Ribbing, of Coca-Cola, USA, as stating his firm had committed $2 million to video cassette training for 150-200 person participation in a one-to-one usage in plant systems.

OURSELVES

So far as we are concerned at Loughborough we have concentrated on two aspects; first with the help of Professor Butters, who researches into laser technology, we explored the potential of three dimensional representation and you may be interested to see the two excerpts we prepared as explanation at the time. These show: (1) the function of a gas laser using interferometry to construct a 3D image of a chess set, and (2) the 'Selectravision' presentation: an extension of our explanation.

It was realized that fascinating as this was, that it would not be likely to affect schools in the immediate future, and although some provision has been made for normal laser investigation to go ahead, our attention was concentrated on the work being done by the Thorn Group in Britain. Because of early association with the production of the well known 8962 monitor distributed by the Radio Rentals Organization we took early steps to produce a colour conversion of such a unit capable, in 1970, of accepting any feed from a video source, be it black or white or colour. The intention was to ally this with the Thorn version of the Philips NM 1500 and it is delay in production of this unit which means our demonstrations will be done with the Philips RF model NM 1500 with our own video adaptation. It is of note that the Thorn version is intended to work at video level to give a better resolution, but to date we cannot report upon this.

Since August 1972 we have had six Philips NM 1500 in regular use. We were at one time held up for cassettes, but this has eased and we have sufficient for our current needs. The cassette recorders have worked to the development of the colour TV received 8744, giving a 22" aspect which we have always found entirely satisfactory. We have also used it with the Hitachi 19" and the Philips 26" A signal at acceptable level has been common throughout. Compatibility has been good and reliability reasonable in that we have only had about 8% withdrawal for technical maintenance. The compatible facility proved very useful when the author was attending a conference on communication in Germany and he was able to employ the rehabilitation cassette made in black and white which you are now to see demonstrated. Further demonstration was achieved by using portable Akai cameras and telecineing the result onto cassette. Thus we are able to demonstrate the function of off-air recording extended by local circumstance, as you will observe. At the conference in Germany, specially called to consider the relevance of new communication media in rehabilitation, I was privileged to see the use of the cassette for hour long recording of surgical technique, some example of which is also included for your inspection. You will have observed that so far black and white has been used and the next demonstration in colour shows the function of the colour cassette. You may be your own judges as to whether the second replay in black and white suffers by comparison.

There has arisen the special need to develop a suitable trolley for the new equipment and we have rejected the earlier version which we produced for video tape machines and which you see demonstrated here. Since the intention is to equip all schools with colour TV and eventually with cassette recorders it is essential to make provision at the outset and a three year plan has been introduced to ensure a simple straightforward conversion. The 8744 or 8750 receiver will be trolley mounted in conjunction with the appropriate cassette recorder.

ESTIMATE OF POTENTIAL

Economic

Seen from the point of view taken in this paper, the economics of the situation are bound to be based upon a comparison with alternatives. Currently the chief of these is the 16mm film. The fact that most institutions possess a projector and that there are libraries of films implies a built-in advantage. This may be illusory. The cost of a colour cassette recorder at the moment is very close to the cost of a 16mm projector. Using magnetic tape which can be reused many times at a preliminary cost of about £16 for an hour, the economics are indubitably on the side of the recorder, for it has access to a constant stream of broadcast material, which, if it is educational in origin, is free for twelve months of copyright restraints. It is true that in the early cases, schools and colleges may use their present black and white sets for replay, but the colour provision is present at any time the intention is taken to replay in colour.

When one considers the cost of making programmes, there is a very distinct split. The construction of a black and white programme such as you have seen today is less costly than expected. Given the possession of industrial type quality cameras (relatively cheap) and acceptance of a somewhat lower picture quality, then the provision of a 'One-off' programme through the video cassette is well within a normal educational budget for even a small secondary or large primary school. The question of colour is at the moment a different question. It is only possible to create the quality of colour needed to play back at acceptable level by the employment of expensive equipment. This could well change over the next few years. Currently any programme to be made in quantity at a local level would require a good quality 35mm or 16mm film to be prepared and the cassettes to be copied professionally. This could be somewhat tedious and the most up-to-date costing forecast is as follows.

196

Programme technical costing per copy in US dollars (mechanical replication)

Number of copies	Type 4 programme
500	$7.50
1,000	$6.00
5,000	$4.80
10,000	$4.65

(Insight: Issue 7. 4. 2.2. December 1972 'Economics of Video Cassettes'
Gunner Birgvall)

The type 4 method referred to is the quoted cost of mechanically reproduced copy made from film for which all copyrights are clear. One needs to differentiate sharply between the local use of the video cassette as a black and white programme maker and its use with off-air and professionally produced cassettes. There is a level at which material can be produced and accepted because it is local and immediate. But if cassettes are to be distributed and replicated in any quantity, then professional standards need to be observed. Because of this it is likely that well produced 35 and 16mm film will form the basis of cassette production for the foreseeable future.

For this reason, in Leicestershire, a three year programme of development will be undertaken with the direction of film and television production in the hands of James Archibald and associates, whose productions have gained international repute. It will be identified with the Loughborough Campus but function freely and experimentally.

Development

This is hard to hazard. It appears that for the next three years the market will be concerned with the development, placing and servicing of the equipment reviewed in this article. There will certainly be developments with cheaper colour cameras, notably the Akai $\frac{1}{4}$" format. The discs using new laser techniques for retrieval will make some strides and holography will certainly make a statement. But all in all the practical and functional outlook for the next five years must be in line with the tape technologies already outlined and with the broadcast of educational programmes via satellites. By that time it is likely that laser technology will have advanced so that some type of scan retrieval from a 'densified page' will be possible, and at that time the possibility of 3D will be much more real.

Educational

There is much built-in resistance to the fast developing technologies concerned with audio visual representation and the video cassette will come in for its share of obloquy. Nevertheless, it appears that the provision of resource areas and the demands of curriculum reform will lead inevitably to the provision of audio visual resources. Since the provision of broadcast material is likely to expand in the field of television, then it is almost sure that video cassettes are likely to become a significant part of the normal academic provision. But this may well be the smaller part of the story. Considered on the stage of world wide education one must bear in mind the likelihood of the domestic provision of cassette recorders as an integral part of a television receiver. This means that extra mural education takes on a new dimension. The take-home facility of the cassette module is already planned and units on language study, home gardening, vocational skills are already intended to be hired from bookstalls and the like. Perhaps the greatest assurance of the employment of the cassette recorder lies in the ready acceptance of its role by the many teachers and lecturers who have seen it in development. If the price remains within its present range its educational potential will undoubtedly be thoroughly explored.

BIBLIOGRAPHY

CNITE (1972) Centro Nazionale Italionio Technologie Educative. Anno 3.
    No. 2. Educational Satellites
Insight (1972) CTV Report Issue 7
Leedham, J. (1972) in 'Aspects of Educational Technology VI'. (Ed)
    K. Austwick and N. D. C. Harris. Pitman, London. Page 161
Leedham, J. (1972) School Based Television. Journal of Programmed
    Learning and Educational Technology, July 1972

Computer Simulation of a Classroom:
An educational game to study
pre-instructional decisions
P D MITCHELL

INTRODUCTION

This paper reviews a programme of research which attempts to link concepts
and methods from several areas of educational technology. Specifically these
facets are system analysis, simulation and gaming, instructional design, and
self-regulated instruction. Presented here is a rationale for, and a description of, a computer simulation of a class of students which can serve both as
laboratory investigating instructional planning and as an educational game.
The game player, cast in the role of teacher, takes pre-instructional decisions and a computer program, simulating a set of students, provides plausible
instructional outcomes for each. Thus an educational technologist or a teacher
trainee can test the effects of alternative instructional strategies and suppor-
tive action without confronting live students.

A PROBLEM IN TEACHER TRAINING

Teacher trainers encounter great difficulty in providing a transition from
relatively abstract teacher training courses to the complex richness of classroom practice. With the exception of practice teaching (which at its best
proves to be a valuable, if not the most valuable, part of teacher training),
few alternatives exist which can be relied upon to provide a relevant practi-
cum situation. And, unfortunately, even the classical approach of observation and practice often leaves much to be desired (Broadbent & Cruickshank,
1965; Cruickshank, 1971). Several recently emerging alternatives or adjuncts
to regular student teaching are interaction analysis (Flanders, 1970; Hough &
Duncan, 1970), microteaching (Allen & Ryan, 1969) and simulation (Boocock
& Schild, 1969; Booth, 1972; Raser, 1969; Tansey & Unwin, 1960).

Interaction Analysis

Interaction analysis provides a systematically reliable tool for recording
and analysing classroom events in which both teacher and student behaviour
can be described and characterized. When student teachers are trained in

this method, teaching ability is said to improve considerably (Coats, 1966; Gustafson, 1969; Twelker, 1966b). Interaction analysis is unquestionably a valuable tool, but it does require a classroom situation.

Microteaching

Not so microteaching which, by involving a small group of pupils, peers, or even a video tape recorder, provides the teacher trainee with an opportunity to practise instruction without the distractions of classroom management. However, it still requires students for realistic training, and by so doing, poses scheduling problems. Ironically, even the special advantage of micro-teaching can easily minimize its pedagogical effect if its users rely unquestioningly upon a small group of primed students whose reactions to this special event may not represent realistic pedagogical situations.

Simulation

Simulations have become popular in pre-service and in-service training. For the most part, these have attempted to portray the classroom scene as accurately as possible, often using sophisticated audio-visual presentations (Kersh, 1963) or a combination of materials — films, role playing, group activity and in-basket techniques (Cruickshank, 1971; Twelker, 1969). But these simulations are inadequate in three important respects.

First, they confuse the role of teacher as classroom manager with that of instructor and initiator. In the former role, the teacher may have to co-operate with parents, principal and colleagues, or cope with health and behaviour problems. As an instructor though, the teacher is concerned solely with initiating educational activities and managing the conditions of learning. Current simulations' fidelity to the classroom is not conducive to simulating purely instructional events or providing practice in theory-based pre-instructional (as contrasted with extemporaneous) planning. If, instead, a simulation could isolate instructional decisions from other classroom decisions, teacher trainees could learn to deal with these quite separate roles.

The second inadequacy of existing simulations is their reliance upon the teacher trainer or peer group to provide reactions to the trainee's decisions. To illustrate, Kersh's (1963) classroom simulator is essentially a tutorial in which the instructor must be present not only to project motion picture sequences to the student, but also to evaluate his response (for innovation, supportiveness and deference to authority), and then select a new film sequence. Cruickshank (1971) relies heavily upon peer interaction. In neither case does the trainee interact independently with a responsive environment for an uninterrupted sequence of decisions.

Thirdly, most existing simulations emphasize classroom interactions to the neglect of instructional planning. Yet it is important to provide practice in taking pre-instructional, not simply extemporaneous, decisions. Since classroom realism is not essential (Twelker, 1966) ideally we need a simulation model of a group of students which will provide opportunities for the teacher trainee or instructional technologist to practise instructional decisions on a responsive environment — responsive in that he can observe and react to the effects of his instruction on each simulated student. Fidelity to a three-dimensional dynamic classroom is less important than flexibility in cognitive strategies and decision-taking on the part of the trainee. Is it possible to develop an instrument to guide the trainee in making the transition from theory to practise by providing opportunities to practice instructional decisions without interfering with live students, but within the context of a responsive environment?

AN INSTRUCTIONAL PLANNING LABORATORY

Such flexibility can be provided by a computer-based simulated classroom. This need not provide an accurate description of how certain phenomena (such as classroom interactions) operate. Rather it will serve both teacher training and research on educational decisions by providing an instrument which includes both a theoretical and an experiential framework for observation and analysis of pre-instructional behaviour. Educational Technologists know precious little about the effects of class size or structure or of alternative instructional strategies. Is it possible to bridge this gap between educational technology theory and instructional practise?

To the extent that the simulated classroom portrays realistically the ways in which people learn, the game-player may learn useful instructional planning. In any event he can practice taking typical decisions and try out several alternatives without going into a real classroom with its confusing demands. Whether such vicarious experience of instructional design will alter behaviour in an ordinary classroom remains to be studied. Naturally this will be an important part of our research. Further, by comparing decisions of experienced teachers, teacher-trainees and others, we can investigate, for example, the components of instructional planning, the effects of studying selected theoretical principles, or behaviour patterns as a function of class size.

THE SIMULATED CLASSROOM

Simulation requires a system analysis leading to a dynamic model of a system or process which permits, and responds to, manipulation of certain variables. The educational simulation or EDSIM Project involves a variant of simulation, operational gaming, in which a human game-player participates as a decision-taker within the structure of the system being simulated. Thus we have a hypothetical class, simulated by the computer program, and a human game-player cast in the role of a teacher or instructional planner. The player's decisions simulate instructional planning and communications within the simulated classroom.

The EDSIM Conceptual Model

Despite the plethora of descriptive and explanatory literature concerned with teaching and learning, slow progress has been made toward quantitative models of instruction. Yet such a model, no matter how crude, is required. Therefore a major step in implementing the EDSIM Project is to devise a crude conceptual model of a student as an adaptive, self-organizing system which responds differentially to educational communications designed to motivate, direct or instruct him. In the interests of simplicity, the model is based on assumptions that do not resemble the class situation; for example, many variables, such as classroom behaviour, are omitted since the aim is to focus only on pre-instructional decisions (ie lesson planning) and their probable effects.

Before describing the theoretical model it is useful to consider the simulation requirements.

Description of the Game

The player's activities determine classroom features to be selected. Players must analyse the educational status of simulated students using the computer's output. Then they must take decisions intended to increase these students' capability. Thus the kind of information presented to the player and the scope of alternative instructional planning strategies jointly establish the level of complexity of the system analysis and simulation. Described in detail in the EDSIM Game Player's Manual, these can only be illustrated here.

To begin playing, the game-player takes several decisions. For example, he specifies what is to be taught in the forthcoming period and how much time should be spent on recall, practice, evaluation, self-management — in other words, his precise teaching strategy. Figure 1 illustrates a few such activities.

Fifteen class periods may be simulated; the unit of play is a simulated fifty minute period consisting of one or more instructional units (the sequence of activities intended to teach a single curriculum objective). The game-player prepares his lesson plan knowing that each teaching act uses up a designated, arbitrarily assigned number of minutes. All decisions enter the machine by card reader.

Reports to Player

Each player receives a record of his instructional decisions plus reports at the end of each simulated period. Although some reports are automatic,

Choose number of Students (S) to teach in this instructional period

Request diagnosis of S: his pre-instructional state of
attention, motivation, self-management capability

State instructional objective: ie the particular concept,
skill or attitude the student should have at the end
of the instructional unit

State standard of mastery expected of S at end of instructional unit

Ask S if he accepts or understands objective

Ask S to state his preferred objective

Initiate substantive information: ie recall or review;
introduce new material; integrate and generalize
material

Arrange examples and illustrations (eg positive or
negative, physical or symbolic, verbal and/or
visual)

Give directions to S for reaching instructional objective

Initiate Student self-management: ie guide S to question
or appraise or to initiate or sustain learning

Solicit response from S: for clarification, diagnosis,
review or reinforcement

Respond to S: in order to clarify, confirm or correct

Figure 1. Illustration of Game Player's Range of Instructional Decisions

others must be requested at the expense of classroom time (eg student response, examination scores; cf Figure 1).

The computer program contains models that alter the capability state of
each student with regard to several curriculum objectives. Each instructional
unit is processed independently for each student. Although a more refined

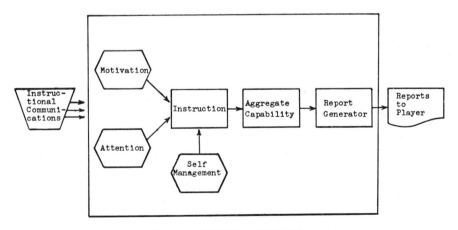

Figure 2. EDSIM Conceptual Model

version is planned, current output is limited. For instance, the player can determine whether or not a student has demonstrated requisite capability with regard to a specified curriculum objective. Naturally it is possible to determine his status for all objectives or conversely the status of all students with regard to any objective. Few additional reports exist; report generators provide statements about student responses to specific questions; when assignments were completed and an evaluation of each; and capricious events such as general student excitement or unrest (resulting from certain player decisions).

The EDSIM conceptual model is illustrated in Figure 2. A discussion of successful game-playing will be found in Mitchell (1972a).

The Curriculum

The artificial curriculum is a set of mathemata (from Greek mathēmata = things learned) organized into a hierarchical structure. The subject-free nature of this curriculum is intended to permit easy interpolation by the game-player to any subject. We assume that only one mathemata can be presented in a single instructional unit but the simulated student may choose to work on a different one or remain idle. The efficiency of instructional communications, and therefore learning, will be low for all but the topic presented by the game-player. Furthermore, we restrict ourselves to a two-state learning model such that at the end of any unit the student has either learned the mathemata or he has not.

A THEORETICAL MODEL

The simulated classroom is extrapolated from the model of a single student described below. Sub-models for updating records such as aggregate capability or generating reports are omitted.

Student's Purposeful State

Russell Ackoff's notions of human communication and purposeful state (Ackoff, 1958; Ackoff & Emery, 1972) permeate the EDSIM model. Following his lead, we assume for each student: (1) a set of mathemata, M_j, to be learned; (2) a set of possible states of each, O_j, such that if O_j is produced the mathemata is learned, otherwise it is not (a planned revision of EDSIM will allow for forgetting); (3) two or more alternative courses of action, A_i, open to the student, each of which has unequal and greater-than-zero probability or producing O_j; and (4) a set of relative values (or utility), V_j, for the jth outcome.

For the sake of brevity, these and other assumptions which describe the student in a purposeful state are shown in Figure 3.

A student is said to be in a purposeful state if he wants to produce a

For any instructional unit, each student (S) may be described by reference to these concepts:

M_j : $1 \le j \le n$ the set of mathemata to be taught

O_j : $1 \le j \le n$ the set of possible outcomes of S's behaviour such that any outcome O_j denotes that the corresponding mathematom M_j is in the learned state

A_i : $1 \le i \le m;$ the set of exclusive and exhaustive activities open to the student
       $m \ge 2$

E_{ij} : $O \le E_{ij} \le 1$ the set of probabilities that A_i, if selected, will produce O_j; thus the efficiency of A_i for O_j, $E_{ij} = P(O_j/S$ chooses A_i in a specified unit)

P_i : $O \le P_i \le 1$ the set of probabilities that S will choose A_i in an instructional unit (u); that is, $P_i = P(A_i/S,u)$

V_j : $O \le V_j \le 1$ the set of relative values or utilities to S of outcomes O_j such that V_j is the probability that S intends to select a course of action having maximum efficiency (E_{ij}) for producing an intended outcome

IC_i^A :   the set of instructional communications received which alters P_i

IC_j^M :   the set of instructional communications received which alters V_j

IC_j^I :   the set of instructional communications received which alters E_{ij}

Figure 3. Abbreviated formulation of the student in a purposeful state

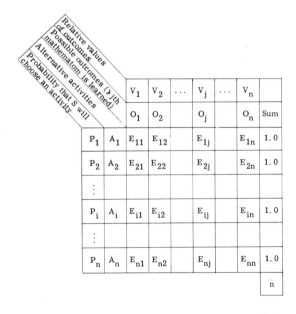

Figure 4. Student's Purposeful State (after Martin, 1963)

preferred outcome, O_j (ie that for which V_j is greatest), and has unequally efficient alternative activities which may produce it. The student's purposeful state is summarized in Figure 4.

We define the probability that a given activity, A_i, will produce an outcome O_j as the efficiency, E_{ij}, of A_i for O_j. Thus $E_{ij} = P(O_j/A_i, S)$. The rational decision of the student is to select the activity which maximizes the probability of producing his preferred outcome; the rational strategy for the game player is to make this possible for all mathemata.

Instruction: A Stochastic Decision Process

Instruction occurs when mathemata undergo a transition from the unlearned to the learned state. Instructional communications are therefore concerned with increasing efficiency E_{ij} for the intended j^{th} outcome until a transition occurs in some instructional unit. Let t_j^S be the probability of such a transition. With probability q_j^S the jth mathemata is in the learned state for student S; thus $q_j^S = P(O_j/S)$. With probability $1 - q_j^S$, M_j is not.

Instructional communications intended to teach the jth mathemata might succeed in a single instructional unit or only gradually raise the value of t_j^S. Once a transition occurs, $q_j^S = 1.0$ for all remaining instructional units (in the present model).

In the model E_{ij} is calculated for each student as a linear function. Thus the algorithm to calculate $E_{ij_u}^S$ for student S is:

$$E_{ij_u}^S = E_{ij_{u-1}}^S + \alpha (IC_j^I)$$

where α = the factor by which each IC_j^I augments E_{ij}. This will be varied in the model.

The probability that M_j will be in the learned state for S at the end of an instructional unit (ie that O_j occurs) is the sum of the probability that it was already in the learned state plus the probability that it was formerly not learned and that a transition occurred. There $q_{j_u}^S = q_{j_{u-1}}^S + t_j^S (1 - q_{j_{u-1}}^S)$ where $q_{j_u}^S \geqq q_{j_{u-1}}^S$

The probability of a transition, t_j^S, is a function not only of instructional communications which alter E_{ij} for some activity but also of the student's self-management capability SM^S. Thus $t_j^S = SM^S \times E_{ij}$ where SM^S is calculated by an algorithm not described in this paper such that $1.0 \leqq SM^S \leqq 1.25$.

Merely increasing the efficiency of some course of action with respect to a specific outcome is insufficient to induce learning. Prerequisite to instruction are motivation (ie the student has a preferred educational outcome in a given instructional unit) and attention (ie he is engaged in the educational activity most likely to produce the desired outcome). Suppose the simulated student receives a set of instructional communications, which action A_i will he choose? In the EDSIM model a selected course of action is intended to achieve a desired outcome. The preference of one outcome over another reflects differential motivation for the several mathemata, each of which has a different utility or value for the individual at a point in time.

Motivation Sub-Model

The notion of motivation generally arises from attempts to explain why some-one chooses a particular course of action. In the simulated classroom the instructional planner determines which mathemata will be dealt with. None-theless, in each instructional unit a student can choose to focus on that mathemata or not; for the latter purpose a dummy mathemata (M_{n+1}) is included in the model. The mathemata which the student intends to learn as a result of choosing some course of action is said to be his preferred mathe-mata. The probability that he intends to select a course of action having maximum efficiency for producing this intended outcome O_k will be termed the relative value to the individual of O_k, viz V_k.

It is quite impossible to estimate realistically the relative values to each simulated student of studying and appropriating to himself the capability im-plicit in any of the mathemata. Yet it is fitting to provide a measure of motivation to be used in simulating transactions for each student. Accordingly relative values will be calculated for each student during each instructional unit. The model assumes minimum motivation initially for all mathemata (ie $V_i = \frac{1}{n}$). Since the student's motivation is altered by certain instructional communications the game player can and should attempt to establish high motivation for the mathemata to be taught.

In the EDSIM model six pre-instructional decisions will increase the relative value of any mathemata: (1) stating the instructional objective; (2) stating the level of attainment or standard expected; (3) demonstrating ex-pected performance; (4) stating reasons for the objective; (5) probing for student's acceptance or understanding of the objective; or (6) asking the student to state his preferred mathemata. Each is assumed in the model to have the same effect, that of producing increments in motivation proportional to the difference between maximum and no motivation.

The relative value of O_j in instructional unit (u), (V_{j_u}) is:

$$V_{j_u} = \begin{cases} V_{j_{u-1}} + IC_j^M \left(\dfrac{1.0 - \frac{1}{n}}{6} \right) & \text{if this calculation is less than or equal to } 1.0 \\ 1.0 & \text{otherwise} \end{cases}$$

Attention Sub-Model

Even if the student is differentially motivated with respect to mathemata he must also attend and respond before instructional communications can induce a change in his capability. Stated otherwise, having acquired a preferred outcome O_j, namely mastery of mathemata M_j whose relative value V_j is greatest, he must identify and select a course of action A_i whose activities have maximum efficiency E_{ij} in producing O_j. The game player can alter the probability of choice (P_i) by directing the student's attention to the activity believed most fruitful, by directing him to question, clarify or appraise the situation or by soliciting a specific behaviour.

Attention, therefore, is the process which modifies probabilities for choosing activities to produce the preferred outcomes as different mathemata are selected for instruction. (Inclusion of a dummy activity A_{n+1}, permits the student to opt out of all potentially successful actions.)

The EDSIM model treats attention as a linear function of the number of repetitions (IC_t^A) of the five instructional decisions which can alter P_i. It is assumed that self-management, SM, leads not only to improvement in motivation and learning rate but also to an increase in attention. Let us assume a rational course of action A_k where V_j is greatest for O_j and E_{kj} is greater than or equal to any other E_{ij}. (This simple case is more complex in practice because of the possibility of polyphasic learning, cf Mitchell, 1972b.)

$$\text{Then } P_k = \begin{cases} \dfrac{1}{m} + SM^S \times IC_i^A \dfrac{(1.0 - \frac{1}{m})}{5} & \text{if this calculation is less than or equal to } 1.0 \\ 1.0 \text{ otherwise} \end{cases}$$

GAME PLAYING

Two administrative approaches exist for playing the EDSIM game. If a time limit (eg a specified number of periods) terminates the game, instructional effectiveness is determined by what the class learned. Alternatively, the game can be played until a specified number of students attains a predetermined criterion and effectiveness is a function of the time required. Either way, the player can compete with his own past performance, with other students or with a required standard.

The game player has access to a variety of learning resources in order to play this game. Thus his own educational activity is guided by a predetermined game structure supported by selected learning resources. Because the exact nature of his participation is not prescribed in detail, the player becomes an active participant in his own education; he sees himself as a producer of events, not merely a spectator. Because the game presents concrete problems in a simplified but dramatic form, the player must take realistic decisions and observe their consequences. Thus the education student, freed from direct instructional control, actively participates in a situation designed to enhance his competence in dealing with realistic problems. Such task-related and role-related problem solving competencies are the mark of the professional who, like the game-player, must set realistic behavioural and experiential goals for himself, monitor his own development toward them, and evaluate his change in capability.

THE EDSIM PROJECT

Of necessity the EDSIM Project encompasses other spheres of activity not reported here. Despite the existence of many non-theory-based games, we find a dearth of information concerning the methodology of simulation and gaming for education. So considerable effort has been devoted to: (1) investigation of system analysis as a tool for educational simulation; (2) investigation of procedures for designing a computable simulation model in the absence of relevant time-series data; (3) investigation of methods of validating simulation models; (4) investigation of algorithms for teaching and learning; and (5) survey of techniques for different kinds of simulation, viz man-model (including games), man-mechanism, and closed loop (ie computer).

Basic research has been necessary to support assumptions included in the model. For instance, we are investigating effects of repetition of instructional communications, self-management strategies for students as educational catalysis, and the differential effectiveness of algorithms, decision tables and flow charts to alter the lesson planner's decisions.

(This research is supported by a grant under the Quebec Minister of Education's 'Programme de formation de chercheurs et d'action concertée'.)

REFERENCES

Ackoff, R. L. (1958) Management Science, 4, 3, 218
Ackoff, R. L. and Emery, F. E. (1972) On purposeful systems.
  Aldine. Atherton, Chicago, Ill
Allen, D. and Ryan, K. (1969) Microteaching. Addison-Wesley Publishing
  Co. Inc., Reading, Mass
Boocock, S. S. and Schild, E. O. (1968) Simulation games in learning.
  Sage, Beverley Hills, California
Booth, R. M. (1972) A case for a computer simulated classroom for teacher
  training. Sir George Williams University, Montreal, Quebec.
  Unpublished manuscript
Broadbent, F. W. and Cruickshank, D. R. (1965) Identification and analysis
  of problems of first year teachers. ERIC # ED 013786
Coats, W. D. (1966) Investigation and simulation of the relationships among
  selected classroom variables. ERIC # ED 029170
Cruickshank, D. R. (1971) ATE Research Bulletin #8, June
Flanders, N. A. (1970) Analysing teacher behavior. Addison-Wesley
  Publishing Co. Inc., Reading, Mass
Gustafson, K. L. (1960) Simulation of anxiety situations and its resultant
  effect on anxiety and classroom interaction of student teachers.
  ERIC # ED 033064
Hough, J. B. and Duncan, J. K. (1970) Teaching: Description and analysis.
  Addison-Wesley Publishing Co. Inc., Reading, Mass
Kersh, B. Y. (1963) Classroom simulation - a new dimension in teacher
  education. ERIC # ED 003613
Martin, M. W. (1963) The measurement of value of scientific information.
  In 'Operations research in research and development'. (Ed) B. V. Dean.
  John Wiley & Sons Inc., New York
Mitchell, P. D. (1972a) Simulating an instructional system for an educational
  game. In 'Proceedings of the Canadian symposium on instructional tech-
  nology'. (Ed) J. Akeroyd. National Research Council, Ottawa, Ontario
Mitchell, P. D. (1972b) in 'Aspects of Educational Technology'.
  (Ed) K. Austwick and N. D. C. Harris. Pitman, London. Page 48

Raser, J. R. (1969) Simulation and society. Allyn and Bacon Inc., Boston, Mass

Tansey, P. J. and Unwin, D. (1969) Simulation and gaming in education. Methuen, London

Twelker, P. A. (1966b) Simulation applications in teacher education. ERIC // ED 025460

Twelker, P. A. (1969) Instructional simulation: a research development and dissemination activity. Final Report. ERIC // ED 032657

The Long-term Development and Evaluation of an Instructional Programme for Marine Engineering Training

J D S MOORE, J F K SMITH

This paper has three main objectives: (a) to describe the development and testing of an unusual programmed package; (b) to discuss the results, collected over several years, of its use in two different training environments, and (c) to consider the effect on training organization structure, of accepting a lengthy course designed in another environment.

The instructional programme deals with auxiliary machinery operator training in the Royal Navy and its main objective is to prepare engineering mechanics to keep specified machinery in a ship in proper running order. The main tasks involved are stopping and starting procedures, routine checks and the logging of readings, fault-finding and remedial action. Additionally, differences in auxiliary machinery characteristics from ship to ship require operators to modify their inputs. Thus a slavish approach to training ship-specific objectives only would probably increase the rigidity of a trainee's behaviour, when adaptability is what the job requires.

It would therefore seem appropriate, at this stage, to describe the development of the programme, bearing in mind these objectives, in order to provide a background for examining the effects of the system.

The latter developed mainly in three phases: (1) audio-programming of two machinery sections (Budgett & Moore, 1969); (2) introduction of data-flow diagrams to replace tape recordings (1969-1970), and (3) modification of the programme for use in a different environment (1970-1973). As the first phase has already been described in the reference, Phases 2 and 3 will be compared in the light of the relevant training organization structures of HMS HERMES, an aircraft carrier (Phase 2) and HMS SULTAN, the Royal Navy's School of Marine Engineering (Phase 3).

In HMS HERMES in 1969, all relevant auxiliary machinery operating activities were listed and were analysed in a hierarchical fashion. Operating skills common to a number of tasks were extracted for learning at the beginning of the course to make the whole repertoire available for trainees, at all other stages of learning (Appendix 1).

The objectives emanating from the tasks and relevant steps were assessed in terms of difficulty and the knowledge needed by the trainee population to perform them was added. (Most steps were easy in that they did not require a trainee either to solve a problem or make a decision.) The 'decision' steps were further analysed in order to record all possible courses of action.

The presentation was as follows:

a) Trainees were given a written sheet which listed the types of auxiliary machinery which they would be required to operate. The purpose of each machine was also described. At this stage trainees had to match a range of services with each auxiliary.

b) Generalizable skills were then taught by an instructor to each trainee in turn, using a list which specified criteria and which was also provided for the trainees. (See Appendix 1)

c) From this stage each item of auxiliary machinery was treated separately, all treatments, however, following a similar routine.

d) Each machine was introduced as a whole system using the constructed response technique with verbal information.

e) Then a similar technique for responding was used with each of the subsystems but presentation of information changed from words to data-flow diagrams. (See Appendix 2). (The main advantages of the latter are that the system always begins on the left, is easy to follow and can be used in relation to any similar machinery.)

f) When all the constructed responses had been made for the particular auxiliary, the trainees showed their booklets to the instructor, who re-explained any facts which had led to errors.

g) Then the trainee went to the appropriate machinery space and used the same set of data-flow diagrams to trace each item in each system. The watchkeeper there acted as a source of confirmation for each identification and also put a X on the diagram for any item not correctly traced. The course instructor, on completion, could then deal tutorially with the problems thus indicated.

h) At this stage, the trainee returned to the machinery space for an entire 4 hour watch, during which time he applied his ability to identify components to logging actual readings under the watchkeeper's supervision. He also compared actual readings with means and extremes and noted whether or not a fault was indicated.

i) Remedial action was then taught individually by the course instructor and the trainees were given, for each machinery area, a sheet of paper describing, partly in algorithmic form, the processes involved in identifying symptoms of faults.

j) Finally, trainees took their lists of objectives dealing with starting and stopping procedures down to the machinery space in question and simulated each step. When a trainee was satisfied that he could carry out all the objectives, as well as ones previously learnt, he contacted the instructor, who tested every item. If performance was less than 100%, the trainee's weaknesses were dealt with tutorially. He was then retested until there were no incorrect responses.

k) When a section had been successfully completed, the trainee was given the next section and the strategies were repeated. The 'bank-building' approach seemed preferable to the option of giving trainees the whole course, thus making the number of pages daunting, rather than positively reinforcing.

The results were encouraging (Tables I and II).

Table I. Overall results (times in hours) — HERMES

Auxiliary	Number of trainees	Number passed	Average time	Slowest	Quickest	Normal time
Turbo Alternators	24	24	21	42	12	30
Diesel Alternators	24	24	18	30	12	30
Air Compressors	24	24	9	24	6	12
Steering Gear	24	24	12	54	6	30
Refrigeration	23*	23*	18	27	6	30
Evaporators	23*	23*	18	24	9	60

*1 trainee went on compassionate leave

Since the standard of performance aimed at was 100%, the results in Table I refer mainly to the times required to achieve the former. As may be seen by comparing average time (new course) with normal time (old course), there was a nil failure rate and considerable savings were made in training times for all sections. It is also significant that the spread of times would have meant, using the conventional course, failure for some trainees ('slowest' column) and long waiting times for others ('quickest' column).

Because the 100% standard was achieved by using section tests initially as a diagnostic medium, the first-attempt scores for each section in Table II illustrate the amount of tutorial work which the course instructor had to undertake (ie 100 - initial score).

Table II. Mean initial scores (per cent)

	Written	Practical
Introduction	100	–
Common Skills	–	100
Turbo Alternators	98	98
Diesel Alternators	95	97
Air Compressors	99	99
Steering Gear	100	99
Refrigeration	100	99
Evaporators	98	99

In view of the promising results, HMS SULTAN decided to evaluate the HERMES system for possible use in its own training environment and hence began appropriate modifications. The latter had to be made bearing in mind not only the new environment but also different conditions of transfer of trainee performance.

The new environment, HMS SULTAN, is a land-based training establishment at Gosport in Hampshire and uses, as an aid to practical training, a harbour training ship, HMS BLACKWOOD. (The latter will put to sea only once more — to go to the breaker's yard.) BLACKWOOD, a frigate, was used for much of the Royal Navy's Auxiliary Machinery Certificate training, and hence was the new environment against which the HERMES system had to be modified (Figure 1).

	Harbour Training Ship (BLACKWOOD)	HERMES
Size	Small	Large
Accommodation	Ashore	On board
Number of machines	1 per Section	Several per section
Running times	0900 - 1600	24 hours a day
Watchkeeper availability	By arrangements	24 hours a day
Annual throughput	Large	Small
Administration	Ashore	On board

Figure 1. Environmental and organizational differences

The second area of difference, concerning external transferability of performance, was that, whereas in HERMES trained ratings worked initially on HERMES machines, the BLACKWOOD trainees leave on completion of training and join ships all over the world, and work on many different types of auxiliary machinery.

A potential third problem area, that of the suitability of the HERMES objectives, did not materialize. SULTAN had already written behavioural objectives for three sections of auxiliary machinery training and these proved almost identical procedurally with the HERMES ones. Hence, the remainder of the HERMES tasks and procedures were accepted by SULTAN (except where machinery was markedly different).

Given acceptance of the HERMES strategies and objectives, modifications entailed:

a) the redrawing of all system diagrams. (Much of the machinery differed, so therefore did the fluid systems. The data flow principle was retained throughout.)

b) rewriting the programmed text to fit these new diagrams

c) inserting all machinery operating limits and means for BLACKWOOD on log heading sheets

d) constructing remedial actions totally in algorithmic form

e) some restructuring and rearranging of some of the sections (BLACK-WOOD had only one machine for each of the latter). Trainees had to be able to start at any one of the eight sections and to move through the course in a variety of sequences, depending on the availability of particular machines at given times.

It was also necessary to revise the administrative system to accept the programmed course. SULTAN management decided that the system should be given a two phase trial. Firstly, a trial of the strategies and the rewritten text within the existing conventional course structure. If the initial trial proved successful, a second trial was to be carried out to assess the effects of a completely free-running system.

Just prior to the initial trial, the seven course instructors and four auxiliary machinery watchkeepers were given a presentation on the new system, dealing with its history, reasons for change and its operation. The presentation was supplemented by a short booklet entitled 'An Instructor's Guide to the Programmed AMC System'.

The first trial was carried out with the 34 trainees Monday 9 November 1970 until Friday 27 January 1971. For the trial the class was divided into four groups of 7 and one group of 6 trainees. Trainees worked through any one section at their own pace, but moved from section to section as a group.

Testing was carried out at the completion of each section; there was no terminal assessment. If a trainee could carry out all section's objectives then he passed that section. During the examination trainees were allowed various job aids, which they would normally be expected to use when operating, such as starting and stopping routines, log heading sheets and remedial algorithms.

All 34 trainees successfully completed the course and were timed over individual sections. The latter times (Table III) compared closely with the learning times in HERMES (in brackets).

Table **III**. Results of initial trial (times in hours) — SULTAN

Section	Number of trainees	Number passed	Average time	Slowest	Quickest
Turbo Generators	34	34	24 (21)	24 (42)	18 (12)
Diesel Generators	34	34	17 (18)	27 (30)	11 (12)
Air Compressors	34	34	12 (9)	33 (24)	5 (6)
Steering Gear	34	34	11 (12)	21 (54)	7 (6)
Refrigeration	34	34	13 (18)	19 (27)	5 (6)
Evaporators	34	34	29 (18)	36 (24)	22 (9)

The success of the first trial showed that, within the limitations of a fixed maximum time for each section, a learning system developed in one environment could be effectively used in a similar (but not identical) one, given modifications to the detail of the system and a similar trainee population.

As a result of feedback from the first trial, about 10% of the programmed text, and a lesser percentage of remedial algorithms, were modified.

Also, since 'waiting-time' developed when machinery was being fully used for practical work, a 'yellow-page' section was added to the end of each main section in order to supply additional (albeit 'nice-to-know' objectives) until the machinery was free. The information thus supplied included references to other books and publications, theory of machine operation, details of the construction of the training ship's machinery and differences between the latter and machinery in the Fleet.

The second trial was free-running and required an extra instructor who was to be known as the AMC Controller. Course Instructors remained for each type of machine but trainees moved freely between instructors as they completed each section. Trainees' movement was regulated by the Controller, who directed trainees between instructors and machinery to optimize instructor and machinery loadings. Any trainee needing to 'mark time' did so in the controller's work space, making use of the colour pages of the programme.

To regulate the movement of the trainees between the various machines the Controller used a Control Board, a 6ft x 4ft wall-mounted peg board, where, by means of a number of coloured pegs and a series of matrices, the Controller could match up 50 trainees at any one time with the machinery sections.

The second trial was carried out with 47 trainees from April until June 1971. The aims of the second trial were (a) to validate minor changes made in the text as a result of feedback from the initial trial; (b) to evaluate the method of training as a fully self-pacing system, and (c) to test the new administration system.

Testing was similar to the method employed in the first trial with the exception that instructors were directed that to pass any section a trainee must not only be able to carry out all the objectives specified but must satisfy the instructor that he had the confidence and judgement necessary to carry out the tasks operationally. The latter objective was measured, quite simply, by an instructor asking himself "Would I employ this man in my watch, on that machine, in a ship at sea?"

Of the 47 ratings who commenced the training course, 46 gained Auxiliary Machinery Certificates. (One trainee did not complete the course for medical reasons.) Four trainees had to be retested on sections, but each passed at the second attempt.

The results of the second trial showed that complete self-pacing could be achieved. The method used to control and administrate the system proved easy to use and flexible and no further changes were deemed necessary in the system or in its method of control.

A major outcome of the trials was that, in place of a block entry of 40/50 trainees, a 'trickle' drafting system has been employed. Each week up to 8 trainees are sent to BLACKWOOD for AMC training and leave as soon as it is practicable after completing their training. In terms of training manpower, this has meant that, although the number of instructors has increased by one (the Controller), the number of trainees obtaining an Auxiliary Machinery Certificate per instructor year, could be increased by 50%.

Table IV. Long term results (times in hours) — SULTAN

Section	Average time	Slowest	Quickest
Turbo Generators	22	50	11
Diesel Generators	22	38	11
Air Compressors	16	27	5
Steering Gear	16	33	5
Refrigeration	16	27	5
Evaporators	27	44	16

Since the first trial, over 300 trainees have successfully completed the AMC Course, achieving the average results shown in Table IV.

The authors consider in conclusion that:

a) It is possible to achieve 100% scores at this level of training.

b) The technique of using transferable strategies within a programmed framework (the objectives being merely immediate criteria for measuring the successful acquisition of the strategies) greatly increases the generalizability of both the usage of the course and trainee performance.

c) The results from the performance of over 400 trainees between December 1969 and January 1973, are stable at a high level. (Minimal differences between HERMES and SULTAN times are probably attributable largely to differences in machinery availability.)

d) Even a training package designed to optimize flexibility required considerable adjustment before it was capable of being used in a second environment. (Although much of the adjustment described in this paper may be attributed to a transition from 'conventional' to 'free-running' training.)

REFERENCE

Budgett, R. E. B. and Moore, J. D. S. (1969) Aspects of Educational Technology, Volume III. (Ed) A. P. Mann and C. K. Brunstrom. Page 272. Pitman, London

APPENDIX 1

ENTRY TEST
Preliminary Watchkeeping Skills

Here is a list of skills which you must be able to perform before beginning
the AMC programme. These skills will be required of you throughout the
complete course. Your instructor will test your performance of each of
these skills and you will not be allowed to begin the next section until he has
initialled all 19 items.

You must be able to:	Instructor's initials
1. OPEN and SHUT VALVES as follows:	
a. **Valves operated by a handwheel**	
(1) When valve wheel is free and cool enough to touch, open and shut it by turning it manually.	
(2) When valve wheel is either tight or hot to touch, open and shut by turning hand wheel with a small wheel spanner.	
(3) Close valve tight using wheel spanner.	
(4) Open valve until it stops and then turn back $\frac{1}{2}$ a turn	
b. **Valves operated by a T-handle**	
As for a. above EXCEPT that, when it is tight or hot, you must tap the T-handle with the wheel spanner (rather than turn it).	
2. OPEN and SHUT COCKS as follows:	
a. **2-way Cocks**	
(1) To OPEN, turn handle of cock IN LINE with the piping.	
(2) To CLOSE, turn handle of cock at RIGHT ANGLES to piping.	
b. **3-way Cocks**	
(1) Turn cock spindle (using spanner provided) to put the flow in the direction required (indicated by a mark).	
(2) Shut off the flow by turning the spindle so that the **blank end** of the cock **faces** the direction of flow.	

APPENDIX 2

DIESEL GENERATORS — CIRCULATING WATER SYSTEM

Use Diagram C   Answers

1. The circulating (cooling) water system of the D/G
   is used to cool **three** fluids:

   (1) **Air**, which keeps the armature cool.

   (2) **Distilled water** which keeps the engine cool.

   (3) **Oil** which lubricates and controls the engine.

2. Sea water is drawn into the system through the   1.
   _____ _____ valve and_____ trap   2.

3. From the weed trap the sea water passed through   3.
   1 of 2 _____ and then to the circulating water pump.

4. From the pump the circulating water passed through   4.
   a _____ valve and _____ valve to the three _____ 5.
                                                            6.

5. The circulating water passes through the three
   coolers and then out of the ship through the _____   7.

   _____ _____.

6. The water leaving the pump is directed two ways,   8.
   either to the generator air _____, or, to the _____ 9.
   _____ cooler and then the _____ _____ cooler.   10.

7. _____ - _____ valves are fitted to all three coolers 11.
   to allow each cooler to be by-passed if required.

8. The circulating water system has three vent points,
   one is situated between the relief valve and _____   12.
   _____ the others are found on the _____ _____   13.
   cooler and the _____ _____ cooler.   14.

9. Fitted into the lub oil cooler is a _____ valve. This 15.
   valve is operated by the watchkeeper in the event of
   the lub oil thermostat being defective. With the
   ported valve in the shut position all the circulating
   water will pass through the cooling pipes in the
   cooler. With the ported valve in the open position
   the circulating water will take the easiest path and
   by-pass the cooler.

10. The _____ valve can be adjusted to give complete   16.
    flow through the cooler (normal condition), no flow
    through the cooler, or a partial flow through the
    cooler, as required.

11. Because the flow through the generator air cooler
    is regulated on the by-pass valve we call this valve
    the _____ _____.   17.

Check your answers on page 118.

(A) If you have more than 13 correct, turn to the next section.
(B) If you have less than 13 correct, see your instructor.

Understanding Selective Perception:
A key to providing readiness for learning
D D PRATT

> All our mental processes depend upon perception.
> Inadequate perceiving results in poor thinking,
> inappropriate feeling, diminished interest in and
> enjoyment of life. Systematic training of percep-
> tion should be an essential element in all education.
> Aldous Huxley (1971)

INTRODUCTION

Most educators would agree on the following two points: (1) traditional classroom environments may have competing stimuli bombarding the learner which
may in turn limit his ability to focus attention on a given learning task; and
(2) readiness to perceive (set induction) is a necessary prerequisite when providing for effective learning.

STATEMENT OF THE PROBLEM

Realistically, the problem for educators is to adapt teaching strategies to
existing classroom environments to affect learning in both the cognitive and
affective domains.

Adaptation of teaching strategies involves an understanding of the process
of selective perception on two levels:

1. objective readiness to perceive (concerned primarily with the
physical nature of the message stimulus and competing stimuli)

2. subjective readiness to perceive (concerned primarily with the
psychological disposition of the perceiver).

REVIEW OF RELEVANT LITERATURE

Contemporary researchers assume three different types of information
storage systems: a sensory register (SR), a short-term store (STS), and a
long-term store (LTS). Figure 1 shows the flow of information between the
three systems (Kumar, 1971).

The selective perception process begins when the perceiver attends to

Raw, undifferentiated stimuli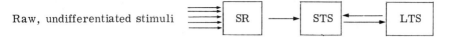

Figure 1. Flow of information between three information storage systems (Kumar, 1971)

The selective perception process begins when the perceiver attends to particular stimuli or messages out of a multiplicity of possible stimuli. Three reasons why people attend to certain stimuli are:

1   characteristics of the stimuli attended to (complexity, intensity, duration, colour, size, shape, pitch, texture, temperature, etc - Witkin, 1969)

2   relation of stimuli, perceived (Figure 1) to other stimuli present (ground - Engel et al, 1968)

3   personal factors such as needs, values, interests, cultural background, stress and psychological set (Bruner, 1965).

OBJECTIVE READINESS TO PERCEIVE

To provide an understanding of the first level of selective perception participants will experience an objective readiness to perceive and a heightened awareness of auditory perception under simulated conditions which focus attention on the auditory channel. Further, they will experience a heightened awareness of normal dependency on visual information. It should become obvious that the physical nature of stimuli present, to a large extent, determine where attention will be focused.

The major premise to be clarified concerning objective readiness to perceive is that a learner may have little or no control over the traditional classroom environment. If he is unable to focus his attention on a given message, because of competing stimuli, his chances for effective learning are diminished.

One way of conceptualizing the problem of attending to one message is to consider it an auditory figure-ground perceptual task (in this instance **Figure** equals attending message and **Ground** competing messages). The problem then becomes one of distinguishing figure from ground and tracking that focus through time until it is processed in the short-term store.

SUBJECTIVE READINESS TO PERCEIVE

In order to actualize the potentialities of learners, teachers must not merely ask students to think, but must also allow them to feel and hopefully more fully experience a given learning task.

In providing for an understanding of selective readiness to perceive, participants will listen to a ten minute tape during which time they will experience a sense of conscious relaxation.

This should provide a psychological readiness to perceive messages which are not only cognitive but also affective in content.

Following this set induction participants will be exposed to auditory messages for subjective valuing during which time they should experience the following:

1   increased awareness of subjective barriers operating when attending to audible message, ie values, needs, cultural background, interest

2   the ability to overcome learned or conditioned patterns of attending and listening

3   increased awareness of previously unnoticed audible stimuli

4   increased subjective valuing of given stimuli or messages.

There is no doubt that individuals have needs, interests and values which lead them to expect and hence to perceive aspects of their environment which others fail to perceive. By the same token they tend to overlook, and sometimes actively avoid, aspects of the environment that are not consonant with their interests. This simply means that what a person perceives is determined to a considerable extent by his 'subjective determinants of perception'.

When an appropriate instructional set is consonant with a person's subjective readiness to perceive he is likely to attend to a given message. If the message is affective in nature and relates directly to feelings experienced by the learner, the match between instructional set and subjective readiness to perceive is vital.

CONCLUSION

This paper and the accompanying experience attempt to explicate selective perception and its relation to providing readiness for learning. The dual format of an experientially based activity in combination with a written paper should add to each participant's understanding and subsequent application of this knowledge in the classroom.

REFERENCES

Bruner, J. S. (1965) The Self in Growth, Teaching and Learning.
  (Ed) D. E. Hamachek. Prentice-Hall Inc., Englewood Cliffs, N.J.
Engel, J. E., Kollat, D. T. and Blackwell, R. D. (1968) Consumer
  Behavior. Holt, Rinehart and Winston, Inc., Toronto
Huxley, A. (1971) Perspectives on the Study of Film. (Ed) J. S. Katz.
  Little, Brown and Co., Boston
Kumar, U. K. (1971) Review of Educational Research, Vol. 41, No. 5
Witkin, B. R. (1969) Journal of Research and Development in Education,
  Vol. 3, No. 1

An Application of Queueing Theory to the Design and Management of Programmed Learning

D REDFEARN

SUMMARY

The provision of self-instructional packages to students, on demand, constitutes a queueing process. Such a process consists of student arrivals, demands for service and, following that service, student departures. Clearly it is not desirable that students should have to queue for lengthy periods of time while waiting for service.

The arguments of this paper are:

a. that for self-instructional packages to be fully effective, attention must be paid at the design stage to their subsequent use in a queueing system, and

b. that attempts should be made to analyse the queueing system to ensure the maximum utilization of self-instructional packages consistent with low queue probabilities.

The paper offers guidelines which will assist in the implementation of the above arguments, and indicates the degree of redundancy in self-instructional resources that may be necessary, and justifiable, in maintaining student waiting times at acceptable levels.

INTRODUCTION

The student demanding self-instructional materials, whether they be textbooks or tape-slide presentations, is seeking to place himself in a situation in which, he hopes, learning will occur and may be said to be motivated to learn. He corresponds to a customer seeking service and the possibility must exist that he will have to wait, or queue, for service. Such an experience is unlikely to enhance his motivation to learn, and the repetition of such experiences must degrade his motivation to learn. 'Programmed Instruction is primarily a scheme for making effective use of reinforcers, not only in shaping new kinds of behaviour but in maintaining behaviour in strength' (Skinner, 1968). The experience of waiting for a program to become available is unlikely to be reinforcing and must negate, to some degree, the time and effort spent in arranging contingencies for reinforcement within the program.

The cost of self-instructional materials may be high, and as a result high utilization is desirable. Unfortunately high utilization conflicts with the requirement for zero, or very short waiting times and some compromise is necessary. The nature of the compromise must depend upon particular circumstances and in many situations low utilizations may well be justified by the requirement to maintain high student motivation. In any event an appreciation of the queueing system is essential if the optimum decisions are to be made.

Queueing systems are defined by the following parameters:

a. an arrival pattern

b. a service mechanism

and c. a queue discipline.

The arrival pattern is determined by the average rate of student arrivals and by the statistical distribution of these arrivals.

The service mechanism determines how many students can undergo self-instruction at the same time and how long they take to complete self-instruction. The former depends upon the number of sets of hardware and software available and the latter is usually specified by the statistical distribution of the time taken to complete self-instruction, ie the service time. In some situations service may occur in more than one phase. For example, it may be desirable to administer a pre-test before self-instruction and a post-test afterwards.

The simplest queue discipline, and the one most likely to be used, is to deal with students in the order in which they arrive.

'The practical world of queues abounds with problems that cannot be solved elegantly but which must be analysed nevertheless.' (Newell, 1971) All but the simplest queues defy complete mathematical analysis and exact solutions to the queueing problems of self-instruction seem unlikely, but it is, at least, possible to isolate and identify those problems. As in other management situations an essential part of the management process is the collection of data upon which decisions may be taken. It is the premise of this paper that, in providing self-instructional resources on demand, adequate decision making is only possible when based upon data which includes that data resulting from an examination of the queueing problems peculiar to the situation under investigation.

SELECTION OF THE QUEUEING MODEL

'It appears that the representation of queueing process by means of high-fidelity mathematical models cannot often be accomplished and that even when it can, the models are likely to defy analysis' (Lee, 1966). Lee goes on to describe three types of approach to queueing problems:

a. approximation using an oversimplified model,

b. simulation,

c. the classical type of approximation exemplified by two techniques, (i) expansion of unmanageable functions in terms of a power series with higher terms assumed negligible and (ii) substitution of initial values in the formulas followed by iteration.

In the case of a self-instructional unit, arrival and service time data is not available until the unit starts to operate. Simulation can only be performed if such data is available, and might be a useful technique once the unit has settled down in operation. However the results of simulation are only likely to be of value in the management of particular self-instructional units, with a particular set of programs and a particular student population.

The third approach infers that at the planning stage sufficient information is available to select an appropriate queueing model. Even were this the case the subsequent analysis is likely to be a laborious business.

What is required is a method which is simple to apply and which will give answers which though inexact may be used as guidelines in the initial planning stage. If the answers can be refined once self-instruction starts and operating data become available so much the better. The method must be usable, and it is suggested that in the majority of cases it must be usable without computer back-up. These arguments lead to the use of approach (a) in the selection of a queueing model for use in self-instructional situations.

THE QUEUEING MODEL

In the introduction it was stated that a queueing system could be defined by a customer arrival pattern, a service mechanism and a queue discipline. At the planning stage it is only possible to state that the queueing system in a self-instructional unit will be multi-channel, ie several students can be served at the same time, and that the queue discipline will be first in first out (FIFO). No data is available relating to the arrival distribution or to the service time distribution.

One of the simplest multi-channel queueing models is the $M/M/c$: (FIFO) model. This coding indicates the following characteristics in the model:

M Arrivals are random occurring at a constant average rate of λ per unit time. The inter-arrival time distribution can be shown to be negative exponential with a constant average value of $1/\lambda$.

M The service time distribution is negative exponential with a constant average value of $1/\mu$.

c The number of channels.

FIFO Customers are served strictly in the order of their arrival.

The assumptions implied by the use of this model are:

a. that the time interval between successive student arrivals ie the inter-arrival time, is distributed negative exponentially,

b. that the times taken for students to complete self-instruction, ie the service time, is distributed negative exponentially.

(This second assumption is likely to be the least satisfactory in practice since, there is a positive lower limit to the service time.)

The differential equations which constitute the mathematical model representing the M/M/c : (FIFO) queueing system are:

$$\frac{d}{dt} P_0(t) = -\lambda P_0(t) + \mu P_1(t)$$

$$\frac{d}{dt} P_n(t) = -(\lambda + n\mu) P_n(t) + \lambda P_{n-1}(t) + (n+1) \mu P_{n+1}(t) ;$$

for $1 \leq n \leq c-1$

and $\quad \frac{d}{dt} P_n(t) = -(\lambda + c\mu) P_n(t) + \lambda P_{n-1}(t) + c\mu P_{n+1}(t) ;$

for $c \leq n$

where $P_n(t)$ is the probability of n customers in the system at time t. Time dependent solutions to these equations can be obtained but in Lee's words "it is not the easiest matter in the world to apply the transient solution" (Lee, 1966). The model may be simplified considerably by writing:

$$\frac{d}{dt} P_n(t) = 0 ; \quad n \geq 0$$

This implies that the probability that n persons are in the system is independent of time, ie the queueing process is in the 'steady state'.

In a self-instructional unit the queueing system will tend to start up daily and to close down at the end of the working day. Lee makes the point that during the starting up periods "the inter-arrival time distributions are unstable.... It would be absurd to attempt to apply a precise time-dependent solution of a model in such circumstances".

Having made the steady state assumption the three equations of the model become:
$$-\lambda P_0 + \mu P_1 = 0$$
$$-(\lambda + n\mu) P_n + \lambda P_{n-1} + (n+1) \mu P_{n+1} = 0 ; \qquad 1 \leq n \leq c-1$$
$$-(\lambda + c\mu) P_n + \lambda P_{n-1} + c\mu P_{n+1} = 0 ; \qquad c \leq n$$

which lead to the steady state probabilities given by the following equations:

$$P_0 = \frac{1}{\sum\limits_{r=0}^{c-1} \frac{(c\rho)^r}{r!} + \frac{(c\rho)^c}{c!} \frac{1}{1-\rho}}$$

$$P_n = \frac{(c\rho)^n}{n!} P_0 ; \quad n \leq c$$

$$P_n = \frac{c^c}{c!} \rho^n P_0 ; \quad n > c$$

226

where $\rho = \lambda/c\mu$

The quantity   is called the 'traffic intensity' and is the ratio of the arrival rate to the service rate. Only values of ρ less than unity are of interest since traffic intensities greater than one imply customers joining the queue faster than they can be served. The probability of the number of customers within the system exceeding the number of channels of service increases as ρ approaches unity.

From the above equations the following rather more useful equations can be derived.

Average number of students in the system

$$N_s = \frac{\rho(\rho c)^c}{c!\,(1-\rho)^2}\,P_0 + c \tag{1}$$

Average time in queue

$$T_q = \frac{(\rho c)^c}{c!\,(1-\rho)^2\,c\mu}\,P_0 \tag{2}$$

Equations (1) and (2) are the basis of Figures 1 and 2.

THE QUEUEING MODEL AS A COURSE DESIGN TOOL

Task analysis may be used to define in behavioural terms the performance ultimately required of a student. Such performances can be expressed as Operational Objectives and collectively form an Operational Performance Standard.

The Course Designers task is to design a course which will lead to the student achieving a number of Training Objectives which collectively form a Training Performance Standard. Clearly it is desirable for the Training Performance Standard to be as close to the Operational Performance Standard as is possible, but in many situations constraints upon the course, time, resources etc will not allow an exact match. In this instance the requirement is to produce a course of self-instructional programs which are to be available, with the associated hardware, on demand. In a real situation, it is likely that the information available to the Course Designer at the start of his work will be limited to the Operational Performance Standard, the resources to be available, ie the number of sets of hardware etc, the size of the student group who will complete the course and quite probably the time period within which the course must be completed by the student group. It follows that before the Course Designer can define his Training Objectives, he must determine a mean self-instructional program length, and it is an argument of this paper that he can not do this without first examining the queueing system he is to set up. A queueing model is required to make use of such information as is available to indicate the number and average duration of units within the overall self-instructional program to allow operation at high utilization without incurring the penalty of unacceptable queueing times.

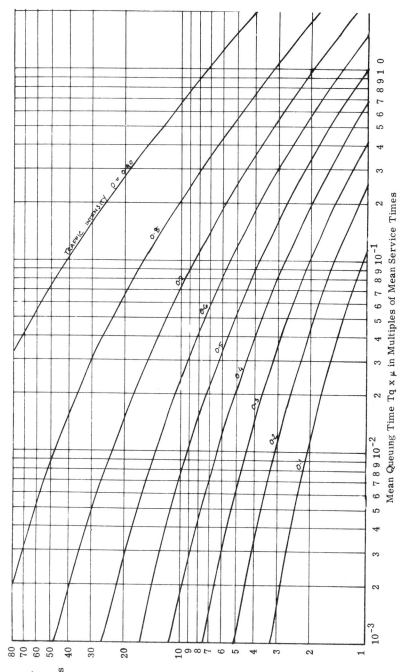

TRAFFIC INTENSITY $\rho = 0.90$

0.8

0.7

0.6

0.5

0.4

0.3

0.2

0.1

C
Number
of
service
channels

80
70
60
50
40
30
20
10 9 8 7 6 5 4 3 2 1

10^{-3} 2 3 4 5 6 7 8 9 10^{-2} 2 3 4 5 6 7 8 9 10^{-1} 2 3 4 5 6 7 8 9 10 0

Mean Queuing Time Tq x μ in Multiples of Mean Service Times

Figure 1

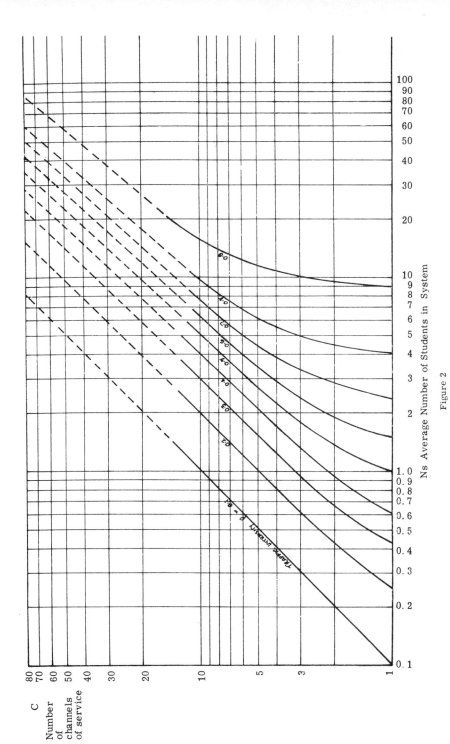

Figure 2

Only when the number and average duration of programs has been established is it possible to define precisely and in detail the Training Objectives of the course.

The queueing model selected for use has been discussed in the previous section. The parameter which may be used to indicate the degree of utilization of equipment is the traffic intensity ρ. For values of traffic intensity approaching unity the average number of people within the queueing system is high, and so equipment utilization will be high, but unfortunately the probability of queueing is also high and average waiting times are long (Figure 2). The requirement is to determine a mean program length which will allow for operation of the system at values of traffic intensity as high as possible consistent with insignificant student waiting times.

As mentioned earlier the queue system is defined by an arrival pattern, a service mechanism and a queue discipline. It is worth examining these characteristics within the context of the data which is likely to be available to the course designer.

The arrival pattern

The arrival pattern is determined by the average rate of student arrivals and by the statistical distribution of these arrivals. The Course Designer is likely to know the maximum number of students required to use his course and the time period within which they must complete the course. He has no guarantee that all these students will use the self-instructional facilities when they are provided. Arrivals will not be uniformly distributed over the allowed time period. The arrival rate will be high at the beginning of the period and will tail off as time passes. Queueing problems are therefore most likely at the beginning of the period.

If self-instructional facilities are to be made available to a student population of N students for a period of n weeks a proportion p of the available students will arrive in week 1 leaving (1-p) N students to arrive in subsequent weeks. If p remains constant Table I can be produced.

Table I

Time interval	Students available	Student arrivals	Students remaining
1	N	pN	$(1-p)N$
2	$(1-p)N$	$p(1-p)N$	$(1-p)^2N$
3	$(1-p)^2N$	$p(1-p)^2N$	$(1-p)^3N$
n	$(1-p)^{n-1}N$	$p(1-p)^{n-1}N$	$(1-p)^nN$

If the course designer assumes that 99% of students will arrive during the n weeks he can determine a value of p which will enable him to calculate the number of student arrivals likely during each week, and in particular in the first week when queueing problems are likely to be at their worst.

In the majority of situations student availability will vary from hour to hour over the working day. A survey of student timetables will indicate those times of day when students are most likely to arrive. Table II shows that in a particular sample studied, 60% of student arrivals were likely between 1200 and 1500.

Table II

EXAMPLE OF STUDENT AVAILABILITY

(Population 300, sample 145)

The main rush period is likely to be between 1200 and 1500 since late afternoon arrivals are unlikely in spite of high availability.

57.5% of availabilities occur between 1200 and 1500.

	Monday		Tuesday		Wednesday		Thursday		Friday		Total possible arrivals
	No	%	No	%	No	%	No	%	No	%	
0900 1000	0	0	0	0	0	0	0	0	33	11	33
1000 1100	30	10	18	6	36	12	24	8	36	12	144
1100 1200	36	12	27	9	57	19	27	9	30	10	177
1200 1300	288	96	288	96	291	97	288	96	297	99	1452
1300 1400	177	59	123	41	177	59	105	35	126	42	708
1400 1500	180	60	117	39	177	59	81	27	138	46	693
1500 1600	183	61	138	46	198	66	63	21	144	48	726
1600 1700	228	76	201	67	228	76	195	65	183	61	1035
											4968

The above data is the result of a questionnaire completed by first year students studying biology as one of their subjects in the University of Glasgow 1971-72.

By following processes such as those described it is possible for the course designer to determine an average arrival rate for the period within which the problems of queueing are likely to be most acute.

The statistical distribution of arrivals can only be determined by collecting data after self-instruction has commenced, and of necessity a distribution has to be assumed during the design phase.

The service mechanism

The service mechanism is determined by the number of students who are able to work at one time, the mean time it takes to complete programs, ie mean service time, and the statistical distribution of service times.

The number of students able to work at the same time is subject to the number of sets of hardware available and the number of program copies.

Mean service time is in fact the quantity which the course designer needs to obtain from the queueing model, before he can define Training Objectives.

As with the arrival distribution, data on the service time distribution will only start to become available once self-instruction commences, and a distribution must be assumed at this stage.

The queue discipline

The simplest queue discipline involves dealing with students in order of arrival on a first come first served basis.

Application of the queueing model

As indicated earlier the most usable queueing model is the M/M/c : (FIFO) model. Its use is most satisfactorily demonstrated by use of an example. Consider the following constraints:

Time allowance for completion of self-study 3 weeks ie 15 working days

Student population   100

Max number of channels (No of hardware   5
                                    sets)

The problem is to determine the mean program duration consistent with no significant queueing.

An investigation of student availability indicates that 60% of arrivals are likely between 1200 and 1500 daily. 90% of students are expected to take advantage of self-instruction on demand. (Table I)

After 3 weeks 10 students remain to complete programs.

$$\therefore \quad (1-p)^3 = 0.1$$
$$p = 0.536$$

In week 1 the number of arrivals is pN ie 53.6 or 54.

60% of these arrivals are likely to occur between 1200 and 1500.

Total week 1 arrivals between 1200 and 1500 = 32

Thus mean arrival rate between 1200 and 1500 = 32 ÷ 15 = 2.13/hr

'Traffic Intensity' $\rho = \dfrac{\lambda}{c\mu}$

where ρ λ = mean arrival rate

c = number of channels of service

μ = mean rate of service, ie reciprocal of mean service time

$$\rho = \frac{2.13}{5\mu}$$

$$\therefore \quad \mu = \frac{0.426}{\rho}$$

The above equation allows columns A, B and C of Table III to be completed. Column D indicates the mean queueing time corresponding to traffic intensity in Column A. These values may be obtained by entering Figure 1 with the value of traffic and the number of channels of service available.

Table III

(A) ρ	(B) μ	(C) $1/\mu$	(D) Tq
0.3	1.42	42.2 min	0.26 min
0.4	1.06	56.5	1.19
0.5	0.85	71.0	3.7
0.6	0.71	84.5	11.0

$1/\mu$ represents the mean programmed time

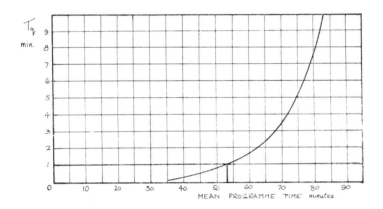

Figure 3

The data in Table III is plotted in Figure 3, and indicates the relationship between the mean program length and mean queueing time. At this point the Course Designer must make a value judgement and decide what is an acceptable mean queueing time. If one minute is taken as an acceptable mean queueing time the graph indicates a mean program time of 53 minutes. Reference back to Table III shows that this implies operation of the system at a traffic intensity rather less than 0.4 which indicates that the average number of students within the system is 2.2 (Figure 2). On average two sets of hardware will be idle, but this low utilization may well be justified by the extremely low desirability of queues.

233

The mean program time in this example has been shown to be 53 minutes. The course designer now has to decide how to use this. If he decides on a program 53 minutes long he will require the same number of program copies as sets of hardware in order to retain a similar mean queueing time. However, if he decides to use two programs each of about 26 minutes mean duration he may well be able to work with fewer program copies, and at a higher traffic intensity.

If the program time is split to form two separate programs the mean arrival rate will be doubled to become 4.26/hr. The number of sets of hardware remains at 5 and the traffic intensity becomes

$$\rho = \frac{4.26}{5\mu}$$

and Table IV may be constructed.

Table IV

ρ	μ	$1/\mu$	Tq
0.3	2.84	21.2 min	0.132 min
0.4	2.12	28.2	0.59
0.5	2.7	35.0	1.35
0.6	1.42	42.2	5.5

Inspection of Table IV and comparison with the values in Table III shows that since the mean arrival rate is doubled, the mean rate of service μ must be doubled to maintain a given value of traffic intensity. It follows that the mean waiting time corresponding to a particular traffic intensity is halved.

Two programmes of mean length 32 minutes produce a mean waiting time of one minute at a traffic intensity of 0.45.

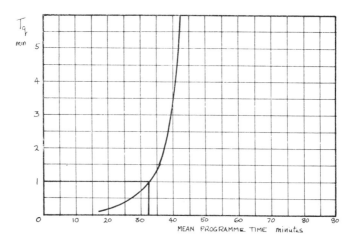

Figure 4

Figure 2 indicates that for a traffic intensity of 0.45 the average number of students in the system is 2.5.

The mean rate of arrival for each program will be 2.13/hr and the mean rate of service is 60/32 ie 1.87/hr. The traffic intensity is now given by

$$\rho = \frac{2.13}{c.1.87} = \frac{1.14}{c}$$

where c now represents the number of program copies required to prevent program based queues.

Table V

ρ	c	Tq . μ	Tq
0.3	3.8	.018	.575 min
0.4	2.85	.091	2.88
0.5	2.28	.28	8.9
0.6	1.9	.62	19.8

The values of Tq.μ are extracted from Figure 1. Figure 5 indicates that for a mean waiting time of one minute 3.5 channels of service are required, ie 3.5 copies of the programs.

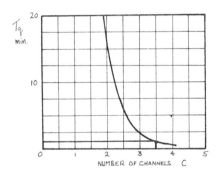

Figure 5

Clearly c must be an integer, so that 4 program copies are required.

The process described could be continued for program times split into 3, 4, 5 etc, parts but clearly there is a minimum mean program length below which it is not reasonable to go. The majority of the student population will be able to complete two programs of mean duration 32 minutes within the time allowance of 3 weeks upon 5 sets of hardware with a mean waiting time of one minute.

The Course Designer now knows that he has a mean program time of 2 x 32 minutes and is now in a position to define his Training Objectives.

If the Training Objectives achievable within that time, are not acceptable it may well be that he can justify additional time or hardware, a position he would have been unlikely to be in had the queueing model not been used.

THE QUEUEING MODEL AS A MANAGEMENT TOOL

Given a course of self-instructional programs, a student population and a period of time within which the majority of students are, hopefully, to complete the programs, management is required to determine the number of sets of hardware and software which are necessary to reduce the probability of queues to an acceptably low value while maintaining as high an equipment utilization as is possible. The author sees the elimination of significant student waiting times as being of first priority which may require that there are periods during the operation of the self-instructional unit when equipment utilization is extremely low in order to ensure that queues are controlled during busy periods. Whatever the priorities it is essential that management be provided with the most useful data available upon which its decisions may be taken.

In this instance the major difficulty is in attempting to provide data for decision making. Decisions on number of copies of software and on the number of sets of hardware are required before self-instruction can begin. As was indicated earlier much of the data required only starts to be generated with the commencement of self-instruction. This lack of firm data is again taken as justification for using a simple queueing model which at best can only be an approximation to the real system. Program validation may yield some data on mean times taken to complete programs, ie mean service time and on the statistical distribution of service times. However it is likely that the actual service time distribution would lead to a model which defies analysis.

Queues will form if no channel of service is vacant. Service may be denied either due to non-availability of a program, or non-availability of hardware. The manager is required to determine how many copies of the program to provide and how many sets of hardware are required.

An example will most conveniently demonstrate the use of the queueing model. One hundred students are to be given the opportunity to make use of a course of self-instructional programs consisting of 5 programs. Program validation indicates that the mean time to complete a program is 30 minutes. Self-instructional facilities are to be available for three weeks (15 working days) and an analysis of student programs indicates that 60% of student arrivals are likely between the hours of 1200 and 1500. It is anticipated that 90% of students will take advantage of the self-instructional facilities.

Reference to Table I $(1-p)^3 . 500 = 50$ *

$$p = 0.536$$

Thus proportion of students using facilities in week 1 is 0.54. Total arrivals week 1 are 270, and total arrivals between 1200 and 1500 in week 1 are 162. Thus mean arrival rate between 1200 and 1500 in week 1 is 10.8/hr.

'Traffic intensity' $\quad \rho = \dfrac{\lambda}{c\mu} = \dfrac{10.8}{c.2} , \quad \dfrac{1}{\mu} = 30$ min

$$c = \frac{5.4}{\rho}$$

Table VI is constructed from the above equation and Figure 1.

Table VI

ρ	c	Tq.μ	Tq
0.3	17.9	< .001	< .03 min
0.4	13.5	< .001	< .03
0.5	10.8	.006	.18
0.6	9.0	.031	.93
0.7	7.7	.12	3.6

If mean waiting is selected not to exceed 1 minute, it can be seen from Table VI that 9 channels, sets of hardware, are required to operate at a traffic intensity of 0.6 to give a mean waiting time of 0.93 minutes. It is emphasized that this large number of sets of hardware is required to overcome the busy periods in week 1. Figure 2 shows that the average number of students within the system during the hours between 1200 and 1500 in week 1 is 5.7 giving some indication of the degree of equipment utilization.

An example to determine the number of program copies has already been completed previously and so there is little point in repeating the process here.

CONCLUSIONS

The use of a queueing model described in the previous pages cannot be expected to produce exact answers, but it is suggested that it provides the Course Designer and Course Manager with some guidance in areas where available information is scant. The methods described can assist in management decision making, and though approximate, they have the virtue of being simple to use without the backing of a computer. The longer the queueing system operates the more data is generated and the easier it becomes to use Monte Carlo methods to simulate the system. However, such simulation does nothing to assist in those early decisions which are so vital in order to get a system into operation.

---

* Each student arrives 5 times since the course is of 5 programs.

Examination of Figure 2, which is derived from the Queueing model, indicates that in operating the queueing system at traffic intensities low enough to avoid significant waiting times, the average number of students within the system at any time is lower than the number of channels of service available. This implies that equipment utilization must of necessity be low in order to avoid queues. However, analysis of the queueing system provides information upon which decisions as to provision of equipment may be based, and low utilizations justified by the avoidance of queues during busy periods.

The examples considered in the paper have looked at requirements during the first week of operation of a self-instruction unit. During this initial phase of self-instruction arrival rates will be high (Table I). As self-instruction continues arrival rates will fall. It follows that the most difficult queue problems occur at the beginning of operations and hardware and software requirements are determined to meet these problems. This clearly leads to extremely low equipment utilization during the later stages of self-instruction when the majority of students have completed their programs.

The conclusion reached by the author, is that the use of sophisticated and expensive hardware at low utilization, negates the use of self-instruction on demand except in those rare situations where self-instruction using such hardware is so appropriate that large expense can be justified. In the majority of situations it is suggested that consideration should be given to the use of cheap, simple hardware to provide as many channels of service as is possible and that low utilization be accepted.

REFERENCES

Cox, D. R . and Smith, W. L. (1961) Queues. Chapman & Hall, London

Lee, A. M. (1966) Applied Queueing Theory. Macmillan, London

McGettrick, B. J. (1971) The identification and prior solution of management problems in the administration of programmes. In 'Aspects of Educational Technology V'. (Ed) Derek Packham, Alan Cleary, Terry Mayes. Pitman, London

Newell, G. F. (1971) Applications of Queueing Theory. Chapman & Hall, London

Skinner, B. F. (1968) The technology of teaching. Appleton Century-Crofts, New York

Which Objectives are Most Worthwhile?
D ROWNTREE

Behavioural objectives still mean a lot to the educational technologist. Most of us continue to feel that education is meant to change the student's behaviour — the way he thinks, feels and acts. Even in areas like the Arts, where objectives are supposedly difficult to formulate, we know that they are nevertheless attained: students acquire new attitudes and capabilities and are judged by their performances. Our 'traditional' role has been to help the 'subject-matter expert' clarify his objectives and develop the learning experience through which they can be attained by students. Thanks to the multiplicity of media and methods now available and the inspired empiricism of the so-called 'systems approach', we have had some success in getting students to the objectives. Unfortunately for our peace of mind, students and academics are now beginning to ask the question_ "Why **these** objectives, and not others?" The suspicion is growing that educational technology is too often being used to find better ways of teaching things that should not be taught at all.

Like the Apollo space programme, a new course or learning package may have been both effective and efficient, but was it really worth doing? Would the resources perhaps have been better employed elsewhere? More and more we are faced with the need, identified by Scriven (1967), to evaluate not only the student's performance against objectives but also the objectives themselves. From being merely the midwives of change we perhaps need to assume a more active role in its conception. We need to enquire a little more critically into where our objectives come from and examine closely their relative claims on the student's time.

OBJECTIVES AND THE CURRICULUM

Indeed it is no longer enough for the educational technologist to concentrate on perfecting this or that component of the curriculum unless it is clearly justified by some cogent view of the curriculum as a whole. If educational technology is truly to serve the learner and society, as well as education, we must soon attempt a more total analysis of the desired outcomes in a **lifetime** of learning — not all of which need take place in educational institutions as we know them today.

Of course, the broad view has been taken before (though rarely by educational technologists), and 'desired outcomes' are to be found in abundance in the writings of the 'great educators' and others. They stress the intellectual, moral and emotional growth of the individual, preparation for adult life in society, acquisition of a common culture, and so on. Unfortunately, the suggested outcomes are usually phrased in the vague and abstract language of goals and aims. Children are expected, for example, to become critical and creative thinkers; to learn how to learn; to develop inquiring minds; to be able to communicate their understandings to others; to become capable of making their own moral judgements; to be able to work cooperatively with others; to be adaptable and capable of adjusting to a changing world; and so on (at considerable length). Buried deep beneath these lofty sentiments are, I suspect, the behavioural objectives we would all value most highly — if only we could dig them out and examine them.

Whatever these hidden objectives, they appear not to be getting achieved at present. Student unrest; appeals for 'relevance'; drop-out; graduate unemployment; all highlight our failure to grasp and give priority to the more worthwhile objectives in education. The malaise is well-documented in the growing literature of what might be called educational pathology (see, for example, Goodman,1971; Henry,1971; Holt,1965; Illich,1971; Reimer,1971; Postman & Weingartner,1971, etc). Not only are the valued behaviours not being attained, but pathological behaviours are being attained instead:

> "They learn that what is worthwhile is what is taught and, conversely, that if something is important, someone must teach it to them."
>
> (Reimer, 1971)

> ".... we have ground out students who can solve problems but who will forever have to be guided by someone else ...."
>
> (Thelen, 1972)

> "At present the only intellectual skill the schools genuinely value is memorising and the student behaviour most demanded is answer-giving ..... giving someone else's answers to someone else's questions."
>
> (Postman, 1970)

> "The usual kind of education ..... is designed to give answers to questions which nobody asked and to inhibit the student in discovering his own truth and insight. The lectures and the texts do all that sort of thing for you. They provide a way in which the student can cover up his true self by finding a vocabulary acceptable to most people and a set of facts which are generally known among people generally considered to be generally educated. Once the skill of covering up has been acquired, the student may never be called upon to say what he

really thinks or feels at any point in his education or later
life. This is what makes bores, and produces college graduates who are ignorant and dull, but successful and plausible."
(Taylor, 1960)

The potency of this unwritten curriculum is surely due, in some measure,
to our failure to 'operationalize' the large and long-term aims of education.
We have neglected to analyse the behavioural features of 'critical thinking',
'moral autonomy', 'self-esteem', 'open and inquiring mind', and the numerous other traits or **life-skills** we hope to see develop in the student. Particularly, we have not spelled out and systematized the **behavioural-objectives**
we would recognize as necessary evidence of the attainment of such life-
skills. Having therefore no basis for constructing and evaluating curriculum
experiences in terms of outcomes that might be most valued, we take refuge
in more easily-measured objectives — in particular, the **content** of traditional
subject-disciplines.

What we manifestly need is a **catalogue** of worthwhile objectives. At present we have no systematic procedure for generating objectives, worthwhile
or otherwise, but we can make a model (Figure 1) to help us explore the
sources from which various kinds of aim and objectives are derived.

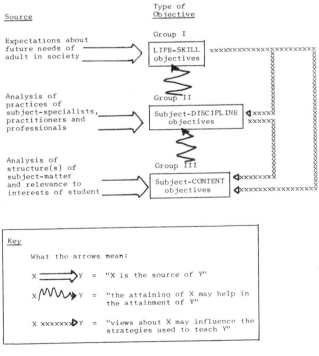

Figure 1. Sources of objectives.
(from Rowntree, D. (1973) **What is Educational Technology**?)

Our views about what is worth learning are largely determined by our beliefs or assumptions about the future roles of adults in society. From such beliefs and assumptions we derive the broad curriculum aims which can then be exemplified behaviourally and operationally as life-skill objectives (Group I). But what life-skills will our students need as adults in the years ahead? What can they conceivably learn now that will be of use to them next year, a decade hence, and in the 21st century — when children now beginning school should be in the prime of life?

Fortunately, some writers are beginning to tease out the behaviours implied by broad curriculum aims. From them we can get some taste of what is needed. For example, Postman and Weingartner (1971) propose an 'inquiry' curriculum in which the teacher:

> "..... measures his success in terms of behavioural changes in students; the frequency with which they ask questions; the increase in the relevance and cogency of their questions; the frequency and conviction of their challenges to assertions made by other students or teachers or textbooks; the relevance and clarity of the standards on which they base their challenges; their willingness to suspend judgements when they have insufficient data; their willingness to modify or otherwise change their position when data warrant such change; the increase in their skill in observing, classifying, generalising, etc; the increase in their tolerance for diverse answers; their ability to apply generalisations, attitudes and information to novel situations. "

Allied skills for exploring and mastering the student's environment are suggested by Whitfield (1971) who wants the student to be able to construct and apply mental models of the real world as follows:

1. Model construction and exploration

(a) To search for, and find, similarities occurring in a variety of situations

(b) To isolate and define the variables underlying these similarities

(c) To determine and define the relationships that exist between the variables

(d) To establish the necessary validity of statements of these relationships

(e) To search for the axioms from which this model can be logically derived

(f) To vary the axioms in order to produce other consistent models

2. Model application

(a) To recognize that a given situation is one in which a certain model is applicable

(b) To make assumptions about the variables defined in the model

(c) To manipulate the model in order to solve the problem

(d) To verify that the chosen model is the best analogue of the given situation

(e) To use the model for making new predictions.

Wilson (1969) considers the aim of "helping pupils to make their own moral judgements". This, he says, demands that pupils:

(a) Understand what is meant by 'moral judgement', ie be able to distinguish between **moral** judgements and those based on expediency, or impulse, or rules, or feelings of guilt, or some form of external authority, and so forth

(b) Possess to an adequate degree the attitude that the feelings, needs and interests of other people are equally important to their own

(c) Possess sufficient knowledge to be able to make a reasonable prediction of the outcome of their actions

(d) Have certain skills of communication with other people

(e) Have sufficient insight into the needs and feelings of other people, and also sufficient insight into their **own** feelings, etc

(f) Have the ability to form their own generalized principles of behaviour

Clearly, more work needs to be done to fully operationalize such objec-tives and the teacher will need sensitive evaluation skills to check that students are attaining them. He may also need to recognize that he must attain some of them himself. So too with the highly affective objectives being suggested by Carl Rogers in **On Becoming a Person** (1961):

> The person comes to see himself differently.
> He accepts himself and his feelings more fully.
> He becomes more self-confident and self-directing.
> He becomes more the person he would like to be.
> He becomes more flexible, less rigid in his perceptions.
> He adopts more realistic goals for himself.
> He becomes more acceptant of others.
> He becomes more open to the evidence, both of what is
> going on outside of himself and what is going on inside
> of himself.

Notice also, in these latter two sets of objectives, the frequent use of the words 'sufficient' and 'more', indicating that each objective must be specified with yet further precision to relate it to the present and possible future states of particular **individual** students. But, and this is the point, despite the rela-tivistic nature of these objectives and the problems they will pose for evalua-tion, they are already far more suggestive of appropriate teaching strategies and learning experiences than are the high-minded platitudes and woolly gene-ralizations that usually preside over curriculum planning.

These few examples suggest what may result when we begin translating into aims and then objectives our views of the adult's future in society.

SUBJECT-DISCIPLINE OBJECTIVES

Until now, not a word about subject-matter. We should **not** begin by taking a 'subject' and asking "What are the relevant objectives? We begin rather with the objectives and ask "Which (**if any**) are the relevant subjects?"

In doing so, of course, we operate within massive constraints. Certain subjects are firmly entrenched in the curriculum, with an integrated exami-nation/career-prospects system acting as a very institutionalized barrier to change. Yet, we must nevertheless ask "Why History, Algebra and Chemistry? Why not Ecology, Astronomy and Criminology? Or why not Psychology, Politics and Anthropology?" Of course the student should be encouraged to follow an interest in such well-defined disciplines where they impinge on his experience and so seem relevant to him. But equally relevant may be non-subjects like pollution, sport, sex, community-development, science-fiction, and car maintenance, and the one subject of direct relevance to students that never gets discussed in school — education!

Meanwhile, the subjects are there — providing data to be manipulated if not facts to be learned. Such writers as Hirst (1968) and Phenix (1964) argue that the established disciplines embody essentially different ways of 'knowing' and coming to terms with experience — different criteria for truth and proof, different modes of investigation, different forms of explanation — all of which are essential to the growth of mind. Unfortunately we are rarely given enough examples from which to determine precisely how the approach of, say, a chemist differs from that of an historian, except in being applied to different 'raw material'. We know especially little of how their supposedly different modes of perception affect their respective approaches to problems outside of their 'subject' (the kind of problem that adults other than academics are facing most of the time) like "Am I doing right by my kids?", "What can we do about the way things are around here?", "Shall I change my job?", or simply "Why won't the car start?".

While Hirst is right to point out that one can't have, say, 'critical thinking' or 'problem-solving' without reference to some subject-matter, this is not to say that the subject-matter must be recognizable as belonging to some one **established** discipline. We should not be surprised if practitioners in the different disciplines have more in common than is sometimes supposed. For example, Whitfield conceived the 'manipulation of models' as mathematics objectives. Yet how many other subject-disciplines (and professions) might also regard these as essential skills? Are they not also appropriate to, say, deciding why the car won't start? Is it so misguided to appropriate them for the curriculum as a whole?

However, insofar as we can isolate distinctive **methods of inquiry** among the disciplines, these are what we mean by subject-discipline objectives (Group II) and on these should lie the emphasis in subject-teaching. Despite examination papers which consistently seem to prove the contrary, educators are more and more committed to the belief that knowledge is becoming obsolete so fast that the only thing worth knowing is how to acquire new knowledge. As Bruner (1960) puts it "Methods of inquiry are more durable than facts and even generalizations".

SUBJECT-CONTENT OBJECTIVES

Finally, Group III objectives. Given that certain **life-skills** are to be aimed for and that students are to learn the subject-**discipline** skills (the specialist modes of inquiry and ways of knowing), what subject-content shall they practise on and what subject-**content** objectives might they acquire as a result?

Bruner is renowned for his assertion that children at almost any age and level of ability can develop a grasp of the nature of a discipline, provided the emphasis in teaching is not on isolated facts but on the fundamental concepts and unifying principles of the subject. At the level of Group III we are asking what the student has to do to demonstrate his grasp of these concepts and principles and their relationships. Such behavioural objectives we can derive from an examination of the structure (or structures) of the discipline.

But Group III objectives can also be decided by the student. To have him learn the teacher's structure would be little better than having him learn isolated facts. Instead he can be encouraged to develop structures of his own, building analogies and examples out of his personal experience. Without this he is unlikely to be developing the over-riding life-skills and subject-discipline skills. Thus, the teacher may either identify subject-content objectives himself, or help the student identify such objectives, appropriate to the thrust of the student's own enquiries.

So, in Figure 1, we see how, from different sources, three broad groups of objectives can be derived. No doubt the model is over-simple. For instance, the division between groups may not be as clear-cut as the diagram suggests. As I have already hinted, I am not entirely convinced that subject-disciplinary skills are separable from life-skills. Some writers lump them both together under the name 'process' objectives. (And if disciplinary skills are not life-skills, how do we justify the compulsory presence of subjects in the curriculum, considering how few people, apart from educators, continue to practice an academic discipline after leaving school?) Again, I am not too happy about the division between disciplinary skills and content skills. How realistic is it to divorce the structure of the discipline from the characteristic modes of inquiry by which that structure is built and extended? On the other hand, perhaps there should be more rather than fewer groups?

My reason for using this model is that curriculum-makers do seem to postulate behaviours in each of the three groups I have described. Unfortunately, they have done too little to specify the behaviours required in Group II and, especially, in Group I. These groups are usually left as broad and amorphous aims that are probably too vaguely articulated even to have the enlightening effect they should have on the teaching — which concentrates mainly on Group III, where objectives **do** get spelled out (in examinations if nowhere else). To my mind, this produces an upside-down curriculum. We could, and it is at least arguable that we often should, specify and teach Group I objectives without touching on Groups II and III. Yet we usually, and without argument, stake our all on Group III, with no more than lip-service paid to Groups I and II. As a result we get the kind of malaise described by Miller (1962) who evaluated teaching and learning in the medical school of the University of Illinois where 'critical thinking' was held to be an important aim (but was never spelled out as objectives); Miller found that students were given little opportunity to question and discuss and act 'critically', and when their overall course grades were compared with their scores on a standard test of critical thinking it turned out that the twenty-five 'most critical' students did worst on the course while the twenty-five 'least critical' did best.

COMPILING THE CATALOGUE OF WORTHWHILE OBJECTIVES

So what about our catalogue of worthwhile objectives? Something of the sort has been tried before, for example by Bobbitt (1918, 1924) whose 'task analysis' of everyday life revealed 160 major objectives, and by the Russell Sage Foundation (Kearney, 1953 and French et al, 1957) whose 'desirable outcomes' filled two volumes. But those lists were never very operational and are anyway long outmoded. If we are to compile our own catalogue — perhaps a job for Schools Council, Nuffield, or NCET? — what characteristics should it have?

The catalogue should list and give examples of behaviours relating to all the overarching aims of education (largely from Group I perhaps, but with illustrations, no doubt, from Groups II and III). It should attempt to establish relationships between these objectives (eg what are the links between affective and cognitive objectives? What is the connection between reading, thinking and writing skills? Can we identify related groups of objectives and learning sequences through them?). It should relate sequences of objectives to other aspects of the learner's development (eg how would 'critical thinking' or 'effective reading' differ at ages 7, 15 and 20?). It should review learning activities (in and out of 'school') and materials appropriate to the various objectives (eg programmes on creative problem-solving (Peel, 1967) or on learning how to learn (Rowntree, 1970); the GCE O-level course on 'thinking' being developed by de Bono (1972); various Nuffield and Schools Council projects, and so on). It should suggest evaluation techniques for observing or testing the attainment of each objective and should consider the implications (probably far-reaching) for the assessment and grading of students (eg are some combinations of objectives really worth more 'marks' than others?).

Needless to say, such a work should not be tackled briefly or lightly. Its compilation would require iterative consultations and debate among teachers, students, academics, philosophers, parents, community leaders and others. Since there can be no beneficial calculus for identifying unarguably worthwhile objectives, it would need to accommodate conflicting viewpoints. Thus it would take away none of the responsibility of teacher and student to make a wise and personal **choice** of objectives. It should be open-ended enough to allow for periodic up-dating, yet structured enough to help the teacher and student develop their own local objectives and relate them to the bigger design. Certainly the catalogue would not be prescriptive. No one student could be expected to attain all its 'desired outcomes'. Rather it would be descriptive of the rich variety of response of which humanity is **capable**. Being expressed in operational terms, it should provide, for those with the motivation to use it, real help in designing worthwhile learning, and avoiding the trivial or undesirable behaviours so widely acquired in education today. Whether it would be so used is another matter. If not, at least we would all know **precisely** what we are missing.

REFERENCES

Bobbitt, F. (1918) The Curriculum. Houghton Mifflin, Boston
Bobbitt, F. (1924) How to Make a Curriculum. Houghton Mifflin, Boston
Bono, E. de (1972) Times Educational Supplement 21 July. No. 2983, pp 16 & 57
Bruner, J. S. (1960) The Process of Education, Harvard University Press, Boston
French, W. et al (1957) Behavioural Goals of General Education in High School. Russell Sage Foundation, New York
Goodman, P. (1971) Compulsory Miseducation. Penguin, London. (First published 1962)
Henry, J. (1971) Essays on Education. Penguin, London
Hirst, P. H. (1968) in Changing the Curriculum (J. F. Kerr). London University Press, London
Holt, J. (1965) How Children Fail. Pitman, London
Illich, I. D. (1971) Deschooling Society, Harper and Row, New York
Kearney, N. C. (1953) Elementary School Objectives. Russell Sage Foundation, New York
Miller, G. (1962) (Ed) Teaching and Learning in Medical School. Harvard University Press, Boston
Peel, E. A. (1967) 'Programmed Thinking' in Problems and Methods in Programmed Learning - Part 1. (Ed) M. Tobin. School of Education, University of Birmingham, Birmingham
Phenix, P. H. (1964) Realms of Meaning. McGraw-Hill, New York
Postman, N. (1970) 'Curriculum Change and Technology' in To Improve Learning. (Ed) S. G. Tickton. Bowker, New York
Postman, N. and Weingartner, C. (1971) Teaching as a Subversive Activity. Penguin, London. (First published 1969)
Reimer, E. (1971) School is Dead. Penguin, London
Rogers, C. (1961) On Becoming a Person. Houghton Mifflin, New York
Rowntree, D. (1970) Learn How to Study. Macdonald, London
Rowntree, D. (1973) What is Educational Technology? (Book in preparation)
Scriven, M. (1967) 'The Methodology of Evaluation' in Perspectives of Curriculum Evaluation (Ed) R. W. Tyler, R. Gagné and M Scriven. Rand McNally, Chicago
Taylor, H. (1960) Art and Intellect. Doubleday, New York
Thelen, H. A. (1972) Education and the Human Quest. Chicago University Press, Chicago. (First published 1960)
Whitfield, R. (1971) (Ed) Disciplines of the Curriculum, McGraw Hill, London
Wilson, J. (1969) Moral Thinking. Heinemann, London

Can Mastery Learning be Realized by Programmed Instruction?

R SCHWARZER

THE IDEA OF MASTERY LEARNING

It is an accepted fact in traditional teaching that one realizes the place of learning objectives. The results achieved at the end of each teaching unit show variances which are generally due to the fact that some scholars profit more from the treatment than others on the grounds of their intellect and motivation. Intelligence, motivation, interest, attitudes, concentration etc are all predictors for successful learning. The criterion is, above all, a dependent variable of such predictors which exist in the participants and which vary inter-individually since, because of its uniformity, traditional teaching has more the character of a constant. The variance of learning achievements gets its codifying by categorizing the variously successful individuals into the valencies of the test-result scale. Here one is careful to see that the frequencies are 'sensibly' distributed over this scale, ie that the extreme valencies are more weakly represented and the central valencies more strongly. This approximately corresponds with the conception of normal distribution which plays an important role in the statistics since very many natural phenomena are distributed in the form of a bell-shaped curve. Since one expects a normal distribution where there are very many personality variables, one might think that quantified learning achievements must be distributed in the same way. This is, however, a basic mistake. Teaching always has a particular aim and data for successful learning cannot be compared accidentally; they are based on the examination of planned learning objectives within a group of participants which has already experienced a suitable treatment. A sign of successful teaching would therefore be a strong distribution to the right-hand peak of the successful learning data, in which there is so little variance that the inter-individual differences are minimized. The personality variables thereby lose their predictor function to a great extent and the criterion is decisively determined by the way in which the instruction is carried out. This programmatic statement represents the basic idea of Mastery Learning.

Mastery Learning as a new conception of learning in schools has its source mainly in Carroll (1963) and has recently been introduced into pedagogic discussion, amongst others, by Bloom (1971) and Block (1971). Bloom considers pedagogic endeavours ineffective if efficiency in learning can be represented in the form of a normal distribution (Block, p. 49).

In normal practice, however, one will find normally-distributed data in both the pre-test and the post-test. Then the increase in learning is characterized by a mere shifting of the inter-individual differences. An approximate normal-distribution is to be expected. It is a fact that some scholars begin the process of learning with a more or less good background of learning experience. If then in lessons all scholars are given equal treatment, which is the case with the traditional group-based instruction, the more intelligent, motivated, concentrated and expert scholars will profit more so than others. Under these circumstances, normally-distributed achievements in pre-tests seem plausible. Many teachers, however, do not realize at all that they have not succeeded in providing the appropriate learning conditions for all scholars. Inter-individual differences with respect to the scholars' intelligence, capacity for concentration, etc, which really exist, serve as a justification for the occurrence of such differences in achievements at school. This obviously is due to a certain educational concept. Many teachers regard the normal distribution of school results as a matter of course and think that the bottom of the curve, which represents the failures, is as inevitable as the bottom of the curve which represents persons of small stature.

In this connection Davies (1972) names three indicators for effective, ie dysfunctional instruction:

1. The deliberate destruction of the normal curve of distribution in achievement scores.
2. The achievement of all or most of the learning objectives.
3. The lack of any significant relationship between learning achievement and general ability.

With this, not only is the normally-distributed curve done away with, but in addition to this the post-test variance is smaller than that of the pre-test — a reversal of the traditional idea that treatment effects, among other things, are manifested in an enlarged variance. The third indicator is a consequence of the other two: if the intelligence is normally-distributed and if there is an extreme case where all the scholars have dealt with all the tasks correctly in the efficiency test, the result is a correlation coefficient of zero — as can be easily seen from a scattergram. As an extreme case such as this is hardly likely to occur, one will probably have to be satisfied with a lower or non-significant correlation in Mastery Learning rather than the otherwise average correlation.

According to Bloom (in Block, p. 50) one can expect a correlation coefficient of r = 0.70 and higher under traditional conditions; if, however, the character and quality of teaching and the conceded period of learning are adapted to the characteristics and requirements of any type of learning, the majority will accomplish the learning objectives and the correlation between aptitude and achievement will tend towards zero.

THE USE OF PROGRAMMED TEXTBOOKS
AS A STRATEGY OF MASTERY LEARNING

Indicators for Mastery Learning

The advantages of programmed teaching can be generally characterized as follows:

1. The scholar works independently and develops a responsibility for his learning process.
2. Self-pacing
3. He checks the process of learning after each frame, in this way receiving an immediate feedback which has the character of a reinforcement.
4. He works concentratedly as he will otherwise not achieve the frame which follows.
5. He is increasingly motivated by his experiences of success.
6. It is an intimate method of learning. No scholar can be compromised because of false reactions.
7. Learning is effective since the evaluated programmes are a reliable guarantee for successful learning.

Because of its objectivity in teaching, individualization and systematic reproducibility of successes in learning (reliability), programmed instruction can best be understood as a possible strategy of Mastery Learning. The question here is as to whether this technological strategy, isolated from others as the only system variable, is capable of realizing Mastery Learning. The results obtained from teaching research which are available on this point are contradictory (Schwarzer, 1973a). Before the question can be answered, it must be decided which indicators have made it possible to recognize whether the introduction of a learning programme has led to a Mastery effect or not:

1. There must no longer be predictors for success in learning which have their foundation in the individual, ie his intelligence, ability to concentrate, appreciation for instruction, fore-knowledge, etc must not affect the post-test efficiency significantly; this means that all correlation coefficients with the post-test must not significantly deviate from zero. In addition to this, the variance analysis should not contain any significant main effects of these predictors on the post-test in the form of a criterion variable. All inter-individual differences which influence success in learning in the conventional form of teaching must be compensated for by the conditions which the teaching programme offers. The only (not quantitative) predictor for successful

learning is, therefore, the teaching itself.

2. The anticipated 'homogenizing effect' of the application of a teaching programme must be manifested in a post-test variance smaller than that of the pre-test. This can, on the one hand, be directly inferred from the elementary statistics and, on the other hand, a similar indication is also given from the number of significant differences between school classes or types of schools before and after the treatment. It is, for example, expected that significant differences present in the pre-test between primary school, secondary modern and grammar schools, disappear in the post-test.

3. A factor analysis must never contain a common factor for intelligence and success in learning. Either the post-test variable should form a specific factor or its saturation should be low and distributed over several factors.

As far as technical research is concerned, the learning programme in the light of investigation into Mastery Learning variables offers considerable advantages: the time needed can be directly observed when applying the frames individually, the quality of instruction is objectified as far as teaching aids are concerned and the time allowed in self-pacing. It is, therefore, expected that the Mastery effects handled here are materialized by learning at one's own rate and rhythm (time adaptivity of the teaching system) and by incremental learning, reinforcement and shaping. Should these effects not materialize in certain teaching programmes and controls, this is an indication for the fact that programmed instruction is not suitable as global strategy and that instead investigations must be made into the role of teaching programmes as a foundation for another type of Mastery Learning strategy.

Empiric Investigations

In order to investigate these problems, the author carried out 8 projects with teaching programmes on more than 1,900 scholars in various types of schools in the period from 1970 to 1972. The findings were not consistent. In only one case was the post-test variance smaller than the pre-test variance and in all cases there was a more or less great number of intelligence sub-tests which correlated significantly with the post-test performance.

The investigations showed that intelligence and subject-restricted learning experience each explain approximately one-quarter of the post-test variance and that the linear combination of these two predictors is the most effective prediction of learning success. These effects are not considerably different from those to be found in traditional teaching. The only exception here is the comprehensive school; here, with a right-hand peak distribution, the post-test variance and correlation coefficients are lower.* One can add

---

*That the one is connected with the other is statistically of slight importance but alters nothing as far as the indicator function for Mastery Learning is concerned.

251

the hypothesis mentioned above to this, namely that the willingness to adopt technological innovations, and in particular for Mastery Learning, is greater in a structurally reformed system than anywhere else; this Mastery effect for comprehensive schools cannot, however, be generalized since this incomplete investigation of the latest project was only carried out on 6 classes of one comprehensive school.

The effects of the two best predictors — intelligence (including ability to understand instruction) and foreknowledge — on successful learning were tested variance-analytically. Significant effects of the two independent variables were evident in all cases. Successful learning in programmed instruction is, to a certain extent, dependent upon the particular and general learning background of the individual. Furthermore, success in learning exhibited a high saturation in one intelligence factor in almost all factor analyses.

The results of the latest investigation which are summarized here may stand for all the other experiments. These findings are connected with the evaluation of experimental scientific teaching programmes 'Umgang mit Waage und Messzylinder' (Use of scales and measuring cylinder) by Hofsommer/Schwarzer (cf. Schwarzer, 1973b). The teaching programme comprises 120 units and requires an average time of 257 minutes. It was applied in 17 classes (N = approx. 500) of all types of schools to scholars in their fourth to sixth school year. The pre-test values were normally distributed, the post-test values right-hand peaked (checking of normal-distribution with Chi-Square-Test). Because of the form of distribution some further parametric calculations were carried out with area-transformed values. Furthermore, the data set of the scholars in comprehensive schools (6 forms; N=173) was treated separately because the instruments used in the investigation in some cases differed. Because of irrepresentative variability a stratified accidental data set (N=90) was derived from the data set of the three traditional types of schools.

In Mastery Learning the post-test variance should be significantly smaller than the pre-test variance. The t-test check of the correlated variance (cf McNemar, p. 282) rendered this effect for the data of the comprehensive school scholars whereas there were no differences with regard to the data of the traditional school types.

According to Mastery Learning the different types of schools ought not to have significantly differed after application of the programme. A simple variance analysis of the post-test with regard to the school types as well as a co-variance analysis for which the pre-test served as a concomitant variate, rendered, however, most significant F-values. The desired homogenity did not occur.

It is furthermore a question of whether the inter-individually varying intelligence has become effective as a predictor for successful learning.

252

a) In the correlation matrix of the traditional types of schools, the 9 P-S-B sub-tests (Horn, 1969) were included as variables. Seven of these had a correlation with the post-test which varied extremely significantly from zero. The highest simple correlations of the post-test are with the pre-test ($r=0.60$) and with the P-S-B 4 ('Reasoning'; $r=0.54$). The linear combination of these two predictors result in $R_{1(23)}=0.68$, which explains almost half of the post-test variance.

b) In the correlation matrix of the comprehensive school, all 6 intelligence sub-tests of the KLI4+ (Schröder, 1970) had an average but very significant correlation with the post-test. The highest simple correlation is that with the sub-test RA ('Arithmetical Comprehension'; $r=0.42$). The pre-test-post-test-correlations coefficient amounts to $r=0.30$ (1% level). The combination of 17 predictors in the regression analysis results in $r=0.55$ (1% level).

An elucidation of only slightly more than 25% of the variance of successful learning in the case of 17 predictors, to which not only the intellectual variables but also subject-restricted learning success, ability to concentrate and performance motivation belong, is rather inadequate. But this is in line with the purpose of the investigation. In this quantity of predictors there is no variable which makes a useful prediction of the criterion possible. From this aspect, it is therefore a Mastery effect.

Each time, the two factor analyses of the data sets resulted, among other things, in a common factor for intelligence and success in learning. All the calculated multi-dimensional analyses of variance with the post-test as a criterion resulted in significant main effects of the predictors 'intelligence' and 'foreknowledge'.

On the whole, therefore, the findings tend not to come up to the expectations which programmed instruction as a strategy of Mastery Learning promised. Even though the interpretation and generalization of some individual investigations may sometimes appear doubtful as far as method is concerned, on the basis of the many completed and incomplete experiments with various teaching programmes on accidental controls from five types of schools and six age groups, a cumulative generalization of the results can be made in so far as linear teaching programmes as a method on its own do not represent a suitable strategy for mastery learning. It must however be mentioned, with reservations, that the situation could change where branched and computerized teaching programmes are employed over a greater period of time, since the present investigations are restricted in three respects: these are (1) linear programmes; (2) book programmes, and (3) it was always a very short learning phase of only approximately 50 to 500 minutes. For this reason the teaching programme as a single instrument of learning can only be rejected in the light of such conditions.

The pedagogic optimism which characterizes the whole concept has nevertheless been depressed and the bright technological hopes have been confronted with sobering findings which point to the necessity of developing other strategies and of investigating on a wider scale as to how to estimate what value teaching objectifying methods such as programmed instruction can have as an element of an optimal strategy of Mastery Learning. This is by no means an attempt to contradict the basic assumption that the inter-individually different social-cultural and anthropogenic qualifications of the scholar can lose their determining function in the process of learning at school by creating particular system variables. The present investigation was necessary to steer the general interest in research within Mastery Learning into regions, the empirical exploration of which has now become extremely urgent.

Subject Specific Resources—a Decentralized Approach

M W STEVENI

A CASE FOR SPECIALIZATION

"69. I suspect that system makers in general are not of much more use, each in his own domain, than, in that of Pomona, the old women that tied cherries upon sticks, for the more portableness of the same. To cultivate well, and choose well, your cherries, is of some importance; but if they can be had in their own wild way of clustering about their crabbed stalks, it is a better connection for them than any others;"

John Ruskin

These words from a great and controversial Art Educator of the nineteenth century should give us all cause to stop and think about the 'beaded symmetry' on the 'exalting stick', that as educators we are often tempted to avail ourselves. I take it that this plea of Ruskin's is one for less use of sequential curricula and the forms of linear indexing that are inevitable for this style of teaching. I often wonder how John Ruskin would have rated as an Educator of the present day. Stripped of all his nineteenth century moralizing, and often overstated opinions, I think that he would emerge as an even greater figure; in present day parlance his thinking was much more lateral than vertical. His operational mechanisms were ones of symbolic analogy, and rather than use a word like 'po' to delay judgment (de Bono, 1970), he used controversy and argument instead (Whistler, 1890).

As much as one is tempted to speculate about the possible educational strategies of John Ruskin in this present age, I think that I can say one thing with certainty, and that is that he would have worked very much within the framework of his own sphere of understanding, that of the arts, and the power of his analogy would have been emasculated by any attempt to use a more generalized form of language or understanding.

In an age where the alternative to educational integration can only be seen by some of our profession as educational disintegration, I am putting forward a plea for specialization. In an age of educational cost effectiveness, and centralization of resources, I am putting forward a plea for decentralization.

THE SMALL DEPARTMENT

The School of Art Education is part of the Birmingham Polytechnic and has always been a small unit in educational terms, as have the other specialist Art Teacher Training establishments in this country. Traditionally they have been associated with Colleges of Art, rather than Colleges of Education or University Departments of Education, and it has often seemed that because of their separateness they have been regarded as rather an uncomfortable anachronism by those who have to direct the course of educational progress. Having had experience in both large and small educational establishments, I think that I can say with confidence that the small unit such as ours, is and always will be an invaluable testing ground for new ideas. We are proud of the fact that if needs be we can change utterly once a year, for our courses are all post graduate and of one year duration. We are large enough (14 members of staff) to be able to employ our own experts in the educational sciences (if they may be so regarded), yet we are small enough to have very little difficulty in communicating with one another. Curriculum reform and re-evaluation is a matter of constant comment that is then crystallized in a more formal kind of meeting. It is only natural that our programme has over the years adjusted itself to the type of student that we receive. In practical terms this means that at present we have a network system of optional courses for the students to choose from, and a strongly structured tutorial system for counselling. We have discovered that there are certain inevitable corollaries to this type of work that have meant a complete reappraisal of our technology and resources.

Newton Harrison, American West Coast artist, recently showed a piece in the Hayward Gallery in London that very neatly typified the situation that we are in; no doubt many of you will remember press comments about Sick and Mangy Catfish in Polythene tanks. In fact what he was doing was to display what was hopefully a complete ecological system of marine life, that had certain food inputs, and procedures associated with keeping it, but to a large extent depended upon one part of it catering for the needs of another part.

Just as he intimated with his fish and marine life that there were certain entry and exit points to the system and methods contained within it, so there are with our own department. To a large extent we feed upon ourselves: both staff and students. The way in which we feed and the entry and exit points of our system are just as definable as Newton Harrison's. Just as it was important to actually see the fish, so it is with us. In terms of the system that we represent, our existential unrealities are as important as the empirical and rational structures that we can describe.

PROBLEMS OF DEFINITION

The classification of what we do, and what we are concerned with is perhaps the most central of our problems. It would be quite possible to say that a re-source does not become a resource until it has been classified as one. But this is only seeing it from one point of view. Norman Beswick says "A resource includes anything which may be an object of study or stimulus to the pupil...". This seems to indicate that somebody has to say that certain things rather than other things are useful resources. The person who usually defines these as being useful is the teacher or librarian. Because of the way that we work, we would prefer to amend the definition to "anything which is **found** to be an object of study or stimulus by the pupil". This would seem to rename resource centres as 'possible' resource centres, and places the onus for declaration of what may, or may not, be a resource on the user rather than the keeper of the centre.

A resource has to possess a certain degree of possibility for fitting with-in the contextural basis of understanding that the user holds. In a school situa-tion, this basis of understanding has been recently given by the staff to the pupil, and it is quite logical for the staff to define what usefully obtains to it. In our own case we know that it is absolutely fundamental for us to be 'user orientated' rather than 'keeper orientated'. We do in fact accept anything that any person working within our establishment, either staff or student, cares to give us.

This is the point where we begin to see the difference between a library and a resource centre. A library is able to accommodate any book item that is given to it because the book has already been ascribed a meaning and an intention by the author. However, this is not so for other resource forms. A slide of an old broken chair may owe its existence to different factors, many of which may be highly specialized or even private to the person presenting it.

To open our argument up a little, we could say that a Martian could not use our centre unless he not only had a good command of English, but was also familiar with the underlying processes that helped us to structure our thought and rationalize about it in language terms. We have been presented with accounts of man's ability to structure languages in recent years, but until we know more about this, and can assume that all men have similar structuring abilities, we must surmize that experience, if nothing else, will force our user to place different constructs upon our wares. How significantly different is a Martian from an Engineer in our terms? We are concerned with the Arts, if a person comes to us asking engineer-like questions, can we help him? A resource can only have significance if it has sense for the person that finds it; the person offering an item to the resource centre will only be able to do so if it fits within the framework of what the centre repre-sents. Resources cannot exist unless they are accommodated within known-about frameworks of meaning, but what kind of meaning?

PROBLEMS OF DESCRIPTION

We are now faced with some fascinating problems of description and procedure. If the user and the keeper of the system were both to have common referential points of understanding, the problem would be easy. Any visual image cannot be interpreted in the same way as a structure of words, because it can have a multiplicity of identity. Merleau-Ponty illuminates some of the difficulties of understanding the visual object when talking about the presence of work of art compared with normal visual reality. "The animals painted on the walls of Lasceau are not there in the same way as the fissures and limestone formations, but they are not elsewhere . . . . . I would be at great pains to say where is the painting I am looking at". (Osbourne, 1972)

I can only comment that a geologist would probably have attempted to describe this phenomena from a rather different point of view.

Library systems usually assume a unity of understanding which is represented by coded linear patterns of reference. They get by on the assumption that most people can assume this linear description of knowledge if they are trained to do so, and they can be trained very quickly, because the present educational structure reflects this pattern. Whether they will continue to do so depends upon the path that education will take. Much is being written about the process of integrating knowledge by educationalists, and this must mean that the structure of educational practice will be much more 'three dimensional' than it has been. Jean Piaget has been investigating the links between a group of subject areas especially concerned with education and can see many difficulties here. He comments that Biology, Chemistry, Physics and also Mathematics are clearly defined in a hierarchical sense, and goes on to say: ". . . in the human sciences, interactions are very much weaker, because they lack a hierarchical structure, and for various other reasons. For example, there is no close relationship of a hierarchical order between structural linguistics, econometrics, experimental psychology, logic and so on, and the total absence of exchange between these disciplines may well prevent us from seeing illuminating connections which would be provided by cybernetics or information theory." (Piaget, 1972)

To this I would add the personal comment that the area with which we are concerned in the Arts is more complex still, because it uses the basically private languages of the arts to manipulate metaphoric and analagistic systems that are not meant to be taken at face value in the first place. We must learn to understand what we have before we can adequately communicate and integrate with other disciplines.

Another problem is one of specific identity as a resource, rather than as information or knowledge. If one accepts a definition of a resource as being "any item or system that is found to be an object of study or stimulus by the pupil" we must now consider the resource as a possible object of study, rather than purely one of stimulus. How can one best structure the description of what one has if it is to be recorded in an index that will provide some indication of a possible educational potential. A method of grouping that is commonly used is that of actually physically boxing groups of linked material. The main difficulty with this procedure is that of blocking the use of materials, unless they are duplicated, for other purposes.

We realize that, although the definitions that we are making are at the moment only very sketchy, and encompass what could be termed the media form as well as indicating linked units of items that can fit within instructional programmes, they do economize on actual material and give some indication of teaching potential.

The start of this process of definition would seem to be a clear one of what you consider an item to be — a book, a paragraph in a book, a whole film, and so on. All this is quite easy. However, it is not quite so easy to describe what it is that you have got because the parameters of this kind of description are rather more subtle than a description of media form. A teacher can be considered in this context as being a very complex advice giving structure with infinite play-back possibility. A book will only give one point of view, a slide will present an ambiguous point of view, because it has no stated authority. All of these items can be appreciated if one is able to physically handle the object, but if one is to use techniques such as microfilming where reliance upon an intermediate indexing vehicle is of paramount importance, these clues to possible educational identity should ideally be considered and commented upon.

To compound this problem of specific possible educational identity of an item, one must also mention that there is a factor of negative identity that plays an important part when one makes choices of this nature. If a positive structure is described, 'known-about' classes of objects that are not this, form part of a mental logical structure concerning the object first considered. Mathematically this is quite a normal concept, and any housewife could adequately describe the process of rejection for positive reasons. Although we have not managed to do anything about this to date, methods of establishing 'negatively structured feature searches' are at least in our minds.

INDEXING PROCEDURES

We use three main methods of indexing — a central resource data card, that is a notched edge Kalamazoo fact finder card, an optical coincidence system, manufactured by Ansons, and a linear findex strip index, manufactured by Kalamazoo.

The central data resource card that we have devised is the subject of an investigation that we are conducting for the Leverhulme Foundation as a major project that will last for one year. Referring to Figure 1 you will

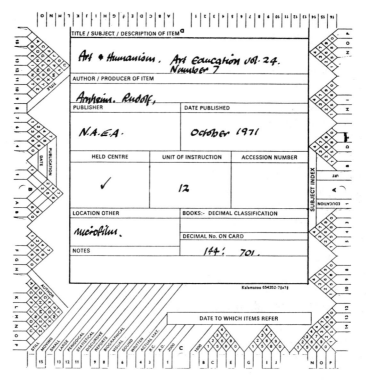

Figure 1

notice that all four sides of the card are capable of notching, the card is then inserted into a machine with rectangular rods fitted into the base, which then vibrates the notched cards downwards. This means that insertion into the machine, and removal from it can be very speedy, and the programme of rods which can include as many as 32 can be left set in the machine while many changes of cards are achieved. We use this system for its relative economy, and ease of use. We have looked at other systems that use needle sort, but have decided that they are not quite so quick as this system. As can be seen, the system is an item one, the most important element of which is on side A, and comprises two sets of pyramid sorts, each one representing the Dewey Decimal system into three figures. The group on the right takes precedence over the group on the left, and works as a subject area. The group on the left works as a predicate, thus, the technology of etching and drypoint for example, would be 600-767. In terms of actually using the system, this will mean that if we want to pick a general heading in the 100s we could just rod for a 6 on the left hand side, and a 7 with the 00 being implied in both cases on the right hand side, and get Technology and the Arts, and the user would browse through the cards that came out in this case. So,

260

it can be seen that this system can be more or less specific as the occasion demands. Noahs Prywes has commented in an article on Information Storage and Retrieval with regard to computer use, that most coordinate indexing lacks the degree of stratification necessary for some kinds of search. He also says that if groups of terms are to be used two groups of more or less equal numbers of terms would also facilitate a computer programme (Prywes, 1969).

As our system is intended for eventual change over to computer use, we consider that this 'colon-like' system is of great advantage to the mechanical and computerized methods of sorting.

Side B on the card is fairly self-explanatory. The left hand side of side C is we feel of some interest, because it is a feature list concerning media forms. We started with a thesaurus list of 82 terms concerning media forms which included physical attributes such as film or book form, as well as an indication of the implied educational (as far as we were concerned) identity of the item, but have now adopted this system as one that will provide greater flexibility. It is backed by a thesaurus authority of terms that we actually use to obviate any need for ambiguity, although it is used as a list of sense terms at the same time. Extension D has the capacity of one of a million seen as a series of five notch unit pyramids, and is used to make a list of unit instruction programmes, and link items such as Ministry Reports, or sets of magazines. In this way, sets and instructional units do not need to be physically assembled in any sense, but can exist as notches on the central data card, with the added possibility of dual entry cards if any one item is considered in more than one programme.

Finally, in many cases, a 6 x 4 microfische sheet is attached to the back of the card on side D, so that an actual item of information is retrieved with the card and can be viewed on the viewing systems that we have. The microfilm camera that we use is a Kodak Starfile RVA2 camera, and we use two heads — one for colour microfilm, and the other black and white, both 16mm. If so desired the microfische sheet can be reproduced in diazzo form on an Atlantic printer and developer unit, and if a full size sheet is required, actual size copies can be made on a PFC 1A unit, both again made by Rekodak. We have maintained close links with Rekodak and also Kalamazoo, and both firms have given us a great deal of assistance in starting the programming. The designing of the central data resource card has taken nearly two years, and is the result of several previous cards in which we have attempted different systems, usually of a thesaurus with a number of other operational and descriptive words that can be applied to the Thesaurus. We have another card which is used in a very specialist capacity concerning information about Art Therapy, and this tends to use this type of system rather than the authority of the Dewey permed against Dewey that we are using for the central one.

We are currently tending to regard the card as an intermediary vehicle rather than use it for an original search every time, and by means of photocopying, we can make up preselections of cards quite rapidly. Feature coordinate systems of reference have recently been seen as at least one answer to the problem of cross fertilization of knowledge. We have looked at these, and use an OCCI feature system for slide classification, but we can see that as a central system it could prove to be very self-justifying in that it would provide the answers that are expected too easily, unless great care is taken. Whether it is really capable of providing a broad enough base of information yet remains to be seen. Ralph Munroe Eaton comments well upon another difficulty of the feature analysis when he says, "But is a description an analysis? ..... I can analyse an object into parts a, b and c, which are related in a certain way. I can discover that my inkwell is composed of a small glass jar with a glass cover, and this seems to be genuine analysis. But if I find that the inkwell is black, and that it is on the table, I am discovering relations and qualities which attach to it, and these do not seem to be parts in the same sense." (Eaton, 1964)

The difference between description and analysis of an item is a problem that will have to be ironed out if the system is going to be capable of much expansion. We have already noticed that the point where a feature sheet of a more analytic nature is being substituted for one of a more descriptive nature instead of them both being used. This practice is quite quickly reached after one gets to a certain optimum size even when working within a discipline area as we are.

Our slide collection is contained in a series of visual wallets of 24, and each set of 24 is referred to on the central data card as well as the individual slides having a reference on an optical coincidence system. We use seven main headings that seem to fit our needs, but have reservations about them for the reasons stated above. The headings are:

1. Date or time produced (eg 1971)
2. Media type or process used (eg Paint, Lithography etc)
3. Mental process implied (eg Art, Maths, Conceptual etc)
4. The group or persons represented (eg Infants, Adolescents, or in the case of persons, Cizek, Marion Richardson etc)
5. Producer of the slide (eg Commercial, Staff, Student etc)
6. Place produced (eg Birmingham, Bridgenorth School, Sidcot School etc)
7. Objective content (eg Figures, animals, houses, clothing, natural form etc).

USE OF THE CENTRE

I have indicated some of the central factors concerning description and specific identity of educational resources that interest us most. It must by now be obvious that resources are going to be handled differently in different places in terms of systems of description, and indeed, what may be a resource for one situation, is not so for another. The ideal form of resources would be a form of telepathy, with a central data bank, plus the possibility of teleporting whatever one needed. Putting aside the political question of who is going to be allowed access to such a system, it would not be a practical possibility because one would still have to define what it was that one wanted, within the framework of a known about tangible world. It is not such a simple problem as transposing the language associated with one discipline area with the language associated with another. We are all placed somewhere between the telepathy idea and the other extreme of a Brownie pack asking direct questions of Brown Owl, and getting direct answers of an idiosyncratic nature. Perhaps the clue to sensible operation of a resource centre is to say that we are all in different places and the differences should indicate the referential clues to procedures of operating the system.

We would like to establish a principle that out of every ten staff members in a department such as ours, at least two of them would be engaged whole time in assembling resources for the other eight, and the students in their charge. Their task would be not so much to involve themselves in all of the procedures but to encourage others to feed in as well as to draw out, so that a cyclical pattern of use would develop with the insertion of fresh material that lies outside the knowledge and understanding of those concerned at various points. Using the microfilm, tape and self-produced slide procedures that we are able to because of our particular skills, it would seem that we are moving in this direction. We would emphasize that we are not a library, and we do not aim to present an authoritative selection of all the material that it is possible to gather in our area. We are biased and our bias not only lies within the way in which we describe our items, but also in the type and extent of material that we have.

Finally, it is our intention to engage in real discourse and exchange with other institutions such as ours as well as individuals; not only in this country but throughout the world. The word discourse is used advisedly, because the relationship of the user to our system can never be a passive one. We have consciously built into our system the ability to transport material cheaply and effectively over long distances, and this was one of our original design intentions. If an old woman from Pomona ever does walk in our midst, we would hope that our very unstraight sticks that the cherries of knowledge we carry are on, are at least not seen as plastic imitations of a real branch.

REFERENCES

Beswick, N. Schools Council Paper No. 43
Bono, E. de (1970) A Text Book of Creativity. Ward Lock Educational, London
Eaton, R. M. (1964) Symbolism and Truth: an introduction to the Theory of Knowledge. Dover Publications, New York. First published by Harvard University Press 1925. Page 127
Osbourne, H. (ed) (1972) from an article 'Eye and Mind in Aesthetics'.

Oxford University Press, London. First published in 'The Primary of Perception', North Western University Press 1964. Translated by Carleton Dallery

Piaget, J. (1972) Psychology and Epistomology towards a Theory of Knowledge, translated by P. A. Wells. Penguin University Books, London

Prywes, N. S. (1969) in 'Survey of Cybonetics' (Ed) J. Rowes. Illiffe Books Ltd., London

Ruskin, J. (1886) Frondes Agrestes Readings in Modern Painters. George Allen, London

Whistler (1890) The gentle art of making enemies. William Heineman, London

A Study on Instruction Programs for CAI System—Problems of Fatigue and Assessment Method in CAI

H SUMI, H ITAYA,
M SHIMADA, K YAGI

This paper describes solutions to the two major problems arisen out of learning courses by the biggest CAI System in Japan, developed by the Japan Society for the Promotion of Machine Industry.

The two major problems are concerned with fatigue involved in study and assessment by the tests.

Eight instruction programs for the CAI system were developed in 1971 by the Society. Each program was prepared for students having scholarship equivalent to senior high school graduates, and was intended to be finished in approximately 20 hours of study. As a result of actual instruction by using these programs for the CAI system and of subsequent surveys of various kinds, it was found that the CAI study was more pleasant and easier to understand than conventional studies by lecture, and that the effects of study by this system were superior to those by lecture. However, at the same time, it was found that the CAI study involves more fatigue than study by lecture.

One of the major problems in the CAI study is fatigue. Why do students get more tired in the CAI study? As a result of analysis of fatigue factors, it was revealed that the item having the highest correlation with fatigue was "Was your study by the CAI system pleasant?" Though this fact tells that the study by the CAI system is more pleasant than the conventional one by lecture, it may be said that the instruction programs still have room for improvement. The item having the second highest correlation with fatigue was concerned with study hours. That is to say, it may be said that appropriate study hours are essential for the reduction of fatigue in study. Then, analysis of study hours was made by questionnaire and flicker tests. In consequence, it was found that appropriate study hours per chapter should be about 40 minutes, and a continuous study session should be limited to one hour or one hour and a half from the viewpoint of reduction of fatigue.

In order to improve instruction programs for the CAI system, it was necessary to assess them in appropriate methods. Various methods were conceivable for assessment such as chapter-end questionnaire, course-end questionnaire, examination of contents of slides, measurements of study hours, simulation of the CAI study, etc. We noticed, however, through actual practices that the assessment method by readiness, pre- and post-tests had some problems. One of them was the necessity of checking whether the contents of readiness tests were really appropriate or not. Second problem was that marks in readiness test should be regarded as a standard to take a student ready to study the subject. This paper suggests a solution for these problems.

PEARL SYSTEM DEVELOPED BY THE JAPAN SOCIETY FOR THE PROMOTION OF MACHINE INDUSTRY AND ITS FEATURES

The Japan Society for the Promotion of Machine Industry decided in November 1968 to develop and promote diffusion of the CAI System as one of its projects for diffusion and promotion of new machines. The Society organized a committee for the project (chairman: Dr Shigeru Watanabe, Professor of the Tokyo University), performed a joint development with co-operation of related companies, and finally completed this CAI System in March 1972. Cost and expenses required for the completion amounted to about US $ 1 mil. This CAI System was named PEARL (Programmed Editor and Automated Resources for Learning).

The greatest feature of this system is that an electronic computer system composed of 3 mini-computers and a magnetic disc memory device of 2.5 MW was designed and manufactured so as to control over 30 units of study terminal devices simultaneously.

Another major feature is that the CAI language and its compiler were also developed as softwares suitable for CAI study. This CAI language can easily be understood and used not only by programmers but also by its instructors – authors of the instruction programs.

Configuration of the CAI system is shown in Figure 1. The terminal devices comprise two kinds, one is called the type-I terminal device, and the other, type-II. This system has 8 type-I terminal devices and each consists of a random access slide device (RAS), a CRT Display device, a random access audio device (RAA), a keyboard (KB), and a light pen (LPN). The system has 22 type-II terminal devices and each consists of a random access slide device (RAS) and a keyboard (KB). All these 30 sets of terminal devices are installed in the Promotion of Machine Industry Building, and the following companies co-operated in completion of this system:

Hitachi, Ltd: Electronic computer system

Nippon Electric Co: Keyboards, printers and booths

Tokyo Shibaura Electric Co: Random access slides and random access
audio devices

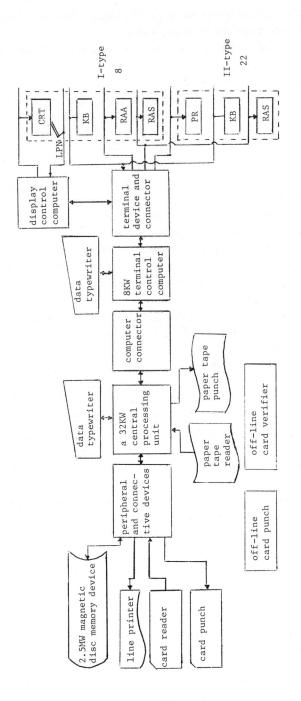

Figure 1. Total network of the CAI system

Matsushita Electric Industrial Co: CRT display devices with light pens
The CAI system has the following features:

(1) All students are able to have a conversation with the system within 3 seconds of access time.

(2) As the form of response to questions, not only multiple choice, but also constructed response, such as answering by use of English letters, Japanese phonetic (KANA) letters and figures are available. Answers also can be made by detecting a specific area on the screen with a light pen.

(3) The system is designed so that students can not only answer questions and explanations presented by the instruction program, but also make requests for hints, correct answers and reference materials when necessary. In other words, this system is designed to meet various requirements of students without forcing instruction materials one-sidedly.

(4) When a student answers a question presented, the computer records his results, the steps of the program he passed and the time he needed. It can judge the ability of the student and present the next question according to his ability. That is, branching is employed for instruction programs as the methods of effective learning.

(5) The process of study is recorded and displayed. Contents of the record include the name of the lesson course, the name of the student, the question presented, the answer and the time spent.

Instruction programs developed so far are for those who have scholarship equal to senior high school graduates, totalling 11 courses, and each program is intended to require 9 to 20 hours for completion of learning. Courses available are: (1) NC Machine Tools, (2) FORTRAN, (3) Introduction to Electronic Computer, (4) COBOL, (5) Repair techniques of Colour Television Sets, (6) Introduction to APT, (7) PERT, (8) Training of Electric Engineers, (9) System Engineering, (10) Public Nuisance, and (11) Technical English.

Among instruction programs mentioned, (1) through (8) were developed in 1971, while those (9) through (11) were developed in 1972.

In preparing these instruction programs, the following original methods and procedures had been employed:

The 1st stage: Compilation of the CAI instruction program, and trial use and debugging by the programmer.

The 2nd stage: First assessment by the assessment group.

The 3rd stage: Revision by the programmers.

The 4th stage: Second assessment by the assessment group.

The 5th stage: Trial use and assessment by the Japan Society for the Promotion of Machine Industry.

The assessment group mentioned above is a group organized for the purpose of assessing instruction programs, and does not include the programmers of the instruction programs. The assessment group adopted an assessment method based on a principle of student testing. That is, the group made students study the courses in practice, and then made assessment for them based on the results of tests, examination of contents of slides, opinions and impressions of the students.

The Japan Society for the Promotion of Machine Industry made reassessment and tried comparison experiments between conventional study by lecture and study by the CAI system.

The following problems of fatigue and an assessment method came out from the process of review of these instruction programs.

PROBLEM OF FATIGUE

ANALYSIS OF FATIGUE FACTORS

As a result of experimental studies performed for the purpose of comparing effects of the CAI study with those of study by lecture, it was found that the CAI study was superior to the conventional one and that the study hours were reduced to almost half of those by lecture. From analysis made on a questionnaire survey conducted after completion of study, it was also found that the CAI study was more pleasant than conventional one by lecture (57%), and easier to understand (56%).

However, as negative opinions for the CAI study, it was pointed out that some students got more tired (38%) than conventional study, or felt like quitting the study halfway (64%). (For further details, refer to the paper 'Computer Assisted Instruction' by ICCC.)

Under these circumstances, much better results of education by the CAI system can be expected by eliminating causes of fatigue. Indeed, some people say that the involvement of fatigue in the CAI study comes from the fact that the study is so condensed, and that this fact is not the essential defect of the CAI study. However, if the causes of fatigue can be eliminated, and so long as the effects of study are not lowered by the elimination of fatigue, it would be unreasonable to leave the study as fatiguing one. From this point of view, analysis of cause of fatigue is a very important theme. Then, what are the factors of fatigue?

Here, we will analyze results of chapter-end questionnaire survey conducted at the end of chapter of studies by CAI as a method to search for possible causes of fatigue. As for concrete items of the chapter-end questionnaire, refer to Table I.

In order to select items having a high correlation with the item (15) 'Tired or bored' in this chapter-end questionnaire, we prepare a 3 x 3 contingency table as seen in Table II, and obtain a coefficient of contingency (c). This coefficient is obtained from the following equation:

$$c = \sqrt{\chi^2 / (\chi^2 + N)},$$
$$= N. \Sigma\Sigma(aij/Ai.A.j + 1)$$

Table I. Chapter-end questionnaire

(1) Could you operate the device easily?

(2) Generally could you see the slides well?

(3) Could you read the typed letters well?

(4) Was the arrangement of instruction materials appropriate?

(5) Could you understand explanations well?

(6) Could you understand the meaning of question well?

(7) Generally could you understand meanings of terms well?

(8) Were instructions for answering easy to understand?

(9) Were the hints easy to understand?

(10) Did you find any errors in the instruction materials contents?

(11) Could you understand presented answers completely?

(12) Did you study by the CAI system arouse your will to study much?

(13) Did you feel study by the CAI system pleasant?

(14) Did you answer the question with confidence?

(15) Did you get tired or bored much?

(16) Did you take any notes during study?

(17) Could you study at your own pace?

(18) Generally did you feel the contents of study difficult?

(19) Did you feel the study hours of this chapter appropriate?

(20) Other remarks, opinions, etc.

Table II. Analysis of causes of fatigue (3 x 3 contingency table)

Fatigue Explanation	Much	Normal	Little	Total
Hard to understand	a_{11}	a_{12}	a_{13}	$A_1.$
Normal	a_{21}	a_{22}	a_{23}	$A_2.$
Easy to understand	a_{31}	a_{32}	a_{33}	$A_3.$
Total	$A._1$	$A._2$	$A._3$	N

Results of analysis:

The values of coefficient of contingency obtained from the chapter-end questionnaire are shown in Tables III and IV. As seen from these tables, the values of coefficient vary depending on each instruction program. It seems that these variations are due to different causes of fatigue by each instruction program, and therefore they are in a certain sense data full of suggestions. Nevertheless, in order to consider the study by the CAI system as a whole, we tried to analyse causes of fatigue by the average values of coefficient of contingency.

Table III. Analysis of causes of fatigue
(Values of coefficient of contingency by items)

Instruction program Item	P1	P2	P3	P4	P5	P6	Average	Total
1. Operation of device	0.162	0.257	0.103	0.254	0.287	0.248	0.218	0.155
2. Slides	0.123	0.239	0.206	0.263	0.330	0.441	0.267	0.155
3. Typed letters	0.126	0.258	0.161	0.196	0.164	0.269	0.196	0.170
4. Arrangement of materials	0.199	0.202	0.358	0.355	0.455	0.402	0.329	0.247
5. Explanation	0.452	0.386	0.285	0.398	0.442	0.378	0.390	0.315
6. Meaning of questions	0.384	0.265	0.280	0.394	0.433	0.355	0.352	0.255
7. Meaning of terms and marks	0.347	0.176	0.278	0.329	0.394	0.415	0.323	0.249
8. Indication of answering method	0.347	0.260	0.346	0.456	0.341	0.413	0.361	0.326
9. Hints	0.205	0.227	0.441	0.259	0.613	0.274	0.337	0.280
10. Error in contents	0.196	0.231	0.168	0.176	0.271	0.386	0.238	0.177
11. Correct answers presented	0.406	0.147	0.289	0.454	0.345	0.445	0.238	0.268
12. Motivation	0.403	0.332	0.359	0.471	0.448	0.253	0.378	0.376
13. Pleasantness of study	0.436	0.437	0.508	0.443	0.366	0.284	0.412	0.451
14. Confidence in answers	0.351	0.402	0.316	0.244	0.513	0.347	0.362	0.333
16. Notes during study	0.260	0.227	0.169	0.145	0.174	0.360	0.294	0.137
17. Tempo of study progress	0.269	0.179	0.201	0.422	0.453	0.588	0.352	0.214
18. Contents of text	0.40	0.417	0.378	0.343	0.436	0.272	0.375	0.364
19. Study hours of this chapter	0.222	0.391	0.417	0.394	0.506	0.527	0.410	0.360
Number of data	191	577	389	240	102	61	1560	1560

Remarks: (1) The average in the table is the simple average of the coefficient of contingencies
(2) The total shows coefficient of contingencies summarized by items from P1 to P6

Table IV. Analysis of factors of fatigue (coefficient of contingencies
and averaged value by items)

Coefficient of contingencies C Item	0.1	0.2	0.3	0.4	0.5	0.6
1. Operation of device						
2. Slides						
3. Typed letters						
4. Arrangement of materials						
5. Explanation						
6. Meaning of questions						
7. Meaning of terms and marks						
8. Indication of answering method						
9. Hints						
10. Error in contents						
11. Correct answers presented						
12. Motivation						
13. Pleasantness of study						
14. Confidence in answers						
15. Notes during study						
16. Tempo of study progress						
17. Contents of text						
18. Study hours of this chapter						

Remarks: (1) The mark 'x' indicates coefficient of contingencies by items on each instruction program
(2) Full line shows simple average value of (1) above
(3) Dotted line indicates coefficient of contingencies summarized by instruction programs
from P1 to P6

It was item (13) 'Did you feel the CAI study pleasant?' that the value of coefficient of contingency (c) was the greatest (c = 0.412485). Items that follow are item (19) 'Did you feel the study hours of this chapter appropriate?' (c = 0.40954), item (5) 'Could you understand explanations well' (c = 0.39023), item (12) 'Did the study by the CAI system arouse your will to study' (c = 0.37770), and item (18) 'Generally, did you feel the contents of study difficult?' (c = 0.37509). These correlations were under the 'significant' level of 0.001 by x^2 test. The item that had the highest correlation with fatigue 'Did you feel the CAI study pleasant?' suggests a very important problem. That is to say, in order to solve the problem of fatigue, any instruction program should be prepared so that the study can be attractive. But, what actions should we take in order to attain this objective? This is a very difficult problem, and it is not easy to present solutions.

Here, we will investigate the problem of study hours, the item that had the second highest correlation with fatigue. How long would be the proper study hour by the CAI system? In order to solve the problem, we made investigation into the actual time required by those who responded to the chapter-end questionnaire that the time was (a) appropriate, (b) too long, and (c) too short respectively for the chapter-end questionnaire, and obtain their averages. The results are shown in Table V. As seen from the Table, the average study hours of those who responded that the time was appropriate were 34.8 to 45.0 minutes. The average study hours of those who responded that the time was too long were 56.0 to 91.6 minutes while those of those who responded as too short were 21.1 to 35.4 minutes. Though study hours per chapter depend on the course, it can be said that the appropriate study hour should be about forty minutes from the viewpoint of fatigue.

Table V

Item Instruction programs	Appropriate			Too long			Too short		
	Number of persons	Average	S.D.	Number of persons	Average	S.D.	Number of persons	Average	S.D.
N.C. Machine Tools	89	39.82	23.82	39	91.59	42.67	12	23.00	12.17
Introduction to electronic computer	123	34.82	25.06	37	80.38	55.95	28	14.32	94.27
FORTRAN	146	39.45	19.43	45	63.36	26.12	4	23.00	11.18
COBOL	120	45.02	20.91	24	56.04	29.72	8	35.38	15.70
Repair techniques of Colour TV	40	35.80	17.45	13	64.85	14.84	17	12.06	13.67

How does the degree of tiredness change, when study hours per chapter are fixed to about 40 minutes and the CAI study continues more than 40 minutes? With regard to this problem, the flicker values obtained from the survey conducted to investigate the degree of tiredness of students would be instructive. Next, we will show the results of these measurements.

MEASUREMENTS OF FATIGUE OF STUDENTS BY FLICKER VALUE

If a light is turned on and off at a certain frequency we can notice flickering. When the frequency gets higher to a certain extent, we come to notice it without flickering. This phenomenon is called 'flicker fusion', and the frequency at which fusion starts is called the 'critical flicker fusion frequency'. This fusion phenomenon has been known for a long time. Also, it has been known that the flicker value varies by individual, and that it becomes smaller as the observer gets tired.

In the nineteen-forties, this value became utilized in examinations of fatigue in industries. In measuring the value, we usually begin with the frequency high fusion phenomenon, lowering it to the level of flickering, and obtain the value of critical flicker frequency, which is called the 'flicker value'.

The flicker value shows the differential threshold of perception dullness due to physiological fusion phenomenon occurring in the centre of ophthalmencephalon. This value increases when neocortex, governing higher mental activities, increases its activities and decreases when the activities are lowered. Namely, the flicker value decreases when one feels sleepy, and increases when you are strained or clear-headed. Therefore, it is possible to measure the degree of tiredness by the flicker value.

When measuring the degree of tiredness by the flicker value, it is necessary to measure it at frequent intervals. However, if measurements are made frequently on each student, study is also interrupted more frequently, and measurement results of time required for study may come to be lacking in reliability. This fact may hamper the original purpose of testing. Consequently, we selected a certain number of students for the measurements of degree of tiredness, and conducted detailed measurements. In this case, we measured flicker values at intervals of 10 minutes so that the relationship between study and degree of tiredness could be grasped well. Measured values shown in Figure 2 are averaged flicker values measured three to four times at intervals of three to four seconds.

We will add some remarks on this Figure. (1) The high value at the beginning of the first chapter shows a possible excitement for the commencement of the study. After the excitement is cooled down, and a normal condition continues from 10.30 am to about noon. (2) At the beginning of the second, third and fourth chapters, some increment is observed; this might be a result of increase in mental activities at the change of chapters. (3) After 12 o'clock, a sudden decrease is seen which clearly seems because of fatigue. Therefore, it is obvious that fatigue increases considerably in a continuous study for about two hours. (4) After taking a lunch time rest for an hour or so, considerable recovery from fatigue is seen and the flicker

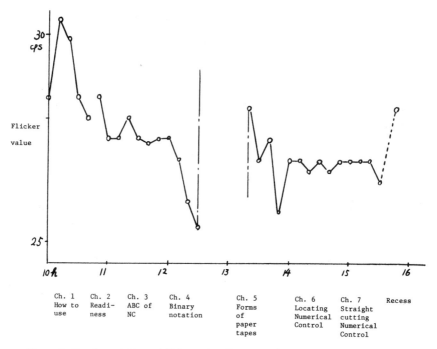

Ch. 1	Ch. 2	Ch. 3	Ch. 4	Ch. 5	Ch. 6	Ch. 7	Recess
How to	Readi-	ABC of	Binary	Forms	Locating	Straight	
use	ness	NC	notation	of	Numerical	cutting	
				paper	Control	Numerical	
				tapes		Control	

Figure 2. Hourly variations of flicker value (Course: NC) effected on August 26, 1971. Subject: A university student (fourth year) (who got full marks in readiness test, and had received flicker test)

value increases. (5) After that, although some variations are observed, a rather constant condition continues until 15.30. (6) Decrease of value is seen near the end of the seventh chapter. It may be a symptom due to the same cause of sudden decrease which occurred at the end of the morning. (7) After a ten minutes' recess at the end of the 7th chapter, the flicker value increased suddenly. This may perhaps be due to the feelings of relief from study and measurements. (8) It may be concluded that in the morning as well as in the afternoon, considerable fatigue occurs as a result of study for two hours.

From the fact above mentioned, it may be given as a conclusion that a continuous study for two hours is the maximum. Although there are differences between individuals, it may also be concluded that the appropriate interval of a continuous study should be limited to one hour or one hour and a half.

ASSESSMENT METHOD BASED ON READINESS TEST, PRE-TEST AND POST-TEST

Various methods such as chapter-end questionnaire, questionnaire after completion of courses, examination of contents of slides, measurements of study hours and CAI study simulation are conceivable for the assessment of the instruction programs for the CAI system. However, it was found from actual practices that the readiness, pre-test and post-test for assessment contained some problems. Now, we will describe these problems first, and then present a tentative method for solution.

Problems

Eight instruction programs for the CAI system developed in 1971 by the Japan Society for the Promotion of Machine Industry are intended to be applicable for those who have scholarship equal to senior high school graduates. Each of them is composed of about 2,000 slides requiring study hours of about 15 hours. On conducting assessment of these instruction programs, we noticed that the assessment method based on tests contained some problems. One of the problems was concerned with the readiness test. Concerning some of these instruction programs, there still remain a lot of difficult problems on preparation of the readiness tests for them. For example, if it is an instruction program like 'Introduction to Electronic Computer' requiring wide share of knowledge, preparation of the readiness test for it is difficult. Though the readiness test for the instruction program was generally prepared by the author himself, it is not sure that it is appropriate for measurement student's readiness. Therefore, it will be an important problem how to check the readiness tests. If it is proved that the readiness test is inappropriate, we have to improve questions for the test. It will be impossible to assess any instruction programs from results obtained by these tests.

Only test results after completion of study by students having readiness are usually employed for assessment of instruction programs. One method for the assessment of instruction programs is to obtain average or standard deviation value of post-test, and another method is to obtain the rate of passing post-test. In Table VI, R stands for readiness test, PRE for pre-test, POST for post-test, + for successful students, - for unsuccessful students, and A, B, C ... H for numbers of students. Assessment of the of the instruction program is made by the equation $(C/(C + D) \times 100)$, and judgement of doubtfulness of readiness test is judged by doubtfulness index of $G/(G + H)$. The larger the doubtfulness index, the less appropriate the readiness test. The first problem that arises from this assessment method is concerned with the standard marks of readiness

Table VI

R	POST PRE	+	-
+	+	A	B
+	-	C	D
-	+	E	F
-	-	G	H

test at which we may judge a student as having readiness for the study. The second problem in this method is the fact that the standard marks of pre-test is fixed to the same marks as those of post-test. If the standard marks of post-test are fixed to 80, then both the students who got 70 marks and less than 10 marks in pre-test are judged as being in the same conditions before the instruction.

Table VII illustrates the results of assessment of four instruction programs developed mainly by the Society, fixing the standard marks in both the readiness test and post-test at 80. In this Table, the mark '?' in doubtfulness column of P3 shows that there were no students who got less than 80 marks in the readiness test. As seen from the Table, both the doubtfulness indices of readiness tests for instruction programs P2 and P4 are comparatively large. However, if we notice the correlation between readiness and post-tests, it cannot be concluded that the questions in the test only have major defects. It may rather be true that the problem comes from fixing the standard marks at 80. Then, is there any way to clarify this point?

Table VII. Assessment based on tests of each instruction program

Instruction program	P1	P2	P3	P4
Successful rate in post-test	40%	100%	80%	67%
Doubtfulness index of readiness test	0.25	0.72	?	0.75
Correlation between R and POST	0.211	0.545	0.309	0.494

A tentative plan for improving assessment method

We divide the students into three groups based on the marks they obtained in pre-test. Here, we propose, as a first step for improvement of a method, to obtain the passing rate and doubtfulness index of readiness test by Group (-) in Table VIII. Standard marks in readiness test should be obtained as follows:

Table VIII. Classification of students based on pre-test

Group (+)	Those who have attained the instruction goals (80 marks or over) in pre-test.
Group ($\pm$)	Those who have not attained the instruction goals in pre-test, but have more than $1/2$ of knowledge of instruction goals.
Group (-)	Those who have less than $1/2$ of knowledge of the instruction goals in pre-test (less than 40 marks).

We first divide the students of the Group (-) into two groups, namely, successful students in post-test (who obtained 80 marks or more) and unsuccessful students (who obtained less than 80 marks), and then obtain the average marks in readiness test on each group. Assign R1 and R2 for the average marks in readiness test for successful group and unsuccessful group in the post-test respectively, then the standard marks in the readiness test will lie between R1 and R2. We thus use the average of R1 and R2 as the standard marks. Table IX shows results of reassessment using this method of the instruction programs shown in Table VII. Assessment of readiness test itself for instruction programs such as P2 and P4 is much better, compared with that on Table VII. However, the fact that there appear such values as 0.667 in P3 and 0.428 in P2 suggests that questions themselves of readiness test have room to be revised. How can we improve questions themselves of readiness test? As an attempt, we work out to utilize post-test.

Table IX. Reassessment of each instruction program

Instruction program	P1	P2	P3	P4
R1	86.6	62.9	94.9	77.3
R2	73.7	46.0	94.5	64.4
R	80.1	54.5	94.7	70.9
Rate of passing post-test	75%	-8.9%	85.7%	60%
Doubtfulness index of readiness test	0.22	0.428	0.667	0.25

We first divide students into two groups, a successful and an unsuccessful ones, from the results of post-tests, and then investigate the correct answer rate for successful and unsuccessful groups on each question composing the readiness test. Table X shows correct answer rates on each question of readiness test of instruction program P2. From this Table, it is found that unsuccessful group obtains higher correct answer rate in questions (1), (6) and (7). That is to say, it suggests that these are not appropriate questions for measuring readiness of students. Therefore, excluding these questions, we determined (3), (4) and (5) as questions for readiness test and make a reassessment by these questions. Then the doubtfulness index of P2 becomes 0.142. Therefore, by this method, it seems that questions of readiness test can considerably be improved.

Table X. Correct answer rates of readiness test for P2

Questions	(1)	(2)	(3)	(4)	(5)	(6)	(7)
Successful group	0.333	0.619	0.917	0.685	0.481	0.422	0.907
Unsuccessful group	0.600	0.452	0.500	0.333	0.111	0.433	0.917

Another method to improve readiness test is to utilize pre-test. This method has an advantage in that the checking of readiness test can be effected before actual instruction. However, we cannot expect in this method such an extent of improvement as has been expected in checking readiness test after the instruction as mentioned above. The basic philosophy of this method is to investigate correct answer rate of the Group (+) or some of the students of the Group ($\pm$) of Table VIII on each question of pre-test, and to exclude questions that had low correct answer rate. Table XI shows correct answer rates of readiness test concerning students who obtained more than 50 marks in pre-test. Judging from the Table, no question seems to contain specific defect in it. Seven questions consist of 39 subquestions. Further investigation on 39 subquestions revealed that 4 subquestions out of 39 needed some improvement. Excluding these subquestions, the doubtfulness index of P2 becomes 0.284. Therefore, it seems that the method to revise readiness test by pre-test is effective to a certain degree, but it is difficult to determine appropriate standard marks in readiness test before making actual study.

Table XI. Correct answer rates of students who obtained
50 marks or more in pre-test

Question	(1)	(2)	(3)	(4)	(5)	(6)	(7)
Correct answer rate	0.70	0.77	1.00	0.73	0.83	0.83	0.81

It seems necessary to prepare a programmed book for instruction program preparation, and to make readiness, pre- and post-tests before and after study for the purpose of checking it, and to review and make necessary amendments on the test questions themselves.

It may be concluded that the methods mentioned in this paper should be employed for improvement as well as assessment of instruction programs on every stage before or after preparation.

REFERENCES

Shigeru Watanabe, Hoichi Itaya, Masayuki Shimada and Kazuo Yagi, (1972) 'Computer Assisted Instruction - A System and its assessment in Japan'. The first International Conference on Computer Communication, **87**, 94

A Case Study of the Development and Use of Teaching Programmes in Life Science Undergraduate Courses

D C B TEATHER, K HARDWICK, J C COLLINS

INTRODUCTION

To experiment with a new technique usually implies dissatisfaction with existing procedure: in this case dissatisfaction with the lecture as a means of introducing large first-year classes to aspects of biological science. The general criticisms to which the lecture, as an all-purpose teaching method, is prone have been cogently expressed by McLeish (1968). But the reasons why the lecture method seems particularly inappropriate to introductory level science teaching are worth considering.

Most science educationalists would agree that a fundamental requirement of scientific education is that it should engender in students an awareness of science as a process of enquiry (Schwab & Brandwein, 1962; Jevons, 1967; Epstein, 1970). While it is possible to achieve this through a lecture, as when a person talks eloquently about his current research, such lectures are probably the exception rather than the rule in the routine of undergraduate teaching. In lectures one can describe the approaches of scientists to problems, one can ask the occasional rhetorical question, but it is probably rare for a student to feel what it is like to be in the position of an investigator. One way towards achieving this would be to present the student with problems, appropriate to his ability, which he then attempts to solve, but 100 students cannot express and have evaluated their own ideas in a lecture context. While it is commonly asserted that this is the function of tutorials and of practical classes, rather than of lectures, there is some evidence to suggest that conventionally taught undergraduate courses, placing undue emphasis on the acquisition of factual knowledge (Jungwirth, 1968), fail to convey even relatively simple principles of scientific methodology (Hutchinson & Martin, 1967). Even if tutorials and practical classes were successful in fostering an awareness of science as a process of enquiry, it is obviously of advantage for this achievement to be reinforced, rather than to be opposed, by other ingredients of the teaching system.

Programmed learning, self-paced and with an inbuilt facility for question asking and answering, seemed to the authors to be a teaching method more appropriate to science education. Descriptions of the scientific process could be replaced by the student actually practising the intellectual skills of scientific investigation under the guidance of a programmed text. We set out to explore the potential of this idea by translating parts of the contents of two introductory-level biology lecture courses into programmed form, and subsequently compared the performances of students who used the programmes with those of students who attended the lectures.

CONSTRUCTION OF THE PROGRAMMES

Two teaching programmes were written to be used in place of four lectures on photosynthesis in preliminary-year biological science (course A) and four lectures on water relations of plants in first-year biological science (course B). As a first step in programme planning, the lecturers' notes on the topics were analysed and the concepts and technical terms which each contained were categorized as follows: (a) those traditionally explained in the lectures, and (b) those with which it was assumed the students would be already familiar.

Pre-tests, requiring short written answers, were used to determine whether essential concepts and terms had been categorized correctly. Both pre-tests contained questions on a range of relevant subjects — mathematics, physics and chemistry in addition to biology.

As the pre-tests were designed only to assist programme construction, the results are not considered in detail. But one feature is noteworthy: of those questions related to concepts and terms in category (b) above, some from each subject area were answered correctly by all students, while others were correctly answered by only a minority. This experience leads the authors to suggest that pre-tests should be used much more often in conventional courses. Besides enhancing feedback about learning, such a procedure alerts students to the fact that tutors are concerned about their learning, which in itself may encourage learning.

After the contents of each programme had been agreed, the first draft of the frames was written by one author (DCBT). A long frame, predominantly linear format, was adopted, but some remedial capacity was introduced by following an answer by a paragraph of supplementary information. The explanation could therefore be used as and if required by each student. The drafts of the frames were then amended by the appropriate co-author (KH in the case of the photosynthesis programme, JCC in the case of the programme on plant water relations) and the first editions were typed and duplicated.

EXPERIMENTAL DESIGN

In order to obtain some comparative measure of the effectiveness of the teaching programmes, some students worked through the programmes appropriate to their course while others attended lectures. The lectures were given at the usual times, and at these times a tutor was present in the laboratory for consultation, if required, by those students who were using a programme; these students were free to work through the programme in the laboratory or at places and times of their own choosing (Stones, 1966).

The design of the experiment is outlined in Table I. This design may

Table I. Outline of Experimental Design

Time	Course A	Course B
4 weeks before course	pre-test	pre-test
Weeks 1 & 2	3 lectures on respiration	introduction to programmed learning division of students into 2 groups: LL group - 4 lectures on water relations PL group - programme on water relations
Weeks 3 & 4	introduction to programmed learning division of students into 2 groups: LL group - 4 lectures on photo-synthesis PL group - programme on photo-synthesis	4 lectures on ionic relations
Week 5	post-test on respiration and photosynthesis questionnaire on teaching and study methods	post-test on water and ionic relations questionnaire on teaching and study methods

appear unnecessarily complex, but its complexity arose from the decision not to allocate students to teaching methods at random. Previous experiments by Leytham, Teather and King (1973) had shown that some first-year students who were required to work through teaching programmes instead of attending lectures reacted emotionally against the novel method. So allocation was based largely on student choice — a procedure which has several precedents in other teaching method comparisons at tertiary level (see Connor, 1968; Engel, Irvine and Wakeford, 1972). Each student was asked to state: (a) a strong preference for the lectures, or (b) a strong preference for the programme, or (c) no strong preference. Students who chose (a) or (b) were allocated to their preferred method. Students who chose (c) were allocated either to the lecture or to the programme group, to equate, as far as possible, the total numbers in each group.

This procedure meant that the two groups might be of unequal ability. Pre-test scores, however, revealed no significant differences between lecture and programme groups, and the experimental design allowed some independent comparison of the abilities of the students in the two groups, for questions relating to the content of the lectures on another section of the course were included in the post-tests and were scored separately. Thus students on course A were post-tested on respiration in addition to photosynthesis; students on course B were post-tested on the ionic relations, in addition to the water relations of plants.

Following the post-test, a questionnaire was administered to provide data on students' attendance and study habits, and their opinions of the teaching methods used in the experiment. Completed copies of the programmes were collected, and data from students' written responses were used to revise the programmes. The revised versions were used in the following year (1972) when the comparison between lectures and programmes was repeated with different groups of students.

RESULTS

These are presented in Tables II - VI. Tables II and III comprise post-test data; Tables IV - VI comprise data obtained from the questionnaire. Pre-tests were used to provide data for the programme construction but they were not comparable in difficulty with the post-tests. Thus, measures of gain (Roebuck, 1972) have not been calculated.

In order to compare the effectiveness of lectures and teaching programmes, the following procedure has been adopted. Consider course A: each student's post-tests score for the part of the course taught exclusively by lectures (respiration) was subtracted from his score for the part of the course taught either by lectures or by teaching programmes (photosynthesis). The mean of these differences for the LL group, indicated by (P-R) in Table

Table II. Means and standard deviations of post-test scores

Course	Year	Group	n	Topic	Teaching method	Post-test score $\bar{x}$ SD	Topic	Teaching method	Post-test score $\bar{x}$ SD
A	1971	LL	32	Respiration	L	10.09 ± 2.90	Photosynthesis	L	9.41 ± 3.28
		LP	24	Respiration	L	9.50 ± 3.11	Photosynthesis	P	10.17 ± 3.32
	1972	LL	34	Respiration	L	7.50 ± 3.87	Photosynthesis	L	12.47 ± 3.86
		LP	28	Respiration	L	9.61 ± 3.93	Photosynthesis	P	15.29 ± 4.15
B	1971	LL	16	Water relations	L	18.19 ± 2.46	Ionic relations	L	19.01 ± 3.93
		PL	41	Water relations	P	19.61 ± 4.11	Ionic relations	L	18.17 ± 3.40
	1972	LL	18	Water relations	L	17.61 ± 4.89	Ionic relations	L	18.17 ± 3.40
		PL	16	Water relations	P	18.75 ± 5.70	Ionic relations	L	19.06 ± 4.92

Table III. Comparisons between lectures and teaching programmes
on the basis of post-test scores (for explanation see text)

Course	Year	Group	n	Mean difference	t	p
A	1971	LL	32	(P-R) = -0.66	1.26	NS
		LP	24	(P-R) = +0.67		
	1972	LL	34	(P-R) = +4.97	0.57	NS
		LP	28	(P-R) = +5.68		
B	1971	LL	16	(W-I) = -0.88	2.46	<0.05
		PL	41	(W-I) = +2.59		
	1972	LL	18	(W-I) = -0.69	0.10	NS
		PL	16	(W-I) = -0.31		

Table IV. Comparisons between lectures and teaching programmes
on the basis of students' total hours worked

Course	Year	Group	n	Topic	Teaching method	Total hours worked* x SD	t	p
A	1971	LL	21	Photosynthesis	L	6.24 ± 1.67	1.4014	NS
		LP	26	Photosynthesis	P	5.47 ± 2.01		
	1972	LL	34	Photosynthesis	L	5.96 ± 2.16	1.1208	NS
		LP	25	Photosynthesis	P	5.34 ± 1.97		
B	1971	LL	16	Water relations	L	6 45 ± 2.21	0.6399	NS
		PL	35	Water relations	P	7.01 ± 3 19		
	1972	LL	22	Water relations	L	10.18 ± 4.31	2.1703	<0.05
		PL	19	Water relations	P	7.59 ± 3.13		

*Total hours worked for teaching method L equals time spent in lectures plus time spent in private study
on the topic (excluding time spent on practical work).
Total hours worked for teaching method P equals time spent on programme plus time spent in private
study on the topic (excluding time spent on practical work).

III, was then compared with the mean for the LP group. A similar comparison was effected with data from course B, and the mean differences between
scores are indicated by (W-I).

These comparisons (Table III) reveal no significant differences between
groups with respect to course A, but students who chose the teaching programme in course B (1971) scored significantly higher in the post-test than
did the students who chose to attend lectures. This difference is not repeated
in 1972, but, as Table IV shows, students of the programmed learning group
achieved (W-I) scores similar to those of the lecture group in significantly
less time.

Several questions on the questionnaire dealt with students' preferences for teaching method, and the results are summarized in Table V. The relevant questions were:

"Q6.   When you were first asked to choose between attending the lectures and studying the learning programme, did you have:

        a strong preference for the lectures?
        a strong preference for the learning programme?
        no strong preferences for either method?

Q10.   If you were invited to participate in a similar experiment how would you choose now:

        a strong preference for the lectures?
        a strong preference for the learning programmes?
        no strong preference for either method?"

Related questions asked the reasons for the original choice and for any change of view.

Table V. Numbers of students preferring each teaching method

Groups	n	L→L	L→O	L→P	O→L	O→O	O→P	P→L	P→O	P→P
All LL groups	96	49	7	5	5	20	10	-	-	-
All LP and PL groups	117	-	-	-	5	28	18	6	11	49

The letter to the left of the arrow indicates the method preferred before the experiment; the letter to the right indicates the method preferred after the experiment. L = 'strong preference for lecture'; P = 'strong preference for learning programme'; O = 'no strong preference for either method'.

From Table V it can be deduced that, in reply to Q6, 29% of all students stated a strong preference for lectures, 31% for the teaching programme, while 40% stated no strong preferences. Comparable percentages for Q10 are 31, 38 and 31 respectively. This difference between students' responses to Q6 and Q10, on the basis of the raw data (n = 213), falls just short of significance at p<0.1 (x^2 = 4.49, df = 2).

Table V shows that 10% of all students view the lecture comparatively more favourably after the experiment, while 21% had a more favourable view of the teaching programme. The preferences expressed by the remaining 69% were unchanged.

Table VI presents data on students' responses to eight pairs of statements presented in the questionnaire. Students were asked to indicate their view of lectures or of teaching programmes by placing a tick in one column in respect of each pair of statements — a Likert-type scale (Likert, 1932). In Table VI, though not in the original test items in the questionnaire, statements often attributed to programmed learning by its protagonists are grouped on the left, and their antonyms are presented on the right.

Table VI. Students' opinions of lectures and of teaching programmes, expressed after the experiment (for explanation see text)

A	strong agreement with A	agree with A	weak agreement with A	weak agreement with B	agree with B	strong agreement with B	B	Differences between distributions (Z value and significance levels)		
								L vs (L)	P vs (P)	L vs P
active way of learning							passive way of learning	0.71 NS	3.07**	6.05***
stimulate curiosity							lead to boredom	-0.06 NS	3.86***	4.35***
demanding							laissez-faire	0.72 NS	0.87 NS	5.49***
lead to self-reliance							lead to dependence	-0.10 NS	0.67 NS	3.46***
motivate							discourage	-0.36 NS	4.61***	4.33***
individual oriented							group oriented	0.85 NS	1.33 NS	6.42***
lead to participation							lead to isolation	0.14 NS	0.12 NS	2.06*
personal							impersonal	0.04 NS	1.92 NS	4.55***

Significance levels: NS $p \geqslant 0.05$.   * $0.05 > p \geqslant 0.01$ ** $0.01 > p \geqslant 0.001$ *** $p < 0.001$

285

Views about teaching programmes are given only by those students who worked through a programme during the experiment (LP and PL groups). These views are subdivided according to the preference for teaching method, which the students expressed after the experiment, in response to Q10 of the questionnaire (see above):

P represents the opinions of students who expressed a strong preference for teaching programmes (n = 60).

(P) represents the opinions of students who expressed either no strong preferences or a strong preference for lectures (n = 46).

Similarly, opinions about lectures are given only by those students who attended the lectures throughout (LL group). These were also subdivided according to expressed preferences for teaching method:

L represents the opinions of students who expressed a strong preference for lectures (n = 51).

(L) represents the opinions of students who expressed either no strong preferences or a strong preference for teaching programmes (n = 39).

The position of the letter L or P in Table VI indicates the position of the median of the distribution. The ends of each horizontal line indicate the positions of the quartiles. The more important comparisons between distribution are made explicit in the three columns on the right of the table. The Mann-Whitney U test (Siegel, 1956), is used to assess the significance of differences with respect to central tendency.

In all eight cases the distributions of the responses of the students who worked through the programme (and subsequently expressed strong preferences for programmed learning) lie significantly to the left of the distributions of the students who attended the lectures (and subsequently expressed strong preferences for the lectures). For example, students who worked through a programme tended to regard programmed learning as a comparatively active way of learning, whereas students who attended lectures tended to regard lectures as a less active way of learning. Moreover, in several cases, those students who experienced programmed learning, and subsequently expressed a strong preference for the method, tended to place it further to the left on the continuum than did those students who worked through the programme but did not express a strong preference for the method.

DISCUSSION

One often undervalued outcome of a study such as this — undervalued because it is difficult to quantify — is the effect upon the tutors who participated. In this case some aspects were seen as particularly relevant to our other teaching. Thus the practice of assessing students' pre-course knowledge came to be regarded as a valuable exercise in its own right, as did the close scrutiny of students' errors in learning, which the revision of the programmes necessitated. The planning and presentation of the programme content was seen to have relevance for the production of other teaching notes, and the responses to the questionnaire gave insights into students' expectations of teaching. (One might postulate that the experience of using the programme would also affect the students' subsequent approaches to learning.)

Moreover, the programme production was not nearly as time-consuming as had, at first, been supposed. Writing the first (1971) editions took approximately 50 man hours for each programme. By comparison, the students' estimates of the length of time they subsequently spent working through each of the programmes averaged 5.5 hours — approximately a 10:1 ratio between tutors' programme preparation time and students' time in learning. However, working from already prepared lecture notes, and in the case of the water relations programme a good review paper (Dainty, 1969), undoubtedly reduced the amount of time needed to prepare such programmes from scratch.

What programmes produced in this way contain, though, is a rearrangement, albeit with some additions and deletions, of the material which was previously put over in lectures. Some students, recognizing this, justified having no preference for either teaching method by "The material learned would be the same in either case", or "I feel that either way of learning would get across the information". The fact that the lectures were given by the tutors who were responsible for programme writing could be expected to produce great similarity between lecture content and programme content (an advantage for the experimental comparison between teaching methods) but could also be expected to produce atypical lectures, ie the lectures benefiting from the thought and effort which the tutors had put into the writing of the programmes. When asked whether the lectures were typical of lectures in the life sciences, the majority of the students answered in the affirmative. Those who thought that they were not typical gave a variety of reasons. For example, Dr Hardwick's lectures "... had more student participation", and "Dr Collins proceeded slower than most lecturers, sticking to the subject and following it through step by step". But, as other students said, "There's no such thing as a typical lecture", and "There are as many different types of lecture as there are lecturers".

So, essentially, we are comparing two methods of putting over to students the same information — either by lectures, or by long-frame, linear teaching programmes with a tutor available to answer queries on the programme during the times which would normally have been allocated to lectures. In fact, as Unwin (1966) found, few students from the programmed learning groups ever approached the tutor, for "There was very little need of explanations by the staff", and "It wasn't really necessary to discuss the programme with staff as there were really no questions to be answered"!

What evidence there is of the comparative effectiveness of these two methods weighs slightly in favour of the teaching programmes — significantly so in the case of course B in that students of the PL group scored higher on the post-test (1971), or took less time to obtain the same post-test scores (1972). But as Bloomer (1972) has pointed out, while the results of comparative experiments have frequently shown no (statistically) significant difference between traditional and innovative teaching methods, it does not follow that no (educationally) significant differences exist: negative results may only indicate that our measuring tools are too crude to detect differences. But one can press the implications of this argument too far: if an innovation requires greater expenditure of time and resources, this should be seen to be justifiable if not by objective, certainly by subjective criteria.

This brings us to consider what students expect from their teaching, and some of their reasons for choosing a particular method are sufficiently revealing to be quoted in some detail. Convenience, for example, would seem to play no small part: "I prefer learning at my own speed and don't like 9.30 lectures". But convenience in this sense brings with it responsibility; several students chose not to attempt the programme because "self-discipline is weak". Another, despite some misgivings, chose the programme and was glad he had done so: "I was undecided; the programme I may have left whereas I am less likely to miss lectures, but I wanted to see how I could cope with it alone... I now feel that I can go at my own rate and understand things as I go along". Again, "There is no pressure and one can take time to think about each stage. Lecturers, in general, are too fast moving", and "A good learning programme makes you think — lectures don't".

But some students find it easier to memorize in lectures: "Can assimilate more in lectures and remember facts visually (ie I can visualize formulae etc as written on the board). Had to be in the right frame of mind and physical surroundings to work through programme — found it difficult to concentrate on". "I find it easier to assimilate a lot of facts when being told them than to read them". "Lectures have a chance of bringing out memorable details".

A conflict of interest sometimes appeared: "There is not sufficient time in lectures both to understand the content and to make notes so that these can be referred to later". Indeed, the desire for "accurate, comprehensive notes" was a major consideration: "Because accurate notes were provided in the programme I was not tied to lecture times". "By going to the lectures I had a fairly good set of notes to refer back to". "I would choose the programme in future because I do not think my lecture notes are adequate". "In a programmed learning course, everything is down in detail so there's no risk of missing anything or copying anything down incorrectly as in a lecture. One can make notes from a textbook, but textbooks contain a lot of irrelevant details".

Notes are, of course, mainly used for exam revision: "I can learn from my own notes better than I can from printed notes", but sometimes they appear to assume a teaching function in their own right: "I chose the programme because I thought it would be more concise and explain the subject better than my notes from lectures"(our emphasis). Part of the trouble with conventional lecture courses is the lack of follow up: "In lectures I continually think 'That's not clear, I'll look it up afterwards', and seldom do".

The end of year examinations, though five months away, obviously influenced students' choice of teaching method. Thus, the teaching programme would be a "good guide to the standard required". Some students were definitely out to beat the system: "In life science courses a particular aspect of the topic is chosen rather than comprehensive teaching on all aspects. The lecturer's emphasis is vital if the right emphasis is to be chosen". (Our stressing). And even more explicitly: "I'd rather attend the lectures by the person who is setting the exam papers so as to get a better idea of what one is expected to produce for answers to examinations".

The students' comments quoted above raise a number of issues about university teaching which could usefully be investigated in future research, but which are outside the immediate scope of this paper. Let us now look at the preferences for teaching method which the students actually expressed. At the end of the experiment more students expressed a preference for programmed learning than had done so at the beginning, though, as we have seen, for a variety of reasons. However, both lectures and teaching programmes had their adherents, and perhaps the inference to be drawn from this is that a greater variety of teaching methods than is commonly employed should be made available — a suggestion supported by the results of comparisons between teaching methods at university level reported by Hartley (1968). If students are given a choice of methods, they should also be given sufficient information about those methods which may be novel to them to make a considered choice. Where the allocation of teaching resources does not allow choice of method to be made available, different sections of a course could, with advantage, be taught by different methods. It is perhaps worth noting that none of the findings of this study indicate that, from the point of view of student learning, the lecture should enjoy the pre-eminence which is today commonplace. Current arguments for a plurality of examining methods have, as natural concomitants, those for a plurality of teaching.

It may, however, be misleading to refer to programmed learning as a specific teaching method. At the more general level, programmed learning becomes a procedure for the design of learning situations and merges into modern teaching methodology (Biran, 1972). The outcome of the procedure may be, say, an educational game rather than a traditional style programmed text. In this investigation we have not attempted to ask fundamental questions about what should be taught and why; instead we have chosen, in the main, to apply programmed learning techniques to the presentation of existing material.

Despite this limitation, which was perhaps implicit in our decision to programme parts of existing courses in piecemeal fashion, our students attributed to programmed learning many of the characteristics claimed by its protagonists. Thus they saw programmed learning as active and motivating; it stimulated curiosity and led to self reliance. Despite the fact that lectures were viewed as more group oriented than programmed learning, they were also seen as more isolating and more impersonal.

One cannot deduce from this study how students' views of programmed learning would change if programmes were used for a larger proportion of the undergraduate course. But the views here expressed indicate that programmed learning may have considerable relevance for what is, in many large and growing departments, a pressing problem: how to counter the tendency towards increasing impersonality of teaching and consequent non-involvement on the part of students. As Niblett stated in 1962: "If a lecturer has 150 or 200 students it is difficult for him to be in touch with more than a few without some quite radical alteration in the teaching system itself." It should, presumably, be possible to alter profoundly the social situation in which teaching and learning occur by making teaching programmes, or other highly structured learning assignments, the focus of work in small groups, and it is in this area that we are undertaking further research.

REFERENCES

Biran, L. A. (1972) APLET Yearbook of Educational and Instructional Technology 1972/3. Kogan Page, London

Bloomer, J. (1972) Evaluating an Educational Game. M.Ed. thesis, University of Glasgow

Collins, J. C. and Teather, D. C. B. (1971) The Water Relations of Plants. Department of Botany/Audio-Visual Aids and Programmed Learning Unit, University of Liverpool

Connor, D. V. (1968) Programmed Learning and Educational Technology, 5, 129

Dainty, J. (1969) The Water Relations of Plants. In 'The Physiology of Plant Growth and Development' (Ed) M.B. Wilkins. McGraw-Hill, London

Engel, C. E., Irvine, E. and Wakeford, R. E. (1972) British Journal of Medical Education, 6, 311

Epstein, H. T. (1970) A Strategy for Education. Oxford University Press, London

Hardwick, K. and Teather, D. C. B. (1971) Photosynthesis. Department of Botany/Audio-Visual Aids and Programmed Learning Unit, University of Liverpool

Hartley, J. R. (1968) Programmed Learning and Educational Technology, 5, 219

Hutchinson, S. A. and Martin, E. (1967) Journal of Biological Education, 1, 261

Jevons, F. R. (1967) The Teaching of Science. George Allen and Unwin, London

Jungwirth, E. (1968) Journal of Biological Education, 2, 39

Leytham, G. W. H., Teather, D. C. B. and King, A. S. (1973) 'The effects of introducing programmed learning into university courses'

Likert, R. A. (1932) Archives of Psychology, No. 140

McLeish, J. (1968) The Lecture Method. Cambridge Monographs on Teaching Methods No. 1. Cambridge Institute of Education

Niblett, W. R (1962) The Expanding University. Faber & Faber, London

Roebuck, M. (1972) Programmed Learning and Educational Technology, 9, 87

Schwab, J. J. and Brandwein, P. F. (1962) The Teaching of Science. Harvard University Press, Cambridge, Mass

Siegel, S. (1956) Nonparametric Statistics for the Behavioural Sciences. McGraw-Hill, New York

Stones, E. (1966) Programmed Learning and Educational Technology, 3, 135

Unwin, D. (1966) Programmed Learning and Educational Technology, 3, 35

The Use of Simulated Exercises (Games) in Biological Education at the Tertiary Level

M A TRIBE, D PEACOCK

INTRODUCTION

For the past three years we have been concerned with designing an Introductory programmed course in Biology for undergraduates as part of the Inter-University Biology Teaching Project (Dowdeswell, 1972; Eraut, 1972; Tribe, 1972).

During this time most of our efforts have been directed towards the problems of individual learning at the Tertiary level in an attempt to provide a conceptual framework for more advanced courses in Biology and to demonstrate that an alternative form of teaching and learning can be used effectively in conjunction with the existing lecture/tutorial courses. Even so, there is still comparatively little opportunity or provision for students to participate in group learning and decision making experiences. This weakness in our present pattern of teaching, together with the desire to find a contrasting, yet complementary, mode of learning to the programmed part of the course, prompted us to examine the use of various group-learning experiences, and in particular the use of simulated research exercises (or games) in Biology.

THE VALUE OF SIMULATED EXERCISES

Games or simulation exercises have been introduced in the last decade for a variety of teaching purposes, including military/political strategy, pure and applied economics, land planning, social administration, medical diagnosis, and management and business studies. As Beard (1970) has pointed out, the history of games is unusual, since it is customary for education to supply both the methods and training for business; with games, however, the process has been reversed. Education has taken from business a method, which in turn, it too has borrowed from military training (for example, it was used by the Germans in the first World War).

With this pedigree and the connotation the word 'game' conjures up with levity and entertainment, it is hardly surprising that institutions of higher education have been, and in the main still are, suspicious of the value of games, especially in subjects with a high factual content.

For this reason, it is worth stating clearly what simulated exercises (games) can offer students who are learning about Science. Simulated exercises provide:

1) Structured situations which encourage scientific discovery and problem solving (ie 'cooperative group learning' as defined by Thompson, 1972);

2) Motivation and stimulation for students to learn about a subject(s) in which they had previously little or no knowledge;

3) Motivation for learning factual information when it is related to a specific problem or task;

4) Effective ways of learning how to get on with other people in a team and the enjoyment which follows;

5) Insight into the social aspects of learning, ie it encourages cooperative learning, frequently establishing working and social friendship which carry over into 'unscheduled hours'.

6) Decision-making opportunities, normally without censure or threat, thus establishing a closer empathy between teacher(s) and taught.

THE STRUCTURE AND OBJECTIVES OF SCIENTIFIC GAMES

Although scientific games may differ with regard to the problem posed and the roles played by students, all games essentially take the following form:

1. INTRODUCTION: (i) to the problem; (ii) roles to be played; (iii) decisions on size of group; (iv) location of resources.

2. EXECUTION: Plans on (i) course of action to be taken on the problem itself; (ii) decisions regarding the organization of each group; (iii) communication of ideas and actions; (iv) cooperation or competition.

3. ANALYSIS: (i) Evaluation of collected observations and data; (ii) presentation of 'original papers'; (iii) presentation of reports; (iv) colloquium presentation and inter-group discussion.

4. FOLLOW-UP: (i) Comparison with real life situation if possible, ie going out into the field, experiments in lab. (ii) supplementary reading.

(The terminology used here is adapted from Boocock & Schild, 1968).

In the two games developed so far our objectives were (a) to provide a task orientated situation similar to a real one in which the students can be actually involved, can take responsibility for their actions and decisions, and can experience the results of these in an environment where the consequence of inappropriate decisions are less threatening.

(b) To provide opportunities for learning effective participation in task orientated groups.

(c) To enable students to explore a real scientific problem in depth and to provide opportunities for using scientific concepts already familiar to them.

(d) To provide an appropriate form of small group learning at suitable

293

points in the introductory programmed course, to offset the isolation sometimes felt by students in working through a series of programmes. We should
add that the simulated exercises are not the only form of group learning in
the Introductory biology course.

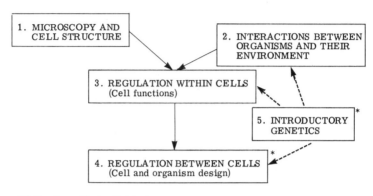

*Units planned but unfinished at present

Figure 1

In Figure 1 the unit structure of the biology course is shown (see also
Tribe, 1972).

So far two simulated exercises have been developed. The first, the
Ecological Research 'game' complements unit 2 "Interactions between living
organisms and their environment"; the second, the Enzyme Research 'game'
complements Unit 3 "Regulation within cells".

OUTLINE OF THE PROBLEM POSED IN THE ECOLOGICAL RESEARCH 'GAME'

At the beginning of this exercise students are shown two colour photographs
of the same piece of rocky coastline, together with the following handout:

1. The Problem

The problem is a very real one, which actually occurs in this country. You
will be shown two photographs of the same piece of coastline taken in July
1958 and July 1967. There are obvious differences between the two. You are
asked to put yourselves in the position of the ecologist who has visited this
coast fairly frequently and who would be interested in trying to find out the
differences between the two situations and the factor(s) which caused them.

2. Objectives

The objectives of the sessions are: (1) to investigate the changes which have occurred in the ecosystem under study, ie from the photographs shown; (2) to suggest possible reasons for the changes; (3) to assess how the environmental changes have affected the stability of this particular ecosystem; (4) to recommend suitable courses of action (if required) for the future, in the event of a similar situation recurring.

3. Solving the Problem

To solve the problem, you will be divided into 'research' groups whose task is to decide on the best way(s) of tackling the problem. For example, the group may wish to carry out field and laboratory investigations or design experiments to test particular hypotheses. Having decided on a particular investigation or experiment you can approach the Tutors, who will play the role of members of the SRC (Science Research Council) for a data sheet giving the results of such an investigation/experiment. The SRC has a bank of some 150 investigations and experiments, but obviously at times they cannot cover all the experiments you may wish to carry out. To make the situation more realistic, we have attempted to cost the investigation in terms of the actual research time taken by a professional ecologist in carrying out each investigation or experiment. This we feel is important because it will impress upon you that time and money are limiting in any research programme. Therefore in designing a series of experiments it is necessary to have an order of priorities so that efficient use is made of these resources.

4. Research Time

The resources of time and money are symbolized by coloured cards which are allocated to each group at the beginning of each session. At the beginning of the first session, 30 weeks of research time are allocated to each group. At the beginning of each subsequent session, further research time may be allocated by the SRC on the basis of: (i) the group's 'Annual Report', and (ii) its record of 'original publications'.

5. Reports and Publications

(a) **The 'Annual Report'**: An annual report should be submitted by the group to the SRC at the end of each session (except the last). It should contain a summary of the progress made in the current session and possible proposals for future research (it should not exceed 100 words).

(b) **The Final Report**: This report should attempt to summarize the group's response to the problem as outlined in the objectives. This written report should not exceed 250 words. The Final Report of each group will be given to the SRC and will also be read at a Conference held at the end of the last session, when all participants will be present and will be encouraged to discuss and question each report.

(c) **Original Papers**: Original papers reporting experiments and findings carried out by a group may be submitted at any time throughout the sessions, and if accepted by the SRC will be published in the "Journal of Ecology" housed in the reference library. Credit in the form of research time (6 weeks) will be given to the group concerned for its original paper. Once published, any paper may be consulted by other groups, but these groups cannot submit the same paper for publication themselves.

6. Functions of the SRC

The Science Research Council (SRC) is represented by two tutors. The SRC functions in four ways:

1) It provides results (if available) in the form of data sheets of experiments suggested by the research groups. The data sheets will be given provided that the SRC is satisfied that the experiment has been sufficiently well-defined.

2) It acts as a referee and editor for any original papers which are submitted.

3) It is the body which eventually decides research time allocation.

4) Members of the SRC may be called into any research group as consultants. Consultancy, however, is costed at two weeks' research time for every five minutes of actual time spent with a group to a maximum of ten minutes. As consultants, the SRC can clarify or provide information on general ecological concepts and experimental techniques. They will not, however, be able to provide any direct answers concerning the interpretation of data sheets.

7. Resources

Each group has free access to a 'library' of reference books, which may be consulted at any time. Published experiments by various groups (as they become available) can also be consulted by any group in the "Journal of Ecology", which is also kept in the library. In addition, a large selection of 2" by 2" colour slides relating to the problem may be seen through the auspices of the SRC and a list of these slides may be consulted freely at any time.

OUTLINE OF THE PROBLEM POSED IN THE ENZYME RESEARCH 'GAME'

Again the construction and working of the exercise is very similar to the ecological one given above, but here the students play the role of biochemical research workers. The group are presented with previously published information about an enzyme as follows:

Previously published information on the enzyme

The enzyme can be isolated from bovine pancreas where it occurs as an inactive proenzyme. The proenzyme can be converted into an active enzyme by incubation with a proteolytic enzyme pepsin. The active enzyme will hydrolyse the following two substrates:

1. The tripeptide -Carbobenzoxy -Glycine -phenylalanine producing Carbobenzoxy -Glycine and Phenylalanine.

2. An ester -hippuryl-Glycine -phenyllactic acid to produce hippuryl-glycine and phenyllactic acid

Hydrolysis

$$\text{\textcircled{} —CONH—CH}_2\text{—CO—OCH—CH}_2\text{—COOH}$$

$$\text{CH}_2$$

Hippuryl-glycine   phenyllactic acid

The objective of the exercise is to design and conduct research to investigate the structure, function and biological role of the enzyme.

MERITS OF THE EXERCISE

It would appear that there is no unequivocal answer to the question "Is group learning more effective than individual learning?" (Thompson, 1972). Indeed, depending on the objectives, both methods have advantages as well as dis-advantages. For example, although learning about the subject matter is of importance, one might well argue that learning how to work effectively with other people is equally important. Games are more likely to achieve this latter objective. In addition, there are a number of skills, which although not unique to this method of learning, are, in our experience, much enhanced by involvement in game simulated exercises, particularly the ability (i) to formulate precise questions appropriate to the problem; (ii) to formulate hypotheses and design appropriate experiments to test them; (iii) to recog-nize the significance of each experiment and its implications to the whole problem; (iv) to interpret experimental data accurately and thoroughly; (v) to write short, concise reports and conclusions on experimental findings.

That these skills are developed in a stimulating and enjoyable way (as indicated by student comments) argues strongly in favour of the careful use of simulated exercises in Higher Education. Other benefits of simulated exercises from the teacher's point of view are that games (a) can be used most effectively with students of mixed abilities and backgrounds; (b) can be adapted to any different academic level (sixth form to postgraduate); (c) allow students to apply their different skills and abilities in a group situation.

ADMINISTRATIVE PROBLEMS

Running simulated exercises properly in a fairly conventional teaching time-table presents its problems. Firstly, the problem of finding available time (preferably two to three hour periods on consecutive days) in an already over-crowded schedule. Secondly, finding a suitable location to carry out the exercise, ie we would advocate 4 or 5 adjacent rooms as an ideal situa-tion. Thirdly, deciding on the number of teaching staff required for smooth running of the exercise. Here again, we suggest that the staff : student ratio ideally should be about 1 : 15.

CRITICISMS, EVALUATION AND ASSESSMENT

Some people object to scientific games, because the game is not the same as actually going out to the seashore to do ecological studies or actually working in a biochemistry laboratory on a research problem. The comment is true, but the objection is based on a misunderstanding of the game objectives. "The object of the game is to involve the student in the types of situation, motives, practical constraints and decisions that are the subject of study, not the specific details. The student should emerge from the game with a better understanding of what it was all about, what was possible and what was not, and why" (Boocock & Schild, 1968, p. 82).

However, there are at least two valid criticisms to the idea of 'games'. The first is the so-called 'Hawthorn effect', ie any novel form of teaching and learning carried out by a small group of enthusiasts is likely to meet with success. The true test of whether games can make a significant contribution to tertiary education is for less committed teachers to try them.

The second major problem is how to evaluate the effectiveness of game simulated exercises? Obviously a student opinion schedule will provide some feedback, but only of a very general kind. It will, for example, show whether the students have enjoyed taking part in the game. However, it is certainly desirable to have a more quantitative analysis of the effectiveness of games and we have in collaboration with Mr Michael MacDonald Ross (Open University) devised a tentative marking schedule for the ecology game, centered round three areas: (i) the problem solving cycle; (ii) group dynamics; (iii) reports and papers.

We do not suggest that this schedule takes into account all the problems, but it is a first attempt at trying to solve some of them. For that matter how rigorously do we analyse the effectiveness of our longer established teaching methods, eg lectures, tutorials, etc?

In conclusion, it should be stated quite clearly that we are not trying to prove that game simulations are better than the more conventional forms of teaching and learning, to quote from Tansey and Unwin, 1969:

"The whole of simulation is merely a means to an end. It is an alternative strategy. If the lecture . . . . . or any other method works there is no need for simulation. If, on the other hand, these methods are not achieving the results that are desired, then it is as well to have an alternative method of presentation. Simulation is merely this method presentation. "

Nevertheless, since other forms of learning rarely make provision for group learning and decision making, we feel that there will be an increasing demand and use made of simulation exercises.

ACKNOWLEDGMENTS

We would like to thank Mr Michael MacDonald Ross (Open University) Mr Stephen Hurry (Open University), and Mrs Janet Peacock for their help in evaluating trials of the "Ecology Game" at the Loughborough Open University Summer School, 1972.

We would also like to acknowledge the encouragement given by our colleagues Dr Michael Eraut and Mr Roger Snook, who have also been involved in the design of the Sussex project.

REFERENCES

Beard, R. (1970) Teaching and learning in higher education. Penguin Education, London

Boocock, S. and Schild, E. O. (1968) Simulation games in learning. Sage Publications

Dowdeswell, W. H. (1972) Nature, **238**, 313

Eraut, M. R. (1972) in 'Aspects of Educational Technology VI'. (Ed) K.Austwick and N.D.H.Harris. Pitman, London. Page 238

Tansey, P. J. and Unwin, D. (1969) Simulation and gaming in education. Methuen Educational Ltd., London

Thompson, G. B. (1972) Educational Research, **15**, 28

Tribe, M. A. (1972) in 'Aspects of Educational Technology VI'. (Ed) K. Austwick and N. D. H. Harris. Pitman, London. Page 98

Syllabus Analysis

T G WYANT

In Further Education greater emphasis is placed on the syllabus and its im-plications than may be thought necessary by other sectors of education. Further Education students are required to complete, or work through, a strictly laid down syllabus: this is usually viewed as an essential require-ment to obtain successful examination results on completion of the course. The syllabus is usually provided by an external examining body or by the College itself.

When the subjects and their constituent topics are viewed in the context of the syllabus, it may be seen that they are stated in the broadest possible terms. Only rarely is some form of Objective given as a guideline. College department and teaching staff are left to interpret the syllabus to the best of their ability relying on their previous experience in running the same or similar courses. For example, in the City and Guilds of London Institute Course No. 730 Further Education Teachers Certificate, one of the topics stated under the subject Methods of Teaching is 'Significance of Programmed Learning'. To what depth should a topic like this be taught? Any length of time from one hour upwards could be allotted: it would be an interesting exercise to ask members of this Conference how much time they think would be appropriate for this topic. Another example occurs in the City and Guilds Course No. 731 Programmed Learning (which is a two year course, one even-ing per week, in itself), where under the heading of Course Management is a topic entitled 'Application of network scheduling to course design and time-tabling'. How long and to what depth should the lecturer responsible develop this subject? Some may be happy to ignore it altogether as a fanciful whim of the syllabus makers. Personally, I would be happy to devote a whole year's work to the topic.

Furthermore, in a syllabus no indication is given of the sequence or logical development of the subject and topics — unless, as some lecturers are known to do, one follows slavishly and blindly the subjects and topics as listed or in the order as it appears in the syllabus.

This paper will try to show how to solve some of the problems which may be met within a syllabus. These problems may be summarized as follows:

1. Interpretation and understanding
2. Entry behaviour requirements
3. Critical concepts and principles
4. The logical relationship between subjects
5. Depth of teaching for each subject or topic
6. The time to be allocated to subjects and topics
7. Student readiness to proceed to new work
8. Setting and selection of examination questions that will test the students' mastery of the subject matter
9. The problems that you have encountered yourself

In a work by Clay (1969) he analysed the number of techniques that are now available to management to solve problems faced by industry: these numbered in the region of 120. An examination of this list suggests that 75% are immediately applicable to educational problems.

One of the techniques, which is used in this paper, is Network Analysis. Other papers by the author (Wyant, 1971,1972) have been given at the last two APLET Conferences. Both were of an individual and personal nature. This paper will be concerned with the application of the technique to a new course being run at Coventry Technical College.

The course is the Ordinary National Diploma in Technology (Engineering). This syllabus is completely new, interdisciplinary and rather complex. It has been produced by a joint committee of the major engineering institutions as a new venture, and the syllabus makers have provided more detail and information for guidance than is usual.

The College offered and started to run this course in September 1972. In the session prior to the course (1971-72) a team of lecturers who were to be involved in the course was selected; it should be stated that this was a major innovation as the members came from various departments in the College, viz Mechanical Engineering, Mathematics, Science, Electrical Engineering and Business and General Studies. The author was appointed as Educational Technology consultant to the team.

The method of tackling the analysis of the syllabus was as follows. A team member from each discipline, in conjunction with the Course Coordinator and the author, compiled a network of his own particular subject matter. The drawing of the network closely followed the discipline imposed by the technique, which asks (in the educational application) "What is the earliest time I could possibly teach this subject or topic?" and also, "What is the latest possible time that I must have taught it by?" For the maximum benefit to be obtained from the resulting network it is essential that these two vital questions are answered honestly.

In some instances the network appeared to have a very linear format (Figure 1); for example, parts of the Electrical Engineering syllabus network

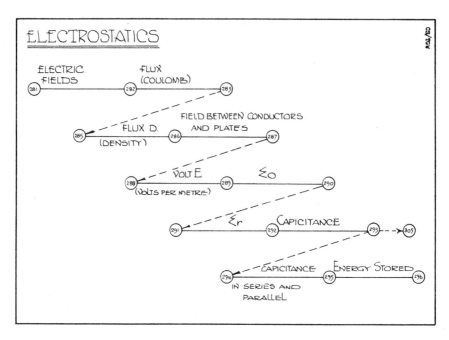

Figure 1

possessed a self-evident and obvious topic progression in a logical order.
(This was later confirmed, in this particular area, by networks drawn by
other Electrical Engineers at a one-day conference held at the Wolverhampton Technical Teachers Training College recently.)

Apart from the Electrical Engineering networks, others showed multiple
starts and a branching aspect. The initial comments made by the tutors were
that the network approach had revealed a completely new view of the syllabus,
which would provide variations of teaching methods differing radically from
the traditional mode.

The tutors have used their networks in varying ways. One has used it as
a referencing device for all the handouts that are produced in his particular
discipline. He can thus ask students to make reference to topics in the syllabus that he knows have been covered by previous handouts, work and teaching.
Another tutor has taken the brave step of issuing the network of his particular
section to the students at the beginning of new segments of work. Another
issues his network at the end of the segment so that students can plan their
revision periods in a systematic and logical manner.

The syllabus-makers requested that colleges should experiment with the
various teaching methods. With this request in mind the team mounted a team
teaching period. For this the members drew a joint network of Basic Science,

which, though successful in showing those topics which lent themselves to the team-teaching approach, unfortunately also showed that the pre-allocation of time-tabled periods was incorrect: from this it became obvious that the time-tabling and scheduling of lectures, lessons, laboratory etc sessions should not be carried out until networks have been completed. However, the flexibility in the network with its multiple starts and activities allowed for adjustments to be made and the exercise ran off with some success.

With the completion of the first phase, ie drawing individual networks, the team itself suggested that it would be beneficial to see a complete network (the network is on display in the Member's Exhibition and is 13' long, perhaps a claimant for an entry in the Guinness Book of Records).

The second phase, which we are now in, is to insert the cross links and dependencies across the subject bands. This should result in a completely subject/topic integrated syllabus network; it is anticipated that this may result in a fresh outlook when another course starts in September 1973.

The future phases we envisage are: to draw a network of the second year of the course, to revise and redraw the first year network in the light of the experience gained after completion of the first full sessions. We are also investigating making use of the referencing facility of the network to produce Synchrofax sheets of those topics in the syllabus where students have experienced difficulty: these will be available for use in the library and will, we hope, form the basis of a learning resources centre. The referencing facility will also play a major part in our intention to use a computer link which is available in the college: information and data would be fed into the computer and that students would be able to obtain access to it, at specified periods of the day, to obtain homework, references, guidance etc.

The College is reluctant to issue copies of the network for general use by other colleges, until it has been validated and de-bugged by the completion of a full course. This policy may seem selfish in some respects, but it is important to realize that the network is peculiar to Coventry Technical College, and has been drawn from a point of view of the availability of resources and each individual team member's approach to his subject. It has been found that though networks or a subject may agree in general outline and development, there is often disagreement with regard to individual topics and aspects. These variations are due to resource availability, the requirements of local industry, students backgrounds, college policy and the varying emphases placed upon subjects/topics within the syllabus due to the methods of learning and teaching adopted by individual students and colleges.

At a recent conference held at Wolverhampton Technical Teacher's Training College attended by staff from colleges in the Midlands area who are offering and running the OND course a desire was expressed for cooperation and resource interchange between colleges. It is hoped that the network approach will facilitate this interaction in a logical and systematic manner.

May I close this paper by summarizing the advantages that we have gained and hope to gain from using the technique of network analysis as a means of Syllabus Analysis. They are:

1. The network provides new insights into the syllabus;

2. The logical development of subjects and their topics can be seen clearly;

3. The dependencies and relationships between different topics in various subject bands can be established;

4. It provides a cross-referencing system that can be used by students, teaching staff and other colleges;

5. It may be used as a basis for developing diagnostic tests or objective questions to establish a student's profile of knowledge;

6. A team-teaching exercise can be planned and executed where it can make the maximum amount of impact;

7. It may be used by students or staff to plan revision schedules;

8. Forms an ideal vehicle for possible application and use of computer facilities;

9. May be used to establish the depth of teaching required for a given subject or topic;

10. The necessary entry behaviour requirements for any section of the syllabus can be established;

11. An evaluation of the subjects/topics can reveal the critical concepts and principles with the syllabus;

12. Alternative solutions to time-tabling problems can be obtained;

13. Enables a complete perspective view of the course to be obtained;

14. Provides a schedule of the importance of handouts, information maps, audio/visual aids etc;

15. Lastly, but by no means least, it provides an opportunity to give papers at APLET Conferences.

REFERENCES

Clay, M. J. (1969) Work Study and Management Services, Vol. 13, Nos. 9-10
Wyant, T. G. (1971) in 'Aspects of Educational Technology V'. (Ed) Derek Packham, Alan Cleary, Terry Mayes. Pitman, London. Page 393
Wyant, T. G. (1972) in 'Aspects of Educational Technology VI'. (Ed) K. Austwick and N. D. C. Harris. Pitman, London. Page 103

Members' Forum

An innovation at this conference was the informal presentation of members' papers and symposia, the organization of which was almost instant, with entries being accepted at the conference itself. This was in response to requests from members after the previous conference, when several 'ad hoc' meetings had occurred. The forum was run in conjunction with the members' exhibition and organized by R J Britton of Eastbourne College of Education.

It should not be thought that instant organization implied haphazard presentation. Some items had received as much preparation as those in the main conference; the authors, however, were spared the discipline of completing their papers in the style and time to permit selection by the convener's panel well before the conference. While space does not permit more than a brief mention of their efforts here, a list of contributors to this forum is appended so that readers can follow up any items that take their interest.

Transatlantic cooperation produced a lively symposium on the Methodology of Simulation and Gaming for Education led by Mitchell and Boyd from Canada with Teather and Gibbs from UK. Brief contributions from each speaker covered both the practice and the problems of innovation. During the discussion which followed, critical attention was paid to the problems of game evaluation in terms of measuring effectiveness and comparing different types of game based on the same model. Further cooperation between McAleese and Griffiths produced a session on Microteaching based on experience in Scottish Universities, which led to such animated discussion that it was agreed to organize a one-day conference to cover this subject alone.

The other sessions contained single papers, including one from France by Dubreuil on the use of CAI for language learning. Eraut contributed to the main theme of the whole conference with his paper on 'Objectives', while Hills described the work of the Educational Technique subject group of the Chemical Society. The papers by Horner, Vaughan, Rees and Wright contained good descriptions of current work which is the backbone of the Association, while Peters contributed an interesting account from Schleswig-Holstein, which helped to put UK work in perspective.

One interpretation of the 'Wandsworth Sound' could be the support given to this forum by the members of the Department of Educational Technology, Wandsworth Technical College. This department is the largest agency for the promotion of educational technology within the Inner London Education Authority and a study of the papers presented by members of staff is an indication of the range of their work.

The contributions to the Members' Forum were:

P D Mitchell G Boyd	Sir George Williams University, Montreal Canada	'Methodology of Simulation and Gaming for Education'
D C B Teather G I Gibbs	University of Liverpool Home Office Unit for Educational Methods	
B Dubreuil	University of Paris	'CAI for teaching English grammar to French University students'
M Eraut	University of Sussex	'Objectives'
R Griffiths	University of Stirling	'Future development in Micro- teaching'
P J Hills	University of Surrey	'The work of the Educational Technique subject group of the Chemical Society'
G Horner	College of Further Education, Harrogate	'Multi-choice questions as a method of learning'
W R McAleese	University of Aberdeen	'Microteaching and University Teaching'
C Peters	Schleswig-Holstein Department of Education	'Programmed Learning for Teachers'
M J Rees M Wright	Home Office Unit for Educational Methods	'Implications of the problems encountered in validation'
B W Vaughan	Parochial School, Trowbridge	'Application of Operational Research Techniques of Net- work Analysis in Education'

and from Wandsworth Technical College, London:

F Dall	'Communication and Television — a pilot CSE Mode 3 school link system'
E Hewett	'The Tape Recorder and the teaching of Reading'
J Maguire	'A systematic approach to language development'
A Russell C Webb	'Teaching Teachers about Educational Technology'
D Taylor	'Using punchboards with slow learners'
G Wilson	'Educational Technology and creative writing'.

Post Conference Comment

ROBIN BUDGETT

The brochure, produced to announce this Conference, hopefully suggested that the Conference might explore on an International basis the new possibilities that Educational Technology may develop in the next ten years. Yet at the same time part of our Association could examine the past ten years and decide in what direction it and Educational Technology might go in the next decade.

Even the most forceful of conveners cannot guarantee that authors of papers will meet his brief and we must leave it to the reader to judge how close in the end this conference came to meeting these objectives.

The conference organizers have certain responsibilities, principal of which is to maintain a standard of paper that will make it worthwhile for an international delegate to travel great distances to hear. This year the papers panel demanded a high standard and only recommended 27 papers for presentation and eventual publication.

However, this was not all the material available to delegates. At one end of the scale were the three international papers published in the first section of this volume, while at the other was the almost-instant Members' Forum which accompanied the Members' Exhibition. Though the main events of this forum had some pre-planning, entries were accepted 'at the post' and the result was a series of most lively occasions. One of the few consistent delegate complaints was that the Forum was so interesting that it clashed with the 'official' papers.

This was the eighth annual conference organized by APLET or its predecessor. The diary reads:

       1966 Loughborough, College of Education
       1967 Birmingham University
       1968 Glasgow University
       1969 London, Goldsmiths' College
       1970 Loughborough University
       1971 Newcastle University
       1972 Bath University
       1973 Brighton, College of Education

London 1969 was the first 'official' international conference, though the delegates had come from many nations in previous years. It seems that the event is now established as a major contribution in the field of Educational Technology.

Up to 1972 the form of the conference had remained virtually unchanged since its inception. The many papers were read concurrently in groups and some wily delegates showed the ability to obtain the gist of a number of papers by moving rapidly between rooms and hearing bits of all. Thus, even while papers were on, the main concourse would seem like a city railway terminus in the rush-hour, with delegates chasing hither and thither. It is true that each conference had some eminent invited speakers to address plenary sessions and symposia were organized to discuss applications of Ed 'Tech' to special areas of learning. However, it was not until last year that a major change in the concept of the Conference was made. It was then that the organizers felt that an attempt should be made to apply the present state of Educational Technology to the Conference, so that the structure of the conference became an attempt to practise what we preach. It was felt that delegates should be given more opportunity for group discussion and that the outcome of each discussion should be fed back to the plenary session by rapporteurs.

At that conference the papers for discussion were not formally presented, but were available, many in audio visual form, for study by delegates before each group met. While the organizers' concept was good, the behaviour of the delegates was not quite as predicted, and subsequent suggestions for improvement were studied at the outset by the organizers of this conference.

Thus the papers by Annett, the Russians and Glaser were each presented in a half-day session consisting of three parts:

1. The presentation of the paper by the author
2. Discussion of the paper by delegates in six groups
3. Plenary session, when the author answered questions put by the group chairmen

The other papers published in this volume were presented in five groups of 5 or 6 parallel sessions and the authors were encouraged to be flexible in their methods of presentation. The lengths of the sessions were sufficient to allow the papers to be read by the delegates, illustrated by the author and finally discussed.

It is a regular complaint of delegates, expressed verbally to the organizers and in 'feedback' questionnaires, that at a conference on educational technology more educational technology should be used in the presentation of papers. While it is hoped that this is not a cry for hardware for hardware's sake, it acknowledges that such technology includes planning and selection of appropriate methods (though see Hawkridge [ibid]), it must be reported that only about half of these published papers were presented with anything more than a simple reading. On the other hand mention should perhaps be made of Baume and Jones's use of dialogue with role-playing to explain the development of their project and Pratt's use of Beethoven's music which this volume, alas, cannot match.